German
Vocabulary
Drills

German Vocabulary Drills

David M. Stillman, PhD,
Daniele D. Godor, MA,
and Ronni L. Gordon, PhD

New York Chicago San Francisco Athens London Madrid
Mexico City Milan New Delhi Singapore Sydney Toronto

1 2 3 4 5 6 7 8 9 10 11 12 13 QVS/QVS 1 0 9 8 7 6 5

ISBN   978-0-07-182614-3
MHID   0-07-182614-9

e-ISBN   978-0-07-182615-0
e-MHID   0-07-182615-7

Library of Congress Control Number 2014935323

McGraw-Hill Education products are available at special quantity discounts
to use as premiums and sales promotions or for use in corporate training
programs. To contact a representative, please visit the Contact Us pages
at www.mhprofessional.com.

Companion Flashcard App
Flashcard sets for additional practice can be found in the McGraw-Hill
Education Language Lab app. Go to mhlanguagelab.com for details on how
to access this free app, which is available for Apple and Android tablet and
mobile devices, as well as computer via web browser (best viewed with
Chrome or Safari browser).

For Alex and Mimi,
whose brilliance and love illuminate and inspire every word we write.
David M. Stillman
Ronni L. Gordon

For my students.
Daniele D. Godor

Contents

Preface

"When I use a word," Humpty Dumpty said in rather a scornful tone, "it means just what I choose it to mean—neither more nor less."
Through the Looking Glass, LEWIS CARROLL

German Vocabulary Drills is designed to provide beginning and intermediate learners of German with essential vocabulary that will enable them to carry on conversations in German, read a wide variety of materials, and write on a broad range of topics in the language. We have selected vocabulary used by the greatest number of speakers in the German-speaking world, and we present commonly used alternative words from Austria and Switzerland.

German Vocabulary Drills goes beyond the basic vocabulary found in most first- and second-year textbooks. To this basic vocabulary, we have added high-frequency words and expressions that make it possible for learners of German to express themselves effectively and confidently on everyday topics such as food, clothing, the house, the daily routine, work, travel, entertainment, and leisure activities, as well as topics of a higher intellectual level—science, the computer, technology, the economy, and intellectual and spiritual life.

Structure and features

German Vocabulary Drills has 15 chapters, each built around a specific theme. Each chapter has titled sections that present groupings of similar words. Instead of presenting words in isolation, we introduce them in a meaningful context that makes learning and remembering new vocabulary easier and more productive.

Language boxes In each chapter, there are brief lexical, grammatical, and cultural explanations prompted by certain words or expressions presented. These explanations enhance the study of German vocabulary by deepening the learner's appreciation of the language and its culture.

Klingen Sie authentisch! and *Ausdrücke, Sprichwörter und Zitate* These unique sections of idiomatic usage are designed to reinforce and expand the vocabulary presented in the chapter by preparing the learner for interaction with native speakers of German. We include expressions, sayings, and quotations in German that enrich and broaden the learner's knowledge of the German language.

Exercises The exercises at the end of each chapter help you master the vocabulary introduced. There is a great variety of exercise types from controlled to free expression: multiple choice, fill-in, matching, classification, word families, composition, oral presentation, and translation.

Answer key An answer key for the exercises facilitates self-study.

App *German Vocabulary Drills* offers an all-purpose vocabulary app that allows the learner to study 450 words and expressions using digital flashcards. The app is compatible with portable devices, so it can be used anytime, anywhere. Visualization of the words on flashcards increases the learner's ability to remember and internalize new vocabulary. This is a very effective and enjoyable way to learn and review vocabulary. See the copyright page for information on how to access the McGraw-Hill Education Language Lab app.

German Vocabulary Drills gives beginners the words and phrases they need to construct simple paragraphs and oral presentations and furnishes intermediate learners with the lexical tools they need to express themselves in more complex writing tasks and oral presentations on a wide variety of topics. Even the most advanced learners will find this book helpful. User-friendly, it is ideal for learners working on their own or as an ancillary for students using a textbook in a classroom setting. Chapters may be covered in any order, making the book compatible with all texts, types of curricula, and classroom approaches, and facilitating the individualization of vocabulary practice.

David M. Stillman, PhD
Daniele D. Godor, MA
Ronni L. Gordon, PhD

Guide to using this book

Gender notation

German nouns are divided into three broad classes called genders: masculine, feminine, and neuter. In vocabulary lists, the gender of a noun is usually indicated by the definite article that accompanies it.

the market	**der** Markt
the post office	**die** Post
the theater	**das** Schauspielhaus

The nominative and accusative singular forms of the definite article are unique in distinguishing gender, but the other singular forms and all the plural forms are not.

	Masculine	*Feminine*	*Neuter*
Nominative	der	die	das
Genitive	des	der	des
Dative	dem	der	dem
Accusative	den	die	das

If a nominative or accusative singular form of the definite article accompanies a noun, it is not necessary to mark the gender of the noun. In some vocabulary drills, however, the dative case of the noun is used, and it is necessary to mark the gender of masculine and neuter nouns. (It is not necessary to mark the gender of a feminine singular noun in the dative case, because **der** marks the noun as uniquely feminine.) The gender is indicated in square brackets after the noun.

They want us to attend <u>the party</u>.	Sie wollen, daß wir an <u>der Party</u> teilnehmen.
the bachelor party	dem Junggesellenabschied [M.]
the family gathering	dem Familientreffen [N.]

The gender of an underlined noun in a vocabulary drill sentence is indicated in square brackets after the sentence.

What's in <u>the backpack</u>?	Was ist in <u>dem Rucksack</u>? [M.]

If a noun appears in plural form, the nominative singular form of the noun is given with its definite article in square brackets.

furniture   Möbel [das Möbel *piece of furniture*]
taxes   Steuern [die Steuer]

If the singular form is never or only rarely used, the notation "[PL.]" is added after the noun.

earmuffs   Ohrenschützer [PL.]
seafood   Meeresfrüchte [PL.]

In some vocabulary drills, a noun is accompanied by the indefinite article. The feminine forms of the indefinite article are distinguishable from the masculine and neuter forms (and therefore the gender of a feminine noun is indicated by the indefinite article), but the masculine and neuter forms are not distinguished from each other except in the accusative case.

	Masculine	*Feminine*	*Neuter*
Nominative	ein	eine	ein
Genitive	eines	einer	eines
Dative	einem	einer	einem
Accusative	einen	eine	ein

There's a pen in the briefcase.   Es liegt ein Stift in dem Aktenkoffer. [M.]
  a checkbook   ein Scheckbuch [N.]
  a pair of eyeglasses   eine Brille

If a noun appears in the accusative case, however, the indefinite article distinguishes the gender of the noun.

The house has a garden.   Das Haus hat einen Garten.
  a lawn   ein Grundstück
  a two-car garage   eine Doppelgarage

In some vocabulary drills, no article accompanies a singular noun; in this case, the noun's gender is indicated in square brackets.

The food tastes better with salt.   Das Essen schmeckt mit Salz besser. [N.]
  cinnamon   Zimt [M.]
  mint   Minze [F.]

If a noun that refers to people does not change in the feminine form but the article does, it is indicated as follows.

domestic worker   der/die Hausangestellte

If the noun changes its form in the feminine, both forms of the noun are given, separated by a slash.

secretary	der Sekretär / die Sekretärin
heretic	der Ketzer / die Ketzerin

Since rules for the regular formation of the feminine noun are given in Chapters 11, 13, and 15, feminine forms are not provided in those chapters' lists unless the forms are exceptions.

farmer	der Bauer / die Bäuerin
firefighter	der Feuerwehrmann / die Feuerwehrfrau

Spelling reform

The German orthography reforms of 1996 (**Rechtschreibreform**) have not been widely adopted by German speakers and the German media in Germany, Austria, and Switzerland.

Most of the words affected by the reform reflect the differences in the use of ß (traditional) vs. **ss** (reform) in syllable-final position. If a text uses **dass** and **muss**, one can be certain that at least some of the spelling reforms are being followed; a traditional text uses **daß** and **muß**, except in Switzerland, where the ß has been seldom used historically.

This book basically follows the traditional, pre-reform spelling rules. A post-reform alternative spelling, however, may be given immediately after the pre-reform spelling; they are separated by a slash.

to graduate	einen Abschluß / Abschluss zu machen
a passport	ein Paß / Pass [M.]
kiss	der Kuß / Kuss
nightclub	der Nachtclub / Nachtklub
photo	das Photo / Foto
still life	das Stilleben / Stillleben
portrait	das Portrait / Porträt
a hard-boiled egg	ein hartgekochtes / hart gekochtes Ei

To avoid confusion in vocabulary drill sentences and in the exercises, the **ss** alternative is not given for common monosyllabic words, such as **daß**, **muß**, and **laß**.

They want us to attend the party.	Sie wollen, daß wir an der Party teilnehmen.
I have to buy a (man's) suit.	Ich muß einen Anzug kaufen.
Let's order the first course.	Laß uns den ersten Gang bestellen.

Grammar and usage abbreviations

M.	masculine	AUS.	Austria
F.	feminine	SWITZ.	Switzerland
N.	neuter		
SG.	singular		
PL.	plural		

1

In der Stadt

In the city

This chapter presents important vocabulary for traveling around the city and shopping. You will learn the German words for places, sights, and stores, and how to ask for and give directions.

German nouns are divided into three classes: masculine, feminine, and neuter. A word that accompanies a noun, such as *a*, *the*, *this*, and *that*, changes form to show the gender of the noun and whether the noun is singular or plural. The word also shows whether the noun is in the nominative, genitive, dative, or accusative case.

The definite article *the* for singular nouns in the nominative case is **der** before a masculine noun, **die** before a feminine noun, and **das** before a neuter noun.

Where is . . . ?	**Wo ist...?**
Where is the bank?	Wo ist die Bank?
the arts center	das Kulturzentrum
the bus station	der Busbahnhof
the bus stop	die Bushaltestelle
the cathedral	die Kathedrale, der Dom, der/das Münster
the cemetery	der Friedhof
the church	die Kirche
the city hall (in a major city)	das Rathaus
the clinic	die Klinik
the concert hall	das Konzerthaus
the consulate	das Konsulat
the department store	das Warenhaus
the embassy	die Botschaft
the funeral home	das Bestattungsinstitut
the gym	das Fitneßstudio/Fitness-Studio
the hospital	das Krankenhaus, das Spital [AUS., SWITZ.]
the hotel	das Hotel
the library	die Bibliothek
the main square	der Hauptplatz

>>>

the market	der Markt
the mosque	die Moschee
the movie theater	das Kino
the museum	das Museum
the nightclub	der Nachtclub/Nachtklub
the opera house	das Opernhaus
the park	der Park
the pawn shop	der Pfandleiher
the police station	die Polizeidienststelle, die Wache
the post office	die Post, das Postamt
the public garden	der öffentliche Garten
the railway station	der Bahnhof
the elementary school	die Grundschule, die Primarschule [SWITZ.]
the middle school	die Sekundarschule [SWITZ.]
the secondary school	das Gymnasium, die Oberschule
the stadium	das Stadion
the stock exchange	die Börse
the subway station	die U-Bahn-Station
the synagogue	die Synagoge
the theater	das Theater, das Schauspielhaus
the tourist office	das Fremdenverkehrsamt
the university	die Universität
the zoo	der Zoo, der Tierpark

The indefinite article *a/an* for nouns in the nominative case is **ein** before masculine and neuter nouns and **eine** before feminine nouns. In the accusative case (as in the section below), the indefinite masculine article changes to **einen**, while the feminine and neuter articles remain unchanged.

What is there around here?

Was gibt es hier in der Nähe?

Is there <u>a drugstore</u> around here?	Gibt es <u>eine Drogerie</u> hier in der Nähe?
an antique store	einen Antiquitätenhändler
an appliance store	einen Elektrofachhandel
an art gallery	eine Galerie
a bakery	eine Bäckerei
a barber(shop)	einen (Herren-)Friseur/(Herren-)Frisör, einen Herrensalon, einen Coiffeur [SWITZ.]
a beauty supply store	einen Schönheitssalon

>>>

a bicycle store	einen Fahrradladen, einen Veloladen [SWITZ.]
a bike rental outlet	ein Fahrradverleih, ein Veloverleih [SWITZ.]
a bookstore	einen Buchladen
a boutique (for trendy clothing)	ein Modegeschäft
a butcher shop	eine Fleischerei, eine Schlachterei [REGIONAL], eine Metzgerei [REGIONAL, SWITZ.]
a café	ein Café, ein Kaffeehaus
a candy store, a sweet shop	einen Süßwarenladen
a caterer, a ready-made food store	ein Bistro, einen Imbiß/Imbiss, eine Imbißstube/Imbissstube
a clothing store	ein Bekleidungsgeschäft
a computer store	ein Computergeschäft
a convenience store	einen Kiosk, einen Minimarkt, einen Spätkauf [REGIONAL]
a dry cleaner's	eine Reinigung, eine Putzerei [AUS.]
an electronics store	einen Elektrofachhandel
a fish store	ein Fischgeschäft
a florist, a flower shop	einen Blumenladen
a food store	ein Lebensmittelgeschäft
a fruit and vegetable store	einen Obst- und Gemüsehandel
a fruit store	einen Obsthandel
a furniture store	ein Möbelgeschäft
a gas station	eine Tankstelle
a gift shop	einen Geschenkartikelladen
a grocery store	ein Lebensmittelgeschäft
a hair salon	einen (Damen-)Friseur/(Damen-)Frisör, einen (Damen-)Salon, einen Coiffeur [SWITZ.]
a hardware store	einen Baumarkt
a health food store	ein Reformhaus
an ice cream parlor	einen Eisladen
a jewelry store	ein Juweliergeschäft
a laundromat	einen Waschsalon
a law firm	eine Anwaltskanzlei, eine Advokatur [SWITZ.]
a leather goods store	einen Lederfachhandel
a mailbox	einen Briefkasten, einen Postkasten [AUS.]
a music store	einen Musikalienhandel
a newsstand	einen Zeitungskiosk
an office supplies store	einen Bürobedarf
an optician('s), an eyeglass store	einen Optiker, einen Brillenladen

an organic food store	einen Bioladen
a parking lot, a parking garage	einen Parkplatz, ein Parkhaus
a pastry shop	eine Konditorei
a perfume store	eine Parfümerie
a pet store	einen Zoofachhandel
a phone store	einen Telefonladen
a real estate agency	eine Immobilienagentur
a restaurant	ein Restaurant
a shoe repair shop	eine Schuhmacherei
a shoe store	ein Schuhgeschäft
a shopping mall	eine Ladenpassage
a sports store	ein Sportgeschäft
a stationery store	eine Schreibwarenhandlung
a supermarket	einen Supermarkt
a superstore	ein SB-Warenhaus, einen Hypermarkt
a tobacco shop	einen Tabakladen, eine Trafik [AUS.]
a toy store	ein Spielzeuggeschäft
a wine store	ein Weingeschäft
a youth hostel	eine Jugendherberge

The definite article in the accusative case is **den** for masculine nouns, while the articles for the other two genders remain unchanged: **die** for feminine nouns and **das** for neuter nouns.

The neighborhood

I know the neighborhood.	Ich kenne die Nachbarschaft.
the alley	die Allee
the apartment house	das Mietshaus, das Zinshaus [AUS.]
the avenue	die Prachtstraße
the boulevard	den Boulevard
the bridge	die Brücke
the building	das Gebäude
the dead-end street	die Sackgasse
the downtown area	das Stadtzentrum
the green spaces	die Grünflächen
the monument	das Denkmal
the old city, the old town	die Altstadt
the shopping area	das Einkaufsviertel

Die Nachbarschaft

the side street	die Seitenstraße
the skyscraper	den Wolkenkratzer
the street	die Straße
the street corner	die Straßenecke
the suburbs	den Vorort
the tunnel	den Tunnel

In German, there is no indefinite article before plural nouns. The indefinite article is also not used before brand names, before nouns referring to substances or materials, or before nouns that cannot be counted.

What do you need?   Was brauchen Sie?

I want to buy aspirin.	Ich möchte Aspirin kaufen. [N.]
beer	Bier [N.]
bottled water	Mineralwasser [N.]
a camera	eine Kamera, einen Fotoapparat
a camera case	ein Kamera-Etui
a coke	Cola [F./N.]
a computer	einen Computer, einen Rechner
envelopes	Briefumschläge [der Briefumschlag]
food	Lebensmittel [N.], Essen [N.]
fruit	Obst [N.]
furniture	Möbel [das Möbel *piece of furniture*]
gas	Benzin [N.]
a guidebook	einen Stadtführer
gum	Kaugummi [N.]
ink cartridges	Tintenpatronen [die Tintenpatrone]
a laptop	einen Laptop
a magazine	eine Zeitschrift
a map of the country	eine Landkarte
medicine	Medizin [F.], Medikamente [das Medikament]
a memory card	eine Speicherkarte
a newspaper	eine Zeitung
paper	Papier [N.]
perfume	Parfum/Parfüm [N.]
postcards	Postkarten [die Postkarte]
a road map	eine Straßenkarte
soap	Seife [F.]

>>>

souvenirs	Souvenirs [das Souvenir]
stamps	Briefmarken [die Briefmarke]
a street map of the city	einen Stadtplan
(a pair of) sunglasses	eine Sonnebrille
suntan lotion	Sonnencreme/Sonnenkrem(e) [F.]
a tablet (computer)	einen Tablet-Computer
a tablet sleeve	ein Tablet-Etui
tissues	Taschentücher [das Taschentuch]
vegetables	Gemüse [das Gemüse]
wine	Wein [M.]

The preposition **in** may take an accusative or dative object. If motion is involved (answering **wohin?** *where to?*), the accusative case is used. If location is involved (answering **wo?** *where?*), the dative case is used. In the following section, the location of the object is at issue and therefore the bag or other container is in the dative case. The definite articles for singular nouns in the dative case are **dem** for masculine and neuter nouns and **der** for feminine nouns.

What's in there?

Was ist darin?

What's in the backpack?	Was ist in dem Rucksack? [M.]
the bag, the handbag	der Handtasche
the box	der Schachtel
the briefcase	dem Aktenkoffer [M.]
the change purse	dem Portemonnaie/Portmonee [N.],
	der Geldbörse [AUS.]
the computer case	der Computertasche
the package	dem Paket [N.], dem Päckchen [N.]
the suitcase	dem Koffer [M.]
the tote bag	der Jutetasche
the (steamer) trunk	der Truhe, dem Überseekoffer [M.]
the wallet	der Brieftasche

In the briefcase

Im Aktenkoffer

There's a pen in the briefcase.	Es liegt ein Stift in dem Aktenkoffer. [M.]
a calculator	ein Taschenrechner [M.]
a CD player	ein CD-Player [M.]
a cell phone	ein Mobiltelefon [N.], ein Handy [N.]
a checkbook	ein Scheckbuch [N.]

>>>

a driver's license	ein Führerschein [M.], ein Führerausweis [M.] [SWITZ.]
an envelope	ein Briefumschlag [M.]
a pair of eyeglasses	eine Brille
a hearing aid	ein Hörgerät [N.]
an ID	ein Personalausweis [M.], eine Identitätskarte [AUS., SWITZ.]
a key ring, a key chain	ein Schlüsselanhänger [M.]
a laptop	ein Laptop [M.]
a marker	ein Filzstift [M.]
money	Geld [N.]
a notebook	ein Notizblock [M.]
a pad, a notepad	ein Schreibblock [M.]
a passport	ein Paß/Pass [M.], ein Ausweis [M.]
a pencil	ein Bleistift [M.]
a pair of sunglasses	eine Sonnenbrille

There are CDs in the handbag.	In der Handtasche liegen CDs. [die CD]
contact lenses	Kontaktlinsen [die Kontaktlinse]
credit cards	Kreditkarten [die Kreditkarte]
documents	Dokumente [das Dokument], Unterlagen [die Unterlage]
earphones, headphones	Kopfhörer [PL.]
files	Akten [die Akte]
keys	Schlüssel [der Schlüssel]
papers	Papiere [das Papier]
photos	Photos/Fotos [das Photo/Foto]
receipts	Belege [der Beleg]

How much is it?   Was kostet das?

How much are the books?	Was kosten die Bücher? [das Buch]
the batteries	die Batterien [die Batterie]
the bus tickets	die Busfahrkarten [die Busfahrkarte]
the cigarettes	die Zigaretten [die Zigarette]
the city tours	die Stadtrundfahrten [die Stadtrundfahrt]
the guided tours	die Führungen [die Führung]
the seats	die Plätze [der Platz]
the tickets	die Eintrittskarten [die Eintrittskarte], die Billets [das Billet] [SWITZ.]

Klingen Sie authentisch!

alternative route	die Umleitung
at the corner	an der Ecke
at the light	an der Ampel
at the next light	an der nächsten Ampel
awning	die Markise, das Vordach
bicycle	das Fahrrad, das Velo [SWITZ.]
bicycle lane	der Fahrradweg
city planner	der Stadtplaner
commuter train	die S-Bahn (Stadtbahn)
construction	der Bau
construction site	die Baustelle
crosswalk	der Zebrastreifen, der Fussgängerstreifen [SWITZ.], der Schutzweg [AUS.]
neighborhood closed to traffic	die Fußgängerzone
neon light	das Neonlicht
neon sign	das Neonleuchtzeichen
the next stop	die nächste Haltestelle
one-way street	die Einbahnstraße
outdoor café seating	die Terrasse
parking meter	die Parkuhr
passerby	der Passant
paved street	die Kopfsteinpflasterstraße
pedestrian	der Fußgänger
pedestrian crossing	der Fußgängerübergang
platform	der Bahnsteig, der Perron [SWITZ.]
sewer	der Abflußkanal/Abflusskanal
sidewalk	der Bürgersteig, das Trottoir [SWITZ.]
streetcar	die Straßenbahn, die Tram, das Tram [SWITZ.]
streetlight, lamppost	die Straßenlaterne
traffic	der Verkehr
traffic circle	der Kreisverkehr
traffic jam	der Stau
traffic lane	die Fahrbahn, die Spur
traffic light, stoplight	die Verkehrsampeln
underground passage (to cross a street)	die Unterführung
urban freeway	die Stadtautobahn
urban infrastructure	die urbane Infrastruktur
walking tour	der Stadtbummel

to ask directions	nach der Richtung fragen
to bicycle	Fahrrad fahren
to cross the street	die Straße überqueren
to get lost	sich verlaufen
to go to all the stores	einen Einkaufsbummel machen
to park the car	den Wagen parken
to stroll around	umherbummeln
to use public transportation	die öffentlichen Verkehrsmittel benutzen
to walk in the crosswalk	über den Zebrastreifen gehen

Which way are you going?	In welche Richtung fahren Sie?
The street is closed.	Die Straße ist abgesperrt.
There's a traffic jam in our neighborhood.	In unserem Viertel ist ein Stau.
All the roads are jammed.	Alle Straßen sind verstopft.
They are going to renovate this industrial neighborhood and make it part of the city.	Sie werden dieses Industriegelände renovieren und es in die Stadt integrieren.
Berlin does not have an underground pedestrian network.	Berlin hat kein unterirdisches Tunnel-System für Fußgänger.

Ausdrücke, Sprichwörter und Zitate

I don't know what he's talking about.	Ich verstehe nur Bahnhof.
Nobody's ever gotten lost on a straight street.	Auf einer geraden Straße ist noch niemand verloren gegangen.
People, not houses, make a city.	Die Menschen, nicht die Häuser, machen die Stadt.

„Alle Hauptstädte sind einander gleich; alle Völker vermischen sich dort."
JEAN-JACQUES ROUSSEAU

„Dörfer sind vom Rhythmus des Tages geprägt, Städte vom Rhythmus der Nacht."
ERHARD BLANCK

„Auf dem Land passiert zu wenig, in der Stadt zuviel."
ULRICH ERCKENBRECHT

„Ich hab' noch einen Koffer in Berlin."
ALDO VON PINELLI

„Wien, Wien, nur du allein
sollst stets die Stadt meiner Träume sein!"
RUDOLF SIECZYŃSKI

Übung 1

Name the type of specialty store where you can buy each item. There may be more than one correct answer for some items.

1. ein Hemd
   _____
2. Briefumschläge
   _____
3. ein Kätzchen
   _____
4. Äpfel
   _____
5. eine Aktentasche
   _____
6. Aspirin
   _____
7. Parfum
   _____
8. eine Brille
   _____
9. Zigaretten
   _____
10. Koteletts
    _____
11. ein Tablet-Etui
    _____
12. Rosen
    _____
13. Vitamine
    _____
14. Benzin
    _____
15. Bücher
    _____
16. Brot
    _____
17. ein Kuchen
    _____
18. eine Flasche Champagner
    _____
19. ein Hammer
    _____
20. ein Fußball
    _____

Übung 2

Match each item or action in the second column with the place where you can buy, get, see, hear, or do it in the first column.

1. _____ im Obst- und Gemüsehandel	a. Skulpturen und Gemälde
2. _____ im Kino	b. den Zug nehmen
3. _____ im Bahnhof	c. Stiefel
4. _____ im Computergeschäft	d. sich die Haare schneiden lassen
5. _____ im Zeitungskiosk	e. ein paar Tennisschläger
6. _____ im Schuhgeschäft	f. Karotten und grüne Bohnen
7. _____ im Sportgeschäft	g. ein Laptop
8. _____ im Museum	h. klassische Musik hören
9. _____ beim Friseur	i. einen Film schauen
10. _____ im Konzerthaus	j. Zeitungen und Zeitschriften

Übung 3

In German, list ten places in the city that you would like to visit.

1. _____
2. _____
3. _____
4. _____
5. _____

6. _____
7. _____
8. _____
9. _____
10. _____

Übung 4

List five stores or places in the city that you like and five that you don't like. Note that **mögen** takes an accusative object.

Ich mag

1. _____
2. _____
3. _____
4. _____
5. _____

Mag ich nicht

6. _____
7. _____
8. _____
9. _____
10. _____

Übung 5

Choose the item you can buy in each of the following stores.

1. im Zeitungskiosk
   - a. Zeitungen
   - b. Aspirin
   - c. eine Flöte

2. im Computergeschäft
   - a. Brot
   - b. Schuhe
   - c. Tintenpatronen

3. im Buchladen
   - a. ein Wörterbuch
   - b. ein Kleid
   - c. Rosen

4. in der Apotheke
   - a. einen Fernseher
   - b. Medikamente
   - c. einen Sessel

5. im Obst- und Gemüsehandel
   - a. ein Tablet-Etui
   - b. Parfum
   - c. Karotten

6. im Lederfachgeschäft
   - a. eine Aktentasche
   - b. Nägel
   - c. Sonnencreme

7. im Zoofachhandel
   - a. ein Fahrrad
   - b. ein Kätzchen
   - c. einen Wagen

8. im Bürobedarf
   - a. Stifte
   - b. eine Hose
   - c. Töpfe

Übung 6

Choose the word that does not belong in each group.

1. a. Synagoge   b. Kirche   c. Baumarkt   d. Kathedrale
2. a. Fleischerei   b. Fischgeschäft   c. Imbiß   d. Juwelier
3. a. Stifte   b. Schuhe   c. Bleistifte   d. Briefumschläge
4. a. Bank   b. Buchladen   c. Zeitungskiosk   d. Bibliothek
5. a. Minimarkt   b. Kino   c. Theater   d. Konzerthaus
6. a. Krankenhaus   b. Klinik   c. Apotheke   d. Bäckerei
7. a. Nachtclub   b. Laptop   c. Koffer   d. Rucksack
8. a. Stadtzentrum   b. Nachbarschaft   c. Stadion   d. Vorort

Übung 7

Translate the following sentences into German.

1. *Where is the computer store?*

   _____

2. *The computer store is near here.*

   _____

3. *Is there a sporting goods store around here?*

   _____

4. *I want to buy a backpack.*

   _____

5. *What's in the wallet?*

   _____

6. *There are money and a driver's license.*

   _____

7. *There are files in the briefcase.*

   _____

8. *Is there a museum in the neighborhood?*

   _____

9. *In this neighborhood there are a library, an arts center, and a tourist office.*

   _____

   _____

10. *I know the old city and the shopping area.*

    _____

2

Kleidung
Clothing

In this chapter, you will learn the German words for clothing, and how to express your likes, dislikes, and preferences in matters of style, color, and fabric. You will be able to describe what you wear for special occasions.

What do you need?	**Was brauchen Sie?**
I need <u>shoes</u>.	Ich brauche <u>Schuhe</u>. [der Schuh]
boots	Stiefel [der Stiefel]
dress shoes	Lederschuhe, Ausgehschuhe
hiking boots	Wanderschuhe
loafers	Slipper [der Slipper]
rubber boots	Gummistiefel
running shoes	Laufschuhe
sandals	Sandalen [die Sandale]
shoelaces	Schnürsenkel [der Schnürsenkel] [REGIONAL], Schuhbänder [das Schuhband] [REGIONAL, AUS.], Schuhbändel [das Schuhbändel] [SWITZ.]
slippers	Hausschuhe, Patschen [der Patschen] [AUS.], Finken [der Fink] [SWITZ.]
sneakers	Turnschuhe
tennis shoes	Tennisschuhe

What does she wear?	**Was trägt sie?**
She always wears <u>boots</u>.	Sie trägt immer <u>Stiefel</u>. [der Stiefel]
clogs	Clogs [der Clog], Holzschuhe [der Holzschuh]
flip-flops	Flipflops [der Flipflop]
high heels	hohe Absätze [der Absatz]
low boots, ankle boots	Ankle Boots [der Boot], knöchelhohe Stiefeletten [die Stiefelette]
pumps	Pumps [der Pump]
slip-ons	Slipper [der Slipper]
wedge-heeled shoes	Keilpumps

In German, the nominative singular forms for *this* are **dieser** before a masculine noun, **diese** before a feminine noun, and **dieses** before a neuter noun. Modern spoken German uses the same word for *this* and *that*. **Jener** *that* has almost disappeared in spoken German; in its place, *this* may be combined with an adverb of place: **dieser dort** *this there*.

What do you like?	**Was gefällt dir?**
I like this shirt.	Mir gefällt dieses Hemd.
this blouse	diese Bluse
these khakis	diese Khakihose
this long-sleeved shirt	dieses Langarmhemd
this short-sleeved shirt	dieses Kurzarmhemd
that pair of pants	diese Hose (dort)
that shirt with French cuffs	dieses Hemd mit Manschetten (dort)
those sweatpants	diese Jogginghose (dort), diese Trainerhose (dort) [SWITZ.]
that sweatshirt	diesen Pullover (dort)
that T-shirt	dieses T-Shirt (dort)
this tank top	dieses Tank-Top, dieses armlose Oberteil
those yoga pants	diese Yoga-Hose (dort)

What can I wrap up for you?	**Was soll ich Ihnen einpacken?**
I'll take these leggings.	Ich nehme diese Leggings. [PL.]
these blouses	diese Blusen [die Bluse]
these shorts	diese Shorts [PL.]
those socks	diese Socken (dort) [die Socke]

The verb **kaufen** *to buy* takes an accusative object.

Shopping	**Einkäufe**
I have to buy a (man's) suit.	Ich muß einen Anzug kaufen.
bathing trunks	eine Badehose
a bathrobe	einen Bademantel
a belt	einen Gürtel
boxer shorts	Boxershorts [PL.]
a cap	eine Kappe
a cape	ein Cape
a coat	einen Mantel

>>>

a down jacket	eine Daunenjacke
a dress	ein Kleid
earmuffs	Ohrenschützer [PL.]
gloves	Handschuhe [der Handschuh]
a handkerchief	ein Taschentuch, ein Nastuch [SWITZ.]
a hat	einen Hut
a hoodie	einen Kapuzenpullover
jeans	eine Jeans
a leather jacket	eine Lederjacke
maternity clothes	Umstandskleidung [F.]
pajamas	einen Schlafanzug, einen Pyjama, ein Pyjama [SWITZ.]
a pants suit	einen Hosenanzug
pantyhose	eine Strumpfhose, eine Feinstrumpfhose
a parka	einen Parka
a rain hat	einen Regenhut, einen Südwester
a rain poncho	einen Regenponcho
a scarf	einen Schal
a shirt	eine Hemdbluse
a skirt	einen Rock
a sweater	einen Pullover
tights	eine Strumpfhose
an umbrella	einen Regenschirm, einen Paraplui [AUS.]
an undershirt	ein Unterhemd
underpants	Unterhosen [die Unterhose]
a winter hat, a winter cap	eine Mütze, eine Wintermütze, eine Haube [AUS.]
a woman's suit	ein Kostüm

The verb **suchen** *to look for* takes an accusative object.

What does she want to buy? | ## Was will sie kaufen?

She's looking for <u>a bathing suit</u>. | Sie sucht <u>einen Badeanzug</u>.

a one-piece bathing suit	einen einteiligen Badeanzug
a bathing cap	eine Badekappe
beachwear	Strandbekleidung [F.]
a bikini	einen Bikini
a bra	einen Büstenhalter, einen BH
a bridal veil	einen Brautschleier
a bridesmaid dress	ein Brautjungfernkleid

a camisole	ein Unterhemd, ein Camisole
a cocktail dress	ein Cocktailkleid
an empire dress	ein Empirekleid
a fur coat	einen Pelzmantel
gaiters	Stulpen [die Stulpe], Gamaschen [die Gamasche]
a girdle	einen Hüftgürtel
a headband	ein Stirnband
a mink coat	einen Nerzmantel
a nightgown	ein Nachthemd
a pants suit	einen Hosenanzug
panties	Höschen [N.]
a slip	ein Unterkleid
a strapless dress	ein trägerloses Kleid
a wedding dress	ein Hochzeitskleid
a wrap, a cover-up	eine Strandtunika

The verb **tragen** *to wear* takes an accusative object. Its present-tense conjugation is as follows: **ich trage, du trägst, er/sie/es trägt, wir tragen, ihr tragt, sie tragen.**

How is he dressed?

He's wearing a raincoat.

a black leather jacket	eine schwarze Lederjacke
a bomber jacket	eine Bomberjacke
a bow tie	eine Fliege, ein Mascherl [AUS.]
a cummerbund	einen Kummerbund
a double-breasted suit	einen Zweireiher
an overcoat	einen Mantel, einen Übermantel
a pin-striped suit	einen Nadelstreifenanzug
a single-breasted suit	einen Einreiher
a suit with wide lapels	einen Anzug mit breitem Revers
tails	einen Frack
a three-button jacket	ein Drei-Knopf-Sakko
a three-piece suit	einen Dreiteiler
a tie	eine Krawatte, einen Schlips
a tie pin	eine Krawattennadel
a trench coat	einen Trenchcoat
a tuxedo	einen Smoking
a two-button jacket	ein Zwei-Knopf-Sakko

Wie ist er gekleidet?

Er trägt einen Regenmantel.

At the jewelry store

I'd like to buy jewelry.
  a charm bracelet
  costume jewelry
  mother-of-pearl cufflinks

  earrings
  a pearl necklace
  a ruby necklace
  a topaz necklace
  a turquoise pendant
  a diamond ring
  an emerald ring
  an engagement ring
  a sapphire and diamond ring
  a wedding ring
  a gold watch
  a platinum watch
  a silver watch
  a diamond tiara

In Juweliergeschäft

Ich möchte Schmuck kaufen. [M.]
  ein Bettelarmband
  Modeschmuck [M.]
  Manschettenknöpfe aus Perlmutt
    [der Manschettenknopf]
  Ohrringe [der Ohrring]
  eine Perlenkette
  ein Halsband mit Rubinen
  ein Halsband mit Topasen
  einen Anhänger aus Türkisen
  einen Diamantring
  einen Smaragdring
  einen Verlobungsring
  einen Ring mit Saphiren/Safiren und Diamanten
  einen Hochzeitsring
  eine goldene Uhr
  eine Uhr aus Platin
  eine silberne Uhr
  ein Diamantendiadem

The verb **bevorzugen** *to prefer* takes an accusative object.

It's a matter of taste.

I prefer sport clothes.
  custom-made clothes
  dark-colored clothes
  designer clothes, haute couture
  formal wear
  light-colored clothes
  natural-fiber clothes
  permanent press clothes
  shrink-proof clothes
  synthetic(-fabric) clothes
  trendy clothes
  washable clothes

Es ist Geschmackssache.

Ich bevorzuge Sportbekleidung.
  maßgeschneiderte Kleidung [F.]
  dunkle Kleidung
  Designermode [F.], Haute Couture [F.]
  formelle Kleidung
  helle Kleidung
  Kleidung aus Naturfasern
  bügelfreie Kleidung
  schrumpffreie Kleidung
  Kleidung aus synthetischen Fasern
  modische Kleidung
  maschinenfeste Kleidung

Fabrics

I'm looking for *a cotton shirt*.	Ich suche ein Baumwollhemd.
corduroy pants	eine Cordhose/Kordhose
a denim skirt	einen Jeansrock
a felt hat	einen Filzhut
a lace blouse	eine Spitzenbluse
leather gloves	Lederhandschuhe [der Lederhandschuh]
a linen jacket	eine Leinenjacke
nylon stockings	Nylonstrümpfe [der Nylonstrumpf]
patent leather shoes	Lackschuhe [der Lackschuh]
a polyester T-shirt	ein T-Shirt aus Polyester
a silk tie	eine Seidenkrawatte
a straw hat	einen Strohhut
suede shoes	Wildlederschuhe [der Wildlederschuh]
a tweed jacket	eine Tweedjacke
a velvet vest	eine Samtweste
a wool suit	einen Wollanzug
woolen socks	Wollsocken [die Wollsocke]
a worsted overcoat	einen Lodenmantel

Der Stoff

The verb **brauchen** *to need* takes an accusative object.

Women's clothing

I need *a dress with buttons*.	Ich brauche ein Kleid mit Knöpfen.
a dress with a belt	ein Kleid mit Gürtel
a dress with pockets	ein Kleid mit Taschen
a dress with ribbons	ein Kleid mit Bändern
a dress with a zipper	ein Kleid mit Reißverschluß/Reißverschluss
a dress with a zipper in back	ein Kleid mit einem Reißverschluß/Reißverschluss auf dem Rücken
a dress with a zipper in front	ein Kleid mit einem Reißverschluß/Reißverschluss auf der Vorderseite
an embroidered dress	ein Kleid mit Stickereien
a low-cut dress	ein Kleid mit tiefem Ausschnitt
a microfiber dress	ein Kleid aus Mikrofaser
a pleated dress	ein Faltenkleid
a polka-dot dress	ein gepunktetes Kleid
a strapless dress	ein schulterfreies Kleid

Damenmode

Sweaters

Do you have any long-sleeved sweaters?
  argyle
  bias-cut
  cashmere
  checked
  short-sleeved
  striped
  turtleneck

What color is it?

Do you also have this suit in white?
  eggshell, off-white
  beige
  light tan
  brown
  black
  gray
  blue
  navy blue
  sky blue
  green
  olive green
  orange
  pink
  red

Die Pullover

Haben Sie Pullover mit langen Ärmeln?
  mit Rautenmuster
  mit Schrägschnitt
  aus Kaschmir
  mit Karomuster
  mit kurzen Ärmeln
  mit Streifenmuster
  mit Rollkragen

Welche Farbe?

Haben Sie diesen Anzug auch in weiß?
  altweiß
  beige
  hellbraun
  braun
  schwarz
  grau
  blau
  marineblau
  himmelblau
  grün
  olivgrün
  orange
  pink
  rot

Klingen Sie authentisch!

article of clothing	das Kleidungsstück
black tie (formal dress)	die Abendgarderobe
brand	die Marke
children's clothing	Kinderkleidung [F.]
designer clothing	Designerkleidung [F.]
dress pants	die Anzughose
dress shoes	klassische Herrenschuhe [der Herrenschuh]
dressing room	die Umkleidekabine
evening dress (item of clothing)	das Abendkleid
eyeglass frame	der Brillenrahmen

fitting room	die Anprobe
lining	das Innenfutter
pajama party	die Pyjamaparty
secondhand clothing shop	der Second-Hand-Shop
nonreturnable	vom Umtausch ausgeschlossen
on sale	im Angebot, im Sonderangebot
too big	zu groß
too small	zu klein
to be badly dressed	schlecht angezogen sein
to be dressed up, to be dressed to kill	herausgeputzt sein, sich in Schale geworfen haben
to be in fashion, to be trendy	modisch sein
to be out of fashion	aus der Mode sein
to be well dressed	gut angezogen sein
to get dressed	sich anziehen
to get undressed	sich ausziehen
to go shopping	shoppen gehen
to go window shopping	einen Schaufensterbummel machen
to iron	bügeln
to sell (something) retail	(etwas) im Einzelhandel verkaufen
to sell (something) wholesale	(etwas) en gros verkaufen
to try on	anprobieren
He prefers to dress casually.	Er bevorzugt es, sich locker anzuziehen.
He prefers casual clothing.	Er bevorzugt Freizeitkleidung.
This jersey doesn't fit him well.	Dieses Trikot paßt ihm nicht gut.
These shoes are tight.	Diese Schuhe sind eng.
This blouse matches the skirt.	Diese Bluse paßt zu dem Rock.
This skirt suits you well.	Dieser Rock steht dir gut.
I'd like to return this blouse.	Ich möchte diese Bluse umtauschen.
I need a new heel.	Ich brauche einen neuen Absatz.
What size do you wear? (clothing)	Welche Größe haben Sie?
What size do you wear? (shoes)	Welche Schuhgröße haben Sie?
I wear a 15½ shirt.	Meine Hemdengröße ist 39.
She wears a size 5 shoe.	Sie hat Schuhgröße 38.

Ausdrücke, Sprichwörter und Zitate

Clothes make the man.	Kleider machen Leute.
Clothes don't make the man.	Das Kleid macht keinen Mönch.
The shoemaker's children go barefoot.	Der Schuster hat die schlechtesten Schuhe.

You know a bird by its feathers.

He who buys what he doesn't need ends up selling what he does need.

You can buy fashion, but you can't buy style.

An den Federn erkennt man den Vogel.

Wer kauft, was er nicht braucht, wird verkaufen müssen, was er nötig hat.

Mode kann man kaufen, Stil muß man haben.

„Die Seele dieses Menschen sitzt in seinen Kleidern."
 WILLIAM SHAKESPEARE

„Eine Dame trägt keine Kleider. Sie erlaubt den Kleidern, von ihr getragen zu werden."
 YVES SAINT LAURENT

Übung 8

In German, name five items that you are wearing today.

1. _____
2. _____
3. _____
4. _____
5. _____

In German, name five items that you wore yesterday.

6. _____
7. _____
8. _____
9. _____
10. _____

Übung 9

Choose the word that does not belong in each group.

1. a. Mantel   b. Bomberjacke   c. Perlenkette   d. Trenchcoat

2. a. Ohrenschützer   b. Flip-Flops   c. Hausschuhe   d. Sandalen

3. a. Strumpfhose   b. Manschettenknöpfe   c. Leggings   d. Stulpen

4. a. Bademantel   b. Strohhut   c. Pyjama   d. Nachthemd

5. a. Sakko   b. Parka   c. Cape   d. Ärmel

6. a. Handschuhe   b. Höschen   c. Unterhose   d. Büstenhalter

7. a. Regenmantel   b. Südwester   c. Ohrringe   d. Gummistiefel

8. a. Perlen   b. Rubine   c. Saphire   d. Seide

9. a. Diadem   b. Schal   c. Ring   d. Halsband

10. a. Schlips   b. Fliege   c. Pullover   d. Krawattennadel

Übung 10

Answer each question about buying clothes for your family or friends.

BEISPIEL   Was kaufen Sie für Ihre Frau?

     Ich kaufe einen Diamantring.

1. Was kaufen Sie für Ihren Bruder?

   _____

2. Was kaufen Sie für Ihre Schwester?

   _____

3. Was kaufen Sie für Ihren Mann oder Ihren Freund?

   _____

4. Was kaufen Sie für Ihre Frau oder Ihre Freundin?

   _____

5. Und für Ihren Sohn oder Ihre Tochter?

   _____

6. Und für Frau Otto?

   _____

Übung 11

Unscramble the letters in each item to create a word related to clothing or jewelry.

1. lentam   _____

2. chcksmu   _____

3. ebuls   _____

4. tilfese   _____

5. halsc   _____

6. türgel   _____

7. migkons   _____

8. hhsecu   _____

Übung 12

Give the German words for the articles of clothing, shoes, and accessories you might use in each situation.

1. Es ist kalt.

   _____

   _____

   _____

   _____

2. Ein Abend in der Oper

   _____

   _____

   _____

   _____

3. Im Büro

   _____

   _____

   _____

   _____

4. Es regnet.

   _____

   _____

   _____

   _____

5. Beim Sport

   _____

   _____

   _____

   _____

6. Am Strand

_____

_____

_____

_____

7. Beim Einschlafen

_____

_____

_____

_____

Übung 13

Translate the following sentences into German.

1. *I have to buy a pair of shoes.*

_____

2. *Do you (Sie) have silk ties?*

_____

3. *I'm looking for a black wool suit.*

_____

4. *I prefer a bias-cut skirt.*

_____

5. *I want to buy a navy blue coat with a belt.*

_____

6. *This striped tie doesn't go with the shirt.*

_____

7. *I like the diamond necklace.*

_____

8. *These pants fit him well.*

_____

9. *I like these earrings.*

_____

10. *She's wearing a turtleneck sweater.*

_____

11. *We would like to go window shopping.*

_____

12. *The designer clothing is on sale.*

_____

3

Lebensmittel
Food

In this chapter, you will learn the German words for foods and beverages, and you will be able to talk about your food preferences, whether you're dining in or out. You will learn vocabulary to describe the ingredients in a dish, and how food looks, smells, and tastes.

What do you like?	**Was mögen Sie?**
Fish and seafood	**Fisch und Meeresfrüchte**
I like fish.	Ich mag Fisch. [M.]
anchovies	Anchovis/Anschovis [die Anchovis/Anschovis]
blue trout, poached trout	Forelle blau [F.]
carp	Karpfen [M.]
catfish	Wels [M.]
clams	Venusmuscheln [die Venusmuschel]
coalfish	Seelachs [M.]
cod	Dorsch [M.], Kabeljau [M.]
crab	Krebse [der Krebs]
cuttlefish	Tintenfisch [M.]
eel	Aal [M.]
flounder	Scholle [F.]
gefilte fish	Gefilte Fisch [M.]
haddock	Schellfisch [M.]
hake	Seehecht [M.]
halibut	Heilbutt [M.]
lobster	Hummer [M.]
mackerel	Makrele [F.]
monkfish	Seeteufel [M.]
mussels	Muscheln [die Muschel]
octopus	Pulpo [M.]
oysters	Austern [die Auster]
perch	Barsch [M.], Egli [M.] [SWITZ.]
red snapper	Schnapper [M.]

〉〉〉

redfish	Rotbarsch [M.]
salmon	Lachs [M.]
sardines	Sardinen [die Sardine]
scallops	Jakobsmuscheln [die Jakobsmuschel]
sea bass	Loup de mer [M.]
filet of sea bass	Filet vom Loup de mer [N.]
sea bream	Dorade [F.], Brasse [F.]
seafood	Meeresfrüchte [PL.]
shellfish	Schalentiere [PL.]
shrimp	Garnelen [die Garnele], Krabben [die Krabbe], Crevetten [die Crevette] [SWITZ.]
smoked salmon	Räucherlachs [M.]
sole	Seezunge [F.]
sprats	Sprotten [die Sprotte]
squid	Tintenfisch [M.]
swordfish	Schwertfisch [M.]
trout	Forelle [F.]
tuna	Thunfisch [M.], Thon [M.] [SWITZ.]
turbot	Steinbutt [M.]
wolffish	Steinbeißer [M.]

Meat

Fleisch

I like meat.	Ich mag Fleisch. [N.]
bacon	Speck [M.]
beef	Rindfleisch [N.]
beef stew	Rindereintopf [M.]
casserole	Auflauf [M.]
cold cuts, luncheon meats	Aufschnitt [M.]
ground beef	Hackfleisch [N.], Gehacktes [N.], Faschiertes [N.] [AUS.]
ham	Schinken [M.]
hamburgers	Hamburger [der Hamburger]
hot dogs	Hot Dogs [der Hot Dog]
lamb	Lamm [N.]
lamb chop	Lammkotelett [N.], Lammkarree [N.] [AUS.], Lammkarré [N.] [SWITZ.]

>>>

lamb stew	Lammeintopf [M.]
leg of lamb	Lammkeule [F.]
liver	Leber [F.]
liverwurst, liver sausage	Leberwurst [F.]
meatballs	Frikadellen [die Frikadelle], Bouletten/Buletten [die Boulette/Bulette] [REGIONAL]
pork	Schwein [N.]
pork chops	Schweinekotelett [N.], Schweinskarree [N.] [AUS.], Côtelette [N.] [SWITZ.]
rabbit	Kaninchen [N.]
rabbit stew	Kanincheneintopf [M.]
red meat	rotes Fleisch [N.]
roast beef	Rinderbraten [M.], Beiried [N.] [AUS.]
salami	Salami [F.]
sausage	Wurst [F.]
sirloin	Lende [F.]
steak	Steak [N.]
stew	Eintopf [M.]
veal	Kalb [N.]
veal chops	Kalbskotelett [N.], Kalbskarree [N.] [AUS.], Kalbskarré [N.] [SWITZ.]
venison	Wild [N.]
leg of venison	Hirschkeule [F.]
wild boar goulash	Wildschweingulasch [N.]

Fowl

Geflügel

I like fowl.	Ich mag Geflügel. [N.]
chicken	Hähnchen [N.], Poulet [N.] [SWITZ.]
duck	Ente [F.]
filet of duck	das Entenfilet
duck liver terrine	die Entenleberterrine
roast goose	Gänsebraten [M.]
ostrich	Strauß [M.]
quail	Wachtel [F.]
partridge	Rebhuhn [N.]
turkey	Puter [M.], Truthahn [M.], Pute [F.]

Vegetables

The asparagus is very good.
  The avocado
  The broccoli
  The cabbage
  The cauliflower
  The chard
  The corn
  The eggplant
  The hummus
  The kale
  The parsnip
  The pumpkin
  The rutabaga
  The spinach
  The squash
  The sweet potato
  The watercress
  The yam

The Brussels sprouts are very good.
  The leafy green vegetables
  The leeks

Fruit

After the meal, I'd like to eat fruit.
  apples
  apricots

  bananas
  blackberries
  blueberries
  cantaloupe
  cherries
  clementines

  coconut
  cranberries
  dates
  figs

Gemüse

Der Spargel ist sehr gut.
  Die Avocado
  Der Broccoli/Brokkoli
  Der Kohl, Das Kraut [AUS.]
  Der Blumenkohl, Der Karfiol [AUS.]
  Der Mangold
  Der Mais, Der Kukuruz [AUS.]
  Die Aubergine, Die Melanzani [AUS.]
  Der Hummus
  Der Grünkohl
  Der Pastinak
  Der Kürbis
  Die Steckrübe
  Der Spinat
  Der Kürbis
  Die Süßkartoffel
  Die Brunnenkresse
  Die Jamswurzel

Der Rosenkohl ist sehr gut.
  Das Blattgemüse
  Der Porree

Obst

Nach dem Essen möchte ich Obst essen. [N.]
  Äpfel [der Apfel]
  Aprikosen [die Aprikose], Marillen [die Marille] [AUS.]
  Bananen [die Banane]
  Brombeeren [die Brombeere]
  Heidelbeeren [die Heidelbeere]
  Cantaloup-Melone [F.]
  Kirschen [die Kirsche]
  Clementinen/Klementinen [die Clementine/ Klementine]
  Kokosnuß/Kokosnuss [F.]
  Cranberrys [die Cranberry]
  Datteln [die Dattel]
  Feigen [die Feige]   >>>

grapefruit	Grapefruits [die Grapefruit]
grapes	Weintrauben [die Weintraube]
lemons	Zitronen [die Zitrone]
limes	Limetten [die Limette]
mandarin oranges	Apfelsinen [die Apfelsine]
mangos	Mangos [die Mango]
oranges	Orangen [die Orange]
papaya	Papayas [die Papaya]
peaches	Pfirsiche [der Pfirsich]
pears	Birnen [die Birne]
pineapple	Ananas [F.]
plums	Pflaumen [die Pflaume]
pomegranates	Granatäpfel [der Granatapfel]
prickly pears	Kaktusfeigen [die Kaktusfeige]
prunes	Zwetschen [die Zwetsche], Zwetschken [die Zwetschke] [AUS.], Zwetschgen [die Zwetschge] [SWITZ.]
quinces	Quitten [die Quitte]
raisins	Rosinen [die Rosine], Weinbeeren [die Weinbeere] [AUS., SWITZ.]
raspberries	Himbeeren [die Himbeere]
strawberries	Erdbeeren [die Erdbeere]
tangerines	Mandarinen [die Mandarine]
watermelon	Wassermelone [F.]

Good side dishes

Gute Beilagen

<u>*The rice is very good.*</u>	<u>Der Reis</u> ist sehr gut.
The brown rice	Der Vollkornreis
The stuffing	Die Füllung
<u>*The peas are very good.*</u>	<u>Die Erbsen</u> sind sehr gut. [die Erbse]
The beans	Die Bohnen [die Bohne]
The beets	Die Rüben [die Rübe]
The carrots	Die Karotten [die Karotte], Die Mohrrüben [die Mohrrübe], Die Rüebli [das Rüebli] [SWITZ.]
The chanterelles	Die Pfifferlinge [M.], Die Eierschwammerl [N.] [AUS.]
The chickpeas	Die Kichererbsen [die Kichererbse]
The french fries	Die Pommes Frites [PL.]

>>>

The green beans	Die Brechbohnen [die Brechbohne], Die Fisolen [die Fisole] [AUS.]
The kidney beans	Die Kidneybohnen [die Kidneybohne]
The lentils	Die Linsen [die Linse]
The mushrooms	Die Pilze [der Pilz], Die Schwammerl [das Schwammerl] [REGIONAL, AUS.]
The potatoes	Die Kartoffeln [die Kartoffel], Die Erdäpfel [der Erdapfel] [AUS.]
The turnips	Die Rüben [die Rübe]
The zucchini	Die Zucchini [PL.], Die Zucchetti [PL.] [SWITZ.]

Some English plural nouns correspond to singular mass nouns in German, and vice versa.

<u>*The greens*</u> *are too old.*	<u>Das Suppengrün</u> ist zu alt.
The bread crumbs	Das Paniermehl
The Brussels sprouts	Der Rosenkohl, Der Sprossenkohl [AUS.]
The chives	Der Schnittlauch
The grains	Das Getreide
The leeks	Der Porree, Der Lauch
The pastries	Das Gebäck
The vegetables	Das Gemüse
The leafy green vegetables	Das Blattgemüse
The shortbread biscuits	Das Sandgebäck
<u>*The oatmeal*</u> *is too old.*	<u>Die Haferflocken</u> sind zu alt.
The convenience food	Die Fertiggerichte [*also*: Das Fertiggericht]
The seafood	Die Meeresfrüchte

German has two words for *some*: **etwas** *some* and **einige** *some, a few*. **Etwas** is used with nouns that are not counted: **etwas Kopfsalat** *some lettuce*. **Einige / ein paar** is used with countable nouns: **einige Tomaten** *some tomatoes*.

For the salad

Für den Salat

Can you put <u>some celery</u> in the salad?	Kannst du <u>etwas Sellerie</u> in den Salat geben? [M.]
some croutons	einige Croutons [PL.]
some cucumbers	einige Gurken [die Gurke]

some lettuce	etwas Kopfsalat [M.]
some mushrooms	einige Pilze [der Pilz]
some olives	einige Oliven [die Olive]
some onions	einige Zwiebeln [die Zwiebel]
some parsley	etwas Petersilie [F.], etwas Petersil [M.] [AUS.], etwas Peterli [M.] [SWITZ.]
some peppers	einige Paprikas [die Paprika], einige Peperoni [die Peperoni] [SWITZ.]
some radishes	einige Radieschen [das Radieschen]
some scallions, some green onions	einige Frühlingszwiebeln [die Frühlingszwiebel]
some shallots	einige Schalotten [die Schalotte]
some tomatoes	einige Tomaten [die Tomate]

Seasonings

Gewürze

The food tastes better with salt.	Das Essen schmeckt mit Salz besser. [N.]
basil	Basilikum [N.]
bay leaf	Lorbeer [M.]
capers	Kapern [die Kaper]
cayenne pepper	Cayennepfeffer [M.]
chervil	Kerbel [M.]
chili	Chili [M.]
chives	Schnittlauch [M.]
cinnamon	Zimt [M.]
cloves	Nelken [die Nelke]
cocoa powder	Kakaopulver [N.]
coriander (leaf)	Koriander (Blätter) [M.]
cumin	Kümmel [M.]
curry powder	Curry [M.]
dill	Dill [M.], Dillkraut [N.] [AUS.]
fennel	Fenchel [M.]
garlic	Knoblauch [M.]
ginger	Ingwer [M.]
marjoram	Majoran [M.]
mint	Minze [F.]
mustard	Senf [M.]
(ground) nutmeg	(gemahlter) Muskatnuß / Muskatnuss [F.]
oregano	Oregano [M.]
paprika	Paprika [M.]

pepper	Pfeffer [M.]
rosemary	Rosmarin [M.]
saffron	Safran [M.]
sage	Salbei [M.]
spices	Gewürzen [das Gewürz]
tarragon	Estragon [M.]
thyme	Thymian [M.]
vanilla	Vanille [F.]

Cooking

Das Kochen

<u>Herbs</u> *are important in cooking.*	<u>Kräuter</u> sind wichtig beim Kochen. [das Kraut]
Broths	Brühen [die Brühe]
Chopped mixed herbs	Kräuter der Provence
Condiments	Gewürze [das Gewürz]
Dressings, Seasonings	Dressings [das Dressing]
Fresh ingredients	Frische Zutaten [die Zutat]
Marinades	Marinaden [die Marinade]
Sauces, Gravies	Saucen/Soßen [die Sauce/Soße]
Stocks	Fonds [der Fond]

The verb **hinzugeben** *to add* takes an accusative object.

What the recipe requires

Was das Rezept verlangt

You have to add <u>the sugar</u>.	Du mußt <u>den Zucker</u> hinzugeben.
the baking powder	das Backpulver
the baking soda	das Natron
the bread crumbs	das Paniermehl, die Brotkrumen [PL.]
the butter	die Butter
the cooking oil	das Speiseöl
the corn starch	die Maisstärke
the eggs	die Eier [das Ei]
the egg white	das Eiweiß, das Eiklar [AUS.]
the egg yolk	das Eigelb
the flour	das Mehl
the honey	den Honig
the jam	die Marmelade

the maple syrup	den Ahornsirup
the mayonnaise	die Mayonnaise/Majonäse
the olive oil	das Olivenöl
the vegetable oil	das Pflanzenöl
the vinegar	den Essig
the yeast	die Hefe, den/die Germ [AUS.]

The preposition **gegen** *to, against* takes an accusative object.

Allergies

Allergien

He's allergic to milk.	Er ist gegen Milch allergisch. [F.]
almonds	Mandeln [die Mandel]
dairy products	Milchprodukte [das Milchprodukt]
gluten	Gluten [N.]
grains	Getreide [N.]
nuts	Nüsse [die Nuß/Nuss]
peanut butter	Erdnußbutter/Erdnussbutter [F.]
peanuts	Erdnüsse [die Erdnuß/Erdnuss]
soy	Soja [F./N.]
wheat	Weizen [M.]

The verb **probieren** *to taste* takes an accusative object.

Taste this!

Probier mal!

Do you want to taste the soup?	Möchtest du die Suppe probieren?
the falafel	die/das Falafel
the hummus	den Hummus
the lasagna	die Lasagne
the macaroni salad	den Nudelsalat
the mashed potatoes	das Kartoffelmus, den Kartoffelstock [SWITZ.]
the noodles	die Nudeln [die Nudel]
the pasta	die Pasta
the pizza	die Pizza
the sandwiches	die Sandwichs [das Sandwich]
the spaghetti	die Spaghetti [PL.]

The verb **bestellen** *to order* takes an accusative object.

Dessert	**Nachtisch**
I'm ordering the apple tart for dessert.	Ich bestelle den Apfelkuchen als Nachtisch.
the brownie	den Brownie
the cake	den Kuchen
the candies	die Süßigkeiten
the cheese	den Käse
the cheese plate	den Käseteller
the cheesecake	den Käsekuchen
the chocolate cake	den Schokoladenkuchen
the custard	den Pudding
the donut	den Donut
the flan	den Pudding
the frozen yogurt	den gefrorenen Joghurt
ice cream	Eis [N.], Eiscreme [F.], Glace [F.] [SWITZ.]
the ice cream	das Eis, die Glace [SWITZ.]
chocolate ice cream	Schokoladeneis [N.]
vanilla ice cream	Vanilleeis [N.]
ice cream cones	Eishörnchen [das Eishörnchen]
ice cream pops	Eis am Stiel [N.]
the lemon tart	den Zitronenkuchen
lollipops	Lollies [der Lollie], Lutscher [der Lutscher]
the marzipan	das Marzipan
the meringue	das Baiser
pastries	das Gebäck
the pear tart	den Birnenkuchen
the pears in syrup	die eingelegten Birnen [die Birne]
red fruit dessert	die rote Grütze
sherbet, sorbet	Sorbet [N.], Fruchteis [N.]
the homemade sherbets	die hausgemachten Sorbets
shortbread biscuits	Butterkekse [der Butterkeks]
the sponge cake	den Biskuitkuchen
the strudel	den Strudel
the waffle	die Waffel

This dish is too . . .

This dish is too <u>*salty*</u>.
  bitter
  cold
  hot
  sour
  spicy, hot
  sweet

Bread to eat

This bread is <u>*good*</u>.
  crisp, crunchy
  fresh
  frozen
  scrumptious
  soggy
  stale
  tasteless
  tasty

Meat that you can't eat

This meat is <u>*rotten*</u>.
  rancid
  spoiled

How would you like your steak?

This steak is <u>*well done*</u>.
  too rare
  rare
  medium rare
  perfectly done
  too well done
  too tough
  very tender
  really juicy
  prepared well
  well seasoned

Dieses Gericht ist zu...

Dieses Gericht ist zu <u>salzig</u>.
  bitter
  kalt
  heiß
  sauer
  scharf
  süß

Brot zum essen

Dieses Brot ist <u>gut</u>.
  knusprig
  frisch
  tiefgefroren
  köstlich
  zäh, weich
  altbacken
  fade, fad [AUS.]
  lecker

Fleisch, das man nicht essen kann

Dieses Fleisch ist <u>vergammelt</u>.
  ranzig
  verdorben

Wie möchten Sie Ihr Steak?

Dieses Steak ist <u>ganz durch</u>.
  zu roh
  blau, englisch
  medium
  genau richtig
  zu durch
  zu zäh
  sehr zart
  wirklich saftig
  gut zubereitet
  gut gewürzt

Other dishes

The stew smells good.
   The chicken fricassee
   The chicken soup
   The crepe
   The cutlet
   The fish soup
   The red cabbage
   The sauerkraut

canned food
comfort food, home cooking
convenience food
fast food
fat-free food
low-fat food
low-calorie food
junk food
organic food
reheated leftovers
vegan food
vegetarian food

Different cuisines

Do you like German cuisine?
   American
   Chinese
   French
   Greek
   Indian
   Indonesian
   Italian
   Japanese
   Mexican
   Spanish
   Thai
   Turkish
   Vietnamese

Andere Gerichte

Der Eintopf riecht gut.
   Das Hühnerfrikassee
   Die Hühnersuppe
   Der Crêpe / Krepp
   Das Schnitzel
   Die Fischsuppe
   Der Rotkohl
   Das Sauerkraut

die Konserven [PL.]
die Hausmannskost
die Fertiggerichte [PL.]
das Fastfood
fettfreie Lebensmittel [PL.]
fettreduzierte Lebensmittel [PL.]
kalorienreduzierte Lebensmittel [PL.]
das Junkfood
Biolebensmittel [PL.]
aufgewärmte Reste [PL.]
vegane Küche [F.]
vegetarische Küche [F.]

Verschiedene Küchen

Magst du deutsche Küche?
   amerikanische
   chinesische
   französische
   griechische
   indische
   indonesische
   italienische
   japanische
   mexikanische
   spanische
   thailändische
   türkische
   vietnamesische

The verb **mögen** *to like* takes an accusative object. Its present-tense conjugation is as follows: **ich mag, du magst, er/sie mag, wir mögen, ihr mögt, sie mögen.**

Something to drink	**Etwas zu trinken**
Do you like wine?	Magst du <u>Wein</u>? [M.]
alcoholic beverages	alkoholische Getränke [das Getränk]
aperitifs	Aperitifs [der Aperitif]
beer	Bier [N.]
beer on tap	Bier vom Faß/Fass
brandy	Weinbrand [M.]
carbonated/sparkling/seltzer water	Sprudelwasser [N.]
champagne	Champagner [M.]
cider	Cider [M.], Apfelmost [M.]
coffee	Kaffee [M.]
black coffee	schwarzen Kaffee [M.]
coffee with milk	Milchkaffee [M.]
coffee with cream	Kaffee mit Sahne [M.]
cream	Sahne [F.], Obers [N.] [AUS.], Rahm [M.] [SWITZ.]
digestives (a dinner drink)	Magenbitter [PL.]
espresso	Espresso [M.]
gin	Gin [M.]
gin and tonic	Gin Tonic [M.]
hot chocolate	heiße Schokolade [F.]
juice	Saft [M.]
lemonade	Limonade [F.]
milk	Milch [F.]
milk shake	Milchshake [N.]
mineral water	Mineralwasser [N.]
noncarbonated water	stilles Wasser [N.]
orange juice	Orangensaft [M.]
red wine	Rotwein [M.]
rosé (wine)	Rosé(-wein) [M.]
rum	Rum [M.]
sherry	Sherry [M.]
sparkling wine	Sekt [M.]
table wine	Tafelwein [M.]
tea	Tee [M.]
iced tea	Eistee [M.]

〉〉〉

>>>

tequila	Tequila [M.]
tonic water	Tonicwasser [N.]
vodka	Vodka [M.]
water	Wasser [N.]
whisky and soda	Whisky mit Soda [M.]
white wine	Weißwein [M.]

Snacks

Imbisse

There is a piece of bread in the basket.	Im Korb ist ein Stück Brot. [N.]
a baguette	ein Baguette [N.]
some bread	etwas Brot [N.]
a cracker	ein Keks [M.], ein Kräcker [M.]
crispbread	Knäckebrot [N.]
popcorn	Popcorn [N.]
a bag of potato chips	eine Packung Kartoffelchips
a roll	ein Brötchen [N.]
a matzo wafer	eine Matze, ein Matzen [M.]
a slice of whole grain bread	eine Scheibe Vollkornbrot

The verb **essen** *to eat* takes an accusative object. Its present-tense conjugation is as follows: **ich esse, du ißt/isst, er/sie/es ißt/isst, wir essen, ihr eßt/esst, sie essen.**

For breakfast

Zum Frühstück

For breakfast, we eat cereal.	Zum Frühstück essen wir Müsli. [N.]
bread	Brot [N.]
a cereal bar	einen Müsliriegel
cheese	Käse [M.]
chocolate spread	Nuß-Nougat-Creme/Nuss-Nougat-Krem [F.]
cornflakes	Cornflakes [PL.]
croissants	Croissants [das Croissant]
eggs	Eier [das Ei]
a hard-boiled egg	ein hartgekochtes/hart gekochtes Ei
a soft-boiled egg	ein weichgekochtes/weich gekochtes Ei
fried eggs	Spiegeleier [das Spiegelei]
scrambled eggs	Rühreier [das Rührei], Eierspeise [F.] [AUS.]
dried fruit	Trockenfrüchte [PL.]
French toast	arme Ritter [M.]
ham and eggs	Eier und Speck [das Ei, der Speck]

>>>

jam	Marmelade [F.]
oatmeal	Haferflocken [PL.]
pancakes, griddle cakes	Pfannkuchen [der Pfannkuchen], Palatschinken [die Palatschinke] [AUS.], Crêpes [der Crêpe] [SWITZ.]
pastries	Gebäck [N.]
rolls	Brötchen [das Brötchen], Semmeln [die Semmel] [AUS.], Weggli [das Weggli] [SWITZ.]
sourdough bread	Sauerteigbrot [N.]
toast	Toastbrot [N.]
whole grain bread	Vollkornbrot [N.]
yogurt	Joghurt [M.] [N.: AUS., SWITZ.]

Meals and Mealtimes

Mahlzeiten und Essenszeiten

We're going <u>to have breakfast</u> at home.	Wir werden zu Hause <u>frühstücken</u>.
to have lunch	zu Mittag essen
to have cake and coffee	Kaffee und Kuchen essen
to have a quick snack/sandwich	eine Kleinigkeit essen
to have an afternoon snack	einen Nachmittagsimbiß/Nachmittagsimbiss essen
to have hors-d'oeuvres	Vorspeisen essen
to have dinner	zu Abend essen
to have a drink	ein Gläschen trinken

The courses of a meal

Die Gänge

Let's order <u>the first course</u>.	Laß uns <u>den ersten Gang</u> bestellen.
the main course	den Hauptgang
a side dish	eine Beilage
the specialty of the house	die Spezialität des Hauses
the fixed-price menu	das Menü
dessert	den Nachtisch

The verb **reichen** *to pass* takes an accusative object.

Seeds and nuts

Samen und Nüsse

Please pass me <u>the nuts</u>.	Reich mir bitte <u>die Nüsse</u>. [die Nuß/Nuss]
the almonds	die Mandeln [die Mandel]
the Brazil nuts	die Paranüsse [die Paranuß/Paranuss]

the cashews	die Cashewnüsse [die Cashewnuß/Cashewnuss]
the chestnuts	die Kastanien [die Kastanie]
the dates	die Datteln [die Dattel]
the dried apricot strips	die getrockneten Aprikosen [die Aprikose]
the dried figs	die getrockneten Feigen [die Feige]
the dried fruit	die Trockenfrüchte [PL.]
the flax seeds	die Leinsamen [der Leinsame]
the hazelnuts, the filberts	die Haselnüsse [die Haselnuß/Haselnuss]
the Macadamia nuts	die Macadamianüsse [die Macadamianuß/ Macadamianuss]
the pecans	die Pecannüsse [die Pecannuß/Pecannuss]
the pine nuts	die Pinienkerne [der Pinienkern]
the pistachios	die Pistazien [die Pistazie]
the poppy seeds	die Mohnsamen [der Mohnsame]
the prunes	die Backpflaumen [die Backpflaume]
the pumpkin seeds	die Kürbiskerne [der Kürbiskern]
the raisins	die Rosinen [die Rosine], Weinbeeren [die Weinbeere] [AUS., SWITZ.]
the seeds	die Samen [der Same]
the sesame seeds	die Sesamsamen [der Sesamsame]
the sunflower seeds	die Sonnenblumenkerne [der Sonnenblumenkern]
the walnuts	die Walnüsse [die Walnuß/Walnuss], die Baumnüsse [die Baumnuß/Baumnuss] [SWITZ.]

All of the verbs in the following section, including **backen** *to bake*, **grillen** *to grill*, and **kochen** *to cook*, take an accusative object.

Food preparation

We have to boil the water.
  to bake the donuts
  to barbecue the chicken legs
  to baste the turkey
  to beat the eggs
  to blend the ingredients
  to bread the slices of eggplant
  to brown the onions
  to chop the onions
  to cook the meat

Speisenzubereitung

Wir müssen das Wasser kochen.
  die Donuts backen
  die Hähnchenschenkel grillen
  den Truthahn begießen
  die Eier schlagen
  die Zutaten vermischen
  die Auberginenscheiben panieren
  die Zwiebeln anbraten
  die Zwiebeln kleinhacken/klein hacken
  das Fleisch kochen

>>>

to cook the fish over low heat	den Fisch bei kleiner Hitze kochen
to cook the pancakes over high heat	die Pfannkuchen bei großer Hitze backen
to deep fry the potatoes	die Kartoffeln frittieren
to defrost the chopped steak	das Hackfleisch auftauen
to dice the mushrooms	die Pilze würfeln
to freeze the leftovers	die Reste einfrieren
to fry the eggs	die Eier braten
to grill the sausages	die Würstchen grillen
to grind the meat	das Fleisch wolfen, das Fleisch faschieren [AUS.]
to knead the dough	den Teig kneten
to look at the cookbook	ins Kochbuch schauen
to marinate the olives	die Oliven marinieren
to mash the banana	die Bananen zerdrücken
to mix the vegetables in the blender	das Gemüse im Mixer vermischen
to peel the potatoes	die Kartoffeln schälen
to pickle the vegetables	das Gemüse einlegen
to poach the eggs	die Eier pochieren
to prepare coffee and cake	Kaffee und Kuchen zubereiten
to puree the peaches	die Pfirsiche pürieren
to put pepper in the broth	die Brühe pfeffern
to reduce the syrup, to boil down the syrup	den Sirup einkochen
to roast the leg of lamb	die Lammkeule braten
to salt the artichokes	die Artischocken salzen
to sauté the potatoes	die Kartoffeln sautieren
to season the dish	das Gericht würzen
to simmer the sauce	die Sauce/Soße köcheln lassen
to slice the gingerbread	den Lebkuchen schneiden
to smoke the meat	das Fleisch räuchern
to spice up the sauce	die Sauce/Soße aufpeppen
to steam the vegetables	das Gemüse dampfgaren
to stew the beef	das Rindfleisch schmoren
to stir the coffee	den Kaffee umrühren
to strain the endives	den Endiviensalat schleudern
to stuff the cabbage leaves	die Kohlblätter füllen
to toast the bread	das Brot toasten
to warm up the soup	die Suppe aufwärmen
to wash the fruit	das Obst waschen
to whip the cream	die Sahne schlagen

Special ingredients

The recipe calls for boneless sardines.

  boneless chicken breasts
  boneless turkey
  pitted cherries
  pitted dates
  pitted olives
  pitted peaches
  pitted prunes

Some popular drinks, dishes, and foods

advocaat (a Dutch alcoholic beverage similar to eggnog)
apple spritzer
apple strudel
Bavarian veal sausage
beef roulade
Black Forest cake
blood sausage
cabbage rolls
chicken roasted on the spit
cola, soda pop
curd cheese
curried sausage
Doner kebab
dumplings
fish cakes
fondue
goulash
grilled sausage
hash browns, potato pancakes, rosti

home fries
hot wine punch
knuckle of pork (cooked), ham hock

Besondere Zutaten

Das Rezept verlangt <u>Sardinen ohne Gräten</u>.
  [die Sardine]
  Hühnerbrust ohne Knochen [die Hühnerbrust]
  Truthahn ohne Knochen [der Truthahn]
  Kirschen ohne Steine [die Kirsche]
  Datteln ohne Kerne [die Dattel]
  Oliven ohne Steine [die Olive]
  Pfirsiche ohne Kerne [der Pfirsich]
  Backpflaumen ohne Kerne [die Backpflaume]

Einige beliebte Getränke, Gerichte und Speisen

der Eierlikör

die Apfelschorle, der Gespritzter [AUS., SWITZ.]
der Apfelstrudel
die Weißwurst
die Rinderroulade
die Schwarzwälder Kirschtorte
die Blutwurst, die Blunzen [AUS.]
die Kohlrouladen
das Brathähnchen, das Brathendl [AUS.]
der/die/das Spezi
der Quark, der Topfen [AUS.]
die Currywurst
der Döner
die Knödel [der Knödel]
die Fischfrikadellen [die Fischfrikadelle]
die/das Fondue
das Gulasch
die Rostbratwurst
die Kartoffelpuffer [PL.], die Rösti [PL.], die Röschti [PL.] [SWITZ.]

die Bratkartoffeln [die Bratkartoffel]
der Glühwein
das Eisbein

knuckle of pork (grilled)	die Schweinshaxe
lard	das Schmalz
lobscouse (lamb/beef stew)	das Labskaus
malt beer	das Malzbier
marinated beef	der Sauerbraten
meat loaf	der Leberkäse, der Leberkäs [AUS.], der Fleischkäse [SWITZ.]
mustard pickles	die Senfgurken [die Senfgurke]
onion tart	der Zwiebelkuchen
pea soup	die Erbsensuppe
Pilsner (beer)	das Pils
potato salad	der Kartoffelsalat
pretzel	die Brezel, die Bretzel [SWITZ.]
pumpernickel	der Pumpernickel
pyramid cake	der Baumkuchen
red fruit dessert	die rote Grütze
roast pork	der Schweinebraten, der Schweinsbraten [AUS.]
salted and smoked pork chop	das Kasseler, das Selchkarree [AUS.], geräuchtes Rippli [SWITZ.]
stollen	der Stollen
streusel cake	der Streuselkuchen
stuffed pig's stomach	der Saumagen
thimble dumplings	die Spätzle, die Spätzli [SWITZ.]
Viennese schnitzel	das Wiener Schnitzel
wheat beer	das Weißbier, das Hefeweizen

Outside Berlin, *a bismarck* (a donut with sugar coating and filled with jam) is **ein Berliner** [M.]. In Berlin, *a bismarck* is **ein Pfannkuchen** [M.], which means *pancake* outside Berlin. If you want a pancake in Berlin, ask for **ein Eierkuchen** [M.]. If you ask for **ein Pfannkuchen**, you'll get a bismarck, and if you ask for **ein Berliner**, they'll tell you off!

Klingen Sie authentisch!

take-out food	Essen zum Mitnehmen
to clear the table	den Tisch abdecken
to go food shopping	einkaufen
to go to the table	sich zu Tisch setzen
to have food allergies	Lebensmittel-Allergien haben
to set the table	den Tisch decken, tischen [SWITZ.]
to wash the dishes	abwaschen
I don't drink tap water.	Ich trinke kein Leitungswasser., Ich trinke kein Hahnenwasser. [SWITZ.]
Is the meat halal?	Ist das Fleisch halal?
Is the meat kosher?	Ist das Fleisch koscher?
Enjoy your meal!	Guten Appetit!

Ausdrücke, Sprichwörter und Zitate

to drink like a fish	trinken wie ein Loch
to eat like a bird	essen wie ein Spatz
to eat like a horse	essen wie ein Scheunendrescher
It's finger-licking good.	Das ist zum Reinlegen.
It's mouth-watering.	Mir läuft das Wasser im Munde zusammen.
Half a loaf is better than none.	Besser ein halbes Ei als gar keins.
Hunger is the best sauce.	Hunger ist der beste Koch.
Life is too short to drink bad wine.	Das Leben ist zu kurz für schlechten Wein.
Man does not live by bread alone.	Der Mensch lebt nicht vom Brot allein.
You are what you eat.	Der Mensch ist, was er ißt.

„Alkohol löst Zungen, aber keine Probleme."
    WERNER MITSCH

„Wir leben nicht um zu essen, sondern wir essen um zu leben."
    SOKRATES

Übung 14

Group the following words into the seven categories given.

Kartoffel	Dorsch	Truthahn	Strauß	Orange
Rübe	Wildschwein	Wasser	Knoblauch	Apfel
Magenbitter	Rind	Pflaume	Zitrone	Lamm
Karpfen	Bier	Nelken	Wachtel	Wild
Sauerkraut	Hähnchen	Karotte	Barsch	Ente
Seelachs	Thymian	Kaffee	Kaninchen	Aprikose
Rosé	Kerbel	Zimt	Broccoli	Forelle

Obst

_____

_____

_____

_____

_____

Gemüse

_____

_____

_____

_____

_____

Fleisch

_____

_____

_____

_____

_____

Fisch

_____

_____

_____

_____

_____

Geflügel

_____

_____

_____

_____

_____

Gewürze

_____

_____

_____

_____

_____

Getränke

_____

_____

_____

_____

_____

Übung 15

Choose the verb that completes each phrase about food preparation.

1. die Eier _____ (rösten / pochieren)

2. die Kartoffeln _____ (wolfen / schälen)

3. das Brot _____ (schneiden / räuchern)

4. die Lammkeule _____ (braten / pürieren)

5. die Sahne _____ (toasten / schlagen)

Übung 16

1. Name five vegetables that are eaten raw.

   _____

   _____

   _____

   _____

   _____

2. Name five vegetables that are cooked before eating.

   _____

   _____

   _____

   _____

   _____

Übung 17

Name five fruits that are sold in your area in the summer.

_____

_____

_____

_____

_____

Übung 18

Choose the word that does not belong in each group.

1. a. Makrele   b. Hummer   c. Dorade   d. Gurken

2. a. Hamburger   b. Muscheln   c. Steak   d. Hackfleisch

3. a. Salz   b. Pfeffer   c. Mehl   d. Koriander

4. a. Zwiebeln   b. Rosenkohl   c. Porree   d. Datteln

5. a. Baguette   b. Donut   c. Käsekuchen   d. Pfannkuchen

6. a. Ente   b. Gans   c. Hähnchen   d. Dorsch

7. a. Leberwurst   b. Kartoffelchips c. Popcorn   d. Kekse

8. a. Mandeln   b. Kürbis   c. Kastanien   d. Erdnüsse

9. a. Schwein   b. Kaninchen   c. Wild   d. Berliner

10. a. probieren   b. pochieren   c. braten   d. schmoren

Übung 19

Translate the following sentences into German.

1. *What are we having for breakfast?*

2. *Do you (du) like scallops?*

3. *What are we going to eat tonight, fish or fowl?*

4. *There is a French restaurant around the corner.*

5. *This meat is rotten.*

6. *The soup is too salty.*

7. *Can you (du) peel the potatoes and fry the eggs?*

8. *She eats only vegan food.*

9. *Let's try the specialty of the house!*

10. *People eat more and more convenience food.*

11. *I really like Vietnamese cuisine.*

12. *Would you (du) like a glass of white wine?*

4

Haus und Heim
House and home

This chapter presents essential vocabulary to describe your house—the rooms, furniture, and appliances. You'll learn the vocabulary needed to talk about repairs and home improvements. You will also learn the terms for household chores and will be able to tell someone to do them.

The rooms	Die Zimmer
The living room is on the right.	Das Wohnzimmer ist rechts.
The den, The study, The office	Das Büro
The dining room	Das Eßzimmer / Esszimmer
The kitchen	Die Küche
The guest room is on the left.	Das Gästezimmer ist links.
The family room	Das Wohnzimmer
The hall, The corridor	Der Flur, Der Korridor
The bedroom	Das Schlafzimmer
The TV room	Das Fernsehzimmer
The house has a garden.	Das Haus hat einen Garten.
twelve rooms	zwölf Zimmer [das Zimmer]
six bedrooms	sechs Schlafzimmer [das Schlafzimmer]
five bathrooms	fünf Badezimmer [das Badezimmer]
an attic	einen Dachboden, einen Estrich [SWITZ.]
a basement	einen Keller
a greenhouse	ein Gewächshaus
a lawn	ein Grundstück
a pool	ein Schwimmbecken
a staircase	ein Treppenhaus
two toilets	zwei Toiletten [die Toilette]
a two-car garage	eine Doppelgarage

Neuter articles and adjectives have the same form in the nominative and accusative. In the following section, a noun phrase consists of the indefinite article **ein** + an adjective ending in **-es** + a neuter noun.

To describe the house	**Das Haus beschreiben**
We're looking for a <u>big</u> house.	Wir suchen ein <u>großes</u> Haus.
light	helles
modern	modernes
new	neues
small	kleines

We're looking for an <u>old</u> house.	Wir suchen ein <u>altes</u> Haus.
airy, open	offenes
environmentally friendly	ökologisches

It's a <u>comfortable</u> house.	Das ist ein <u>komfortables</u> Haus.
calm	ruhiges
cozy	gemütliches
delightful	reizendes
peaceful	friedliches
pleasant	angenehmes
warm	warmes
welcoming	einladendes

In certain contexts, the preposition **aus** means *made of.*

What is the house made of?	**Aus was ist das Haus?**
That house is made of <u>brick</u>.	Dieses Haus ist aus <u>Backsteinen</u>. [der Backstein]
concrete, cement	Beton [M.]
stone	Stein [M.]
wood	Holz [N.]

The verb **anschauen** *to look at* takes an accusative object.

In the kitchen

Look at the kitchen appliances.
  the blender, the mixer
  the bottle opener
  the butter dish
  the cabinet
  the cans

  the cocktail shaker
  the coffee grinder
  the coffee pot
  the corkscrew
  the dishwasher
  the food processor
  the freezer
  the frying pan
  the jars
  the kitchen towel
  the kitchen utensils
  the microwave oven
  the pantry
  the peeler
  the pepper shaker
  the pot, the saucepan
  the refrigerator
  the saltshaker
  the sink
  the stove, the range
    the electric range
    the gas range
  the teapot

Other appliances

The radio isn't working.
  The air conditioning
  The central heating
  The dryer
  The humidifier

In der Küche

Schau dir die Küchengeräte an. [das Küchengerät]
  den Mixer
  den Flaschenöffner
  die Butterdose
  den Schrank
  die Dosen [die Dose], die Konservendosen
    [die Konservendose]
  den Cocktail-Shaker
  die Kaffeemühle
  den Kaffeekocher
  den Korkenzieher
  die Spülmaschine
  die Küchenmaschine
  den Tiefkühlschrank
  die Bratpfanne
  die Einmachgläser [das Einmachglas]
  das Küchentuch
  die Küchenutensilien [das Küchenutensil]
  die Mikrowelle
  die Speisekammer, die Speis [AUS.]
  den Schäler
  den Pfefferstreuer
  den Kochtopf, die Pfanne [SWITZ.]
  den Kühlschrank
  den Salzstreuer
  die Spüle, den Schüttstein [SWITZ.]
  den Herd
    den Elektroherd
    den Gasherd
  die Teekanne

Übrige Geräte

Das Radio geht nicht.
  Die Klimaanlage
  Die Zentralheizung
  Der Wäschetrockner, Der Tumbler [SWITZ.]
  Der Raumbefeuchter   ❯❯

The vacuum cleaner	Der Staubsauger
The washing machine	Die Waschmaschine

In the living room

Im Wohnzimmer

I like this set of furniture a lot.	Diese Möbelgarnitur gefällt mir sehr.
this armchair, this easy chair	Dieser Sessel, Dieser Fauteuil [AUS.]
this bookcase	Dieses Bücherregal
this carpet(ing)	Dieser Teppich
this coffee table	Dieser Kaffeetisch
this couch, this sofa	Diese Couch, dieses Sofa
this lamp	Diese Lampe
this painting	Dieses Gemälde
this rug	Dieser Vorleger
this stereo	Diese Anlage
this television	Dieser Fernseher
I like these curtains/drapes a lot.	Diese Vorhänge gefallen mir sehr.

In the dining room

Im Eßzimmer / Esszimmer

We still have to buy a table.	Wir müssen noch einen Tisch kaufen.
a buffet, a sideboard	einen Serviertisch
some chairs	einige Stühle [der Stuhl], einige Sessel [der Sessel] [AUS.]
a chandelier	einen Kronleuchter, einen Luster [AUS.]
a china cabinet, a display cabinet	eine Vitrine
a wine rack	ein Weinregal

To express the English verb *to put* in German, use **legen** for objects that lie on the table and **stellen** for objects that stand.

To set the table

Den Tisch decken

Put the cups on the table.	Stell' die Tassen auf den Tisch. [die Tasse]
the glasses	die Gläser [das Glas]
the plates	die Teller [der Teller]
the saucers	die Unterteller [der Unterteller]
the serving dish	die Schale
the soup bowls	die Suppenteller [der Suppenteller]
the wine glasses, the goblets	die Weingläser [das Weinglas]

Put *the forks* on the table.	Leg' die Gabeln auf den Tisch. [die Gabel]
the knives	die Messer [das Messer]
the napkins	die Servietten [die Serviette]
the placemats	die Tischsets [das Tischset]
the tablecloth	die Tischdecke
the tablespoons	die Eßlöffel/Esslöffel [der Eßlöffel/Esslöffel]
the teaspoons	die Teelöffel [der Teelöffel]

In the bedroom
Im Schlafzimmer

There's *a bed*.	Dort gibt es ein Bett.
bed linen	Bettwäsche, Leintücher [das Leintuch] [AUS., SWITZ.]
a bedside rug	einen Bettvorleger
a bedspread	eine Tagesdecke
a blanket	eine Decke
a box spring, a bed base	ein Bettgestell
a chest of drawers	eine Kommode
a closet	einen Wandschrank
a double bed	ein Doppelbett
a mattress	eine Matratze
a night table	einen Nachttisch
a pillow	ein Kissen
a pillow case	einen Kissenbezug

There are *hangers*.	Dort gibt es Kleiderbügel. [der Kleiderbügel]
sheets	Bettlaken [das Bettlaken], Leintücher [das Leintuch] [AUS., SWITZ.]

In the bathroom
Im Badezimmer

There's *a bathtub*.	Dort gibt es eine Badewanne.
a bar of soap	ein Stück Seife
a bath mat	eine Badematte
a bath towel	ein Badetuch
a bidet	ein Bidet
a hand towel	ein Handtuch
a medicine chest	ein Arzneischränkchen
a mirror	einen Spiegel
a plunger	einen Pümpel, eine Saugglocke
a scale	eine Waage
shaving cream	Rasiercreme/Rasierkrem [F.]

〉〉〉

a shower	eine Dusche
a sink	ein Waschbecken, ein Lavabo [SWITZ.]
soap	Seife [F.]
a sponge	einen Schwamm
a toilet	eine Toilette
toilet paper	Toilettenpapier [N.]
a toothbrush	eine Zahnbürste
toothpaste	Zahnpasta [F.], Zahncreme/Zahnkrem [F.]
a towel	ein Handtuch
a washcloth	einen Waschlappen
a wastepaper basket	einen Papierkorb

Do-it-yourself projects

Heimwerken

battery	die Batterie
broom	der Besen
brush	die Bürste
ceiling	die Zimmerdecke, der Plafond [SWITZ.]
door	die Tür
faucet	der Wasserhahn
flashlight	die Taschenlampe
fuse	die Sicherung
hammer	der Hammer
light	das Licht
light switch	der Lichtschalter
lightbulb	die Glühbirne
nail	der Nagel
pipe	die Rohrleitung
pliers	die Zange [SG.]
rain	der Abfluß/Abfluss
saw	die Säge
screw	die Schraube
screwdriver	der Schraubenzieher
smoke detector	der Rauchmelder
socket, plug	die Steckdose
tools	das Werkzeug [SG.]
wall	die Wand
window	das Fenster
wrench	der Schraubenschlüssel

to flush the toilet	spülen
to paint	streichen

Problems

Probleme

Oh, my goodness! There's smoke.	Oh Gott! Dort ist Rauch. [M.]
a fire	ein Feuer [N.]
a hole	ein Loch [N.]
a leak	ein Leck [N.]

The preposition **in** takes a dative object when it expresses location.

Where do they live?

Wo wohnen sie?

They live in a house.	Sie leben in einem Haus. [N.]
an apartment	einer Wohnung
an apartment building	einem Mietshaus [N.]
a retirement community	einer Rentnersiedlung

Household chores

Hausarbeit

It's my turn to cook.	Ich bin dran mit kochen.
to do the gardening	die Gartenarbeit verrichten
to do the housework	die Hausarbeit erledigen
to do the laundry	Wäsche waschen
to iron	bügeln
to make the bed	Betten machen
to mow the lawn	Rasen mähen
to recycle the newspapers	Altpapier wegbringen
to sweep	fegen, wischen [SWITZ.]
to take out the garbage	Müll rausbringen
to vacuum	staubsaugen, Staub saugen
to water the flowers	Blumen gießen

Klingen Sie authentisch!

furnishings, furniture	Möbel [das Möbel *piece of furniture*]
handyman	der Heimwerker
household goods/items/furniture	der Hausrat
landlady	die Hauswirtin
landlord	der Hausbesitzer
mortgage	die Hypothek

real estate agency	das Immobilienagentur
roommate, apartment mate	der Mitbewohner / die Mitbewohnerin
tenant	der Mieter

to fix up the kitchen	die Küche renovieren
to have a housewarming party	eine Einweihungsfeier machen
to live next door to someone	Haus an Haus mit jemandem wohnen
to make oneself at home	tun, als ob man zuhause wäre
to move, to relocate	umziehen, zügeln [SWITZ.]
to rent an apartment	eine Wohnung mieten
to show someone around the house	jemanden durch das Haus führen

| The rent is low/reasonable/high. | Die Miete ist niedrig/angemessen/hoch., Der Mietzins ist niedrig/angemessen/hoch. [AUS., SWITZ.] |

The lightbulb blew.	Die Glühbirne ist kaputt.
The light has gone out.	Das Licht ist ausgegangen.
The toilet is clogged.	Die Toilette ist verstopft.
We have to unclog the sink.	Wir müssen die Verstopfung beseitigen.
Where is the janitor?	Wo ist der Hausmeister?, Wo ist der Abwart? [SWITZ.]
They're always fighting in that house.	Da drüben streiten sie andauernd.

Ausdrücke, Sprichwörter und Zitate

Home sweet home!	Trautes Heim, Glück allein.
My home is my castle.	Daheim bin ich König.
Men build a house, women make it a home.	Männer bauen ein Haus, Frauen schaffen ein Zuhause.
A house without children is like a church without music.	Ein Haus ohne Kinder ist wie eine Kirche ohne Orgel.

„Mit dem Liebsten kann man auch in der kleinsten Hütte glücklich sein."
   LEO TOLSTOJ

„Gerade die großen Häuser sind voll mit Sklaven."
   JUVENAL

„Nicht da ist man daheim, wo man seinen Wohnsitz hat, sondern wo man verstanden wird."
   CHRISTIAN MORGENSTERN

„Man ist glücklich verheiratet, wenn man lieber heimkommt als fortgeht."
   HEINZ RÜHMANN

„Der Friede beginnt im eigenen Haus."
   KARL JASPERS

Übung 20

Match each place in the first column with the activity in the second column that takes place there.

1. _____	Küche	a.	lesen
2. _____	Schlafzimmer	b.	Blumen gießen
3. _____	Schwimmbecken	c.	schlafen
4. _____	Fernsehzimmer	d.	sich waschen
5. _____	Bibliothek	e.	arbeiten
6. _____	Esszimmer	f.	den Tisch decken
7. _____	Büro	g.	mähen
8. _____	Badezimmer	h.	Fernsehen gucken
9. _____	Rasen	i.	schwimmen
10. _____	Garten	j.	kochen

Übung 21

Choose the word or phrase that does not belong in each group.

	a.	b.	c.	d.
1.	Wohnzimmer	Kommode	Küche	Korridor
2.	fegen	bügeln	Blumen gießen	telefonieren
3.	Holz	Hammer	Schraubenzieher	Zange
4.	Bettgestell	Decke	Wasserhahn	Laken
5.	Backstein	Miete	Stein	Beton
6.	Laken	Matratze	Kissenbezug	Einmachglas
7.	Sessel	Löffel	Messer	Gabeln
8.	Spiegel	Waschbecken	Briefkasten	Seife
9.	Dusche	Toilette	Bidet	Kronleuchter
10.	Bücherregal	Pümpel	Sessel	Kaffeetisch

Übung 22

Complete each German phrase so that it expresses the meaning of the English phrase.

1. *to do laundry* Wäsche _____

2. *to make the bed* Betten _____

3. *to mow the lawn* den _____ mähen

4. *to recycle the newspapers*   das _____ wegbringen

5. *to water the flowers*   die _____ gießen

6. *to vacuum*   _____ saugen

7. *to take out the garbage*   den _____ rausbringen

8. *to fix up the kitchen*   die _____ renovieren

9. *to rent an apartment*   eine _____ mieten

10. *to unclog the sink*   die _____ beseitigen

Übung 23

In German, name the items you might use or the things you might do in each situation.

1. Küchengeräte

_____

_____

_____

_____

2. Wohnzimmermöbel

_____

_____

_____

_____

3. Den Tisch decken

_____

_____

_____

_____

4. Werkzeug

_____

_____

_____

_____

5. Hausarbeit

_____

_____

_____

_____

Übung 24

What is necessary in each case?

BEISPIEL   Um Kaffee zu kochen, braucht man _einen Kaffeekocher_.

1. Um Bratwurst zu braten, braucht man _____.

2. Um sich die Hände abzutrocknen, braucht man _____.

3. Damit die Pflanzen im Winter nicht sterben, braucht man _____.

4. Um einen Nagel in die Wand zu schlagen, braucht man _____.

5. Um die Wäsche zu waschen, braucht man _____.

6. Um die Verstopfung zu beseitigen, braucht man _____.

7. Um den Boden zu fegen, braucht man _____.

8. Um eine Schraube zu lösen, braucht man _____.

Übung 25

Translate the following sentences into German.

1. _There is a leak in the attic._

_____

2. _I need a hammer and a screwdriver._

_____

3. _Your (ihr) house is welcoming and quiet._

_____

4. _There's a bar of soap in the medicine chest._

_____

5. _The cans are in the cabinet._

_____

6. The light went out. I think the bulb burned out.

   _____

7. That house is made of stone.

   _____

8. The bottle opener is on the wine rack.

   _____

9. The bedroom is on the right.

   _____

10. I still have to buy a chest of drawers.

    _____

5

Das Büro, der Rechner, die Geschäfte und die Wirtschaft
The office, the computer, business, and the economy

This chapter presents vocabulary to describe the office, the functions of the computer, the running of a business, and elements of the economy. You will also learn vocabulary that will enable you to talk about finances, the stock exchange, and marketing, as well as the people who work in these fields.

At the office	**Im Büro**
answering machine	der Anrufbeantworter
appointment book	der Terminkalender
calendar	der Kalender
cell phone	das Mobiltelefon, das Handy, das Natel [SWITZ.]
cubicle	der Arbeitsplatz
desk	der Schreibtisch
electronic device	das elektronische Gerät
fax machine	das Faxgerät
file cabinet	der Aktenschrank
landline	der Festnetzanschluß / Festnetzanschluss
laptop	der Laptop
notebook	das Notebook
paper	das Papier
paperwork	die Büroarbeit, der Papierkram
pen	der Stift
pencil	der Bleistift
phone number	die Telefonnummer
photocopier	das Kopiergerät
scanner	der Scanner
stapler	der Tacker, die Klammerlmaschine [AUS.], der Bostitch [SWITZ.]
telecommuting	die Telearbeit
workstation	der Arbeitsplatz

The telephone

app	die App
area code	die Ortsvorwahl
cell phone display	der Handy-Bildschirm
country code	die Ländervorwahl
dial tone	das Freizeichen
handset	das Mobilteil
keypad	der Tastenwahlblock
ring tone	der Klingelton
speed dialing	die Kurzwahl
telephone call	der Anruf
wrong number	die falsche Nummer
to dial	wählen
to hang up	auflegen
to make a phone call	anrufen, einen Anruf machen
to pick up the receiver, to take the call	abheben, den Anruf entgegennehmen
It's busy.	Es ist besetzt.
The telephone is out of order.	Das Telefon ist außer Betrieb.
Who's calling?	Wer ist am Apparat?
We got cut off.	Wir wurden unterbrochen.

Das Telefon

The computer

attachment	der Anhang
data processing	die Datenverarbeitung
disk	die Disk, die Disc
e-mail	die E-Mail
an e-mail	eine E-Mail
file	die Datei
folder	der Ordner
Internet	das Internet
Internet user	der Nutzer, der User
junk mail	die unerwünschte Post, die Junkmail
keyboard	die Tastatur
laptop	der Laptop
link	der Link
memory card	die Speicherkarte
online	online

Der Rechner

operating system (OS)	das Betriebssystem
printer	der Drucker
screen	der Bildschirm
search engine	die Suchmaschine
software	die Software
toolbar	die Toolbar
website	die Internetseite
word processing	die Textverarbeitung

Verbs for the computer / Verben rund um den Rechner

to click (on)	klicken (auf)
to copy	kopieren
to create a file	eine Datei erstellen
to cut and paste	ausschneiden und einfügen
to download	runterladen
to drag a file	eine Datei verschieben
to drag and drop	ziehen und ablegen
to go back	rückgängig machen
to install a program	ein Programm installieren
to keep in touch through social media	über soziale Medien in Kontakt bleiben
to log in/on	sich einloggen
to log off/out	sich ausloggen
to make a backup	eine Sicherung erstellen, ein Backup machen, sichern
to save the file	die Datei speichern
to surf the web/Internet	im Internet surfen
to upload	hochladen

Who is attending the meeting? / Wer ist bei dem Meeting anwesend?

The boss is attending the meeting.	Der Chef ist anwesend.
The analyst	Der Analyst
The CEO (chief executive officer)	Der Geschäftsführer
The CFO (chief financial officer)	Der Finanzchef
The consultant	Der Berater
The financial advisor	Der Finanzratgeber
The project manager	Der Projektmanager
The receptionist	Die Empfangsdame
The secretary	Der Sekretär / Die Sekretärin
The web designer	Der Webdesigner

Who has just left?

The employees have just left.

    executives

    experts
    office workers

Banking

bank
bank account
bank card
bank statement
bill (currency)
bill (to pay)
check
checkbook
checking account
e-banking
interest
loan
money
savings account

to deposit
to transfer money
to withdraw money
to write a check

Business

board of directors
branch, branch office
business
businessman
businesswoman
company
consulting
consumer

Wer ist eben gegangen?

Die Angestellten sind eben gegangen.
    [der/die Angestellte]
    Geschäftsführer [der Geschäftsführer /
        die Geschäftsführerin]
    Experten [der Experte] / Expertinnen [die Expertin]
    Büroangestellten [der/die Büroangestellte]

Bankwesen

die Bank
das Bankkonto
die Bankkarte
der Kontoauszug
die Banknote, der Geldschein
die Rechnung
der Scheck, der Check [SWITZ.]
das Scheckbuch, das Scheckheft
das Girokonto, das Gehaltskonto
das E-Banking
die Zinsen [USUALLY PL.]
das Darlehen, der Kredit
das Geld
das Sparkonto

einzahlen
Geld überweisen
Geld abheben
einen Scheck ausstellen

Geschäfte

der Aufsichtsrat, das Direktorium
die Filiale, der Ableger [SWITZ.]
das Unternehmen, die Unternehmung [SWITZ.]
der Geschäftsmann
die Geschäftsfrau
die Firma
die Unternehmensberatung
der Verbraucher

customer	der Kunde
debt	die Schulden [USUALLY PL.]
development	die Entwicklung
dividend	die Dividende
e-commerce	der E-Commerce
earnings	die Einnahmen [PL.]
growth	das Wachstum
management	das Management
merger	die Fusionierung
personnel	das Personal
price	der Preis
profit and loss	Gewinn und Verlust
retail	der Einzelhandel, der Detailhandel [SWITZ.]
salary	das Gehalt, das Salär [SWITZ.]
taxes	Steuern [die Steuer]
wholesale	der Großhandel
to draft a budget, to draw up a budget	budgetieren, einen Haushalt aufstellen
to fire	entlassen
to go bankrupt, to declare bankruptcy	Bankrott machen, Konkurs anmelden
to grow	wachsen
to hire	einstellen
to make a business plan	einen Geschäftsplan machen
to produce	herstellen

Marketing — Vermarktung

ad, advertisement	die Anzeige
advertising	die Werbung, die Reklame
advertising agency	die Werbeagentur
brand	die Marke
cost	die Kosten [PL.]
product	das Produkt
sample	das Arbeitsmuster
to launch an ad campaign	eine Werbekampagne starten, eine Werbekampagne lancieren
to promote something	für etwas werben
to test	testen

Finance and the stock exchange

bear market, falling market	der Bärenmarkt, die fallende Kurse [PL.]
bond	das Anleihepapier
broker	der Börsenmakler
bull market, rising market	der Bullenmarkt, die steigende Kurse [PL.]
diversified portfolio	das gestreute Depot
dividend	die Dividende
investment	das Investment, die Anlage
investor	der Investor, der Anleger
market forces	die Marktkräfte [PL.]
portfolio management	die Bestandsverwaltung
risk management	das Risikomanagement
security, commercial paper	das Wertpapier
seller	der Verkäufer
stock	die Aktie
stock exchange	die Börse
stock portfolio	die Aktienbestände [PL.]
stockholder	der Aktionär / die Aktionärin
ups and downs	die Höhen und Tiefen [PL.]
world market	der Weltmarkt
to invest	investieren, anlegen
to sell	verkaufen
to sell off	abstoßen

The economy

Die Wirtschaft

capitalism	der Kapitalismus
cost of living	die Lebenshaltungskosten [PL.]
debt	die Schulden [USUALLY PL.]
employment	die Beschäftigung
factory	die Fabrik
free enterprise system	die freie Marktwirtschaft
free market	der freie Markt
global financial crisis	die Weltfinanzkrise
goods and services	Güter und Dienstleistungen [PL.]
government	die Regierung
growth	das Wachstum
income	das Einkommen, der Lohn
income tax	die Einkommensteuer

Internal Revenue Service (IRS)	die Finanzbehörde, das Steueramt [SWITZ.]
job	die Arbeit, der Job
pension	die Rente
prosperity	der Wohlstand
public sector	der öffentliche Sektor
recession	die Rezession
rule of law	der Rechtsstaat
underemployment	die Unterbeschäftigung
unemployment	die Arbeitslosigkeit, die Erwerbslosigkeit
value-added tax (VAT)	die Mehrwertsteuer (MWSt.)
to raise taxes	die Steuern erhöhen

Klingen Sie authentisch!

expiration date of the contract	der Ablauf des Vertrags
power of attorney	die Vollmacht
You can send text messages.	Sie können SMS schicken.
I'd like to make a withdrawal.	Ich möchte Geld abheben.
One can use online banking for all bank operations.	Sie können sämtliche Bankgeschäfte online erledigen.
Investors are playing it safe.	Die Anleger gehen auf Nummer Sicher.

Ausdrücke, Sprichwörter und Zitate

to lose everything one has	Haus und Hof verlieren
It's selling like hotcakes.	Es geht weg wie warme Brezeln.
The reputation of a good thing precedes it.	Gute Ware lobt sich selbst.
There's nothing wrong with money.	Geld stinkt nicht.
Never borrow from your friends.	Wo Geld kehrt und wendt, hat die Freundschaft bald ein End.
You can have too much of a good thing.	Allzu viel ist ungesund.

„Wenn ein Mensch dir sagt, er sei durch harte Arbeit reich geworden, frag ihn, durch wessen Arbeit."
  DON MARQUIS

„Wir haben teure Autos und niedrige Lebensmittelpreise. Das ist typisch für die Deutschen."
  BÄRBEL HÖHN

„Zeit ist Geld."
  BENJAMIN FRANKLIN

„Zeit ist Leben."
  MICHAEL ENDE

Übung 26

Complete each German phrase so that it expresses the meaning of the English phrase.

1. *electronic devices*   elektronische _____

2. *to raise taxes*   _____ erhöhen

3. *free market*   der freie _____

4. *wrong number*   falsche _____

5. *to withdraw money*   _____ abheben

6. *to declare bankruptcy*   _____ anmelden

7. *ups and downs*   Höhen und _____

8. *diversified portfolio*   gestreutes _____

Übung 27

Choose the word that does not belong in each group.

1. a. Börse   b. Investor   c. Steuern   d. Verkäufer
2. a. Filiale   b. Wertpapier   c. Aktien   d. Dividende
3. a. Bankkonto   b. Geldschein   c. Kredit   d. Webdesigner
4. a. Papier   b. Fabrik   c. Stift   d. Bleistift
5. a. Produkt   b. Arbeitsmuster   c. Bildschirm   d. Marke
6. a. Rechner   b. Scanner   c. Drucker   d. Link
7. a. Arbeitnehmer b. Darlehen   c. einstellen   d. entlassen
8. a. Banknote   b. Tacker   c. Kopiergerät   d. Telefon
9. a. Einkommen   b. Dividende   c. Verlust   d. Lohn
10. a. Aktien   b. Wertpapiere   c. Anleihepapiere   d. Konkurs

Übung 28

Group the following words into the five categories given.

Einzelhandel	Rechnung	überweisen	Aufsichtsrat	Geschäftsführer
Bildschirm	Großhandel	Banknote	einzahlen	Tacker
Berater	Datei	Terminkalender	Preis	Finanzchef
Software	Kopiergerät	Produkt	Chef	Arbeitsplatz
Zinsen	Betriebssystem	Tastatur	abheben	Schreibtisch

Büro	**Rechner**	**Handel**	**Bank**	**Personal**
_____	_____	_____	_____	_____
_____	_____	_____	_____	_____
_____	_____	_____	_____	_____
_____	_____	_____	_____	_____
_____	_____	_____	_____	_____

Übung 29

Complete each expression with the missing verb from the following list.

schicken	erhöhen	ausstellen	installieren
starten	machen	erstellen	überweisen

1. einen Geschäftsplan _____

2. eine Werbekampagne _____

3. die Steuern _____

4. Geld _____

5. ein Programm _____

6. SMS _____

7. einen Scheck _____

8. eine Datei _____

Übung 30

Match each word in the first column with its synonym in the second column.

1. _____ starten   a. Ratgeber

2. _____ Arbeitsplatz   b. Abgaben

3. _____ Verwalter   c. deponieren

4. _____ Rente   d. Preis

5. _____ Berater   e. lancieren

6. _____ Kosten   f. Konjunkturrückgang

7. _____ Einkommen   g. Pension

8. _____ Steuern   h. Lohn

9. _____ Rezession   i. Manager

10. _____ einzahlen   j. Arbeitsstelle

Übung 31

Translate the following sentences into German.

1. You (Sie) *must back up all your files.*

   _____

2. *We will launch our advertising campaign on social media.*

   _____

   _____

3. *Investors must pay attention to the ups and downs of the stock market.*

   _____

   _____

4. *The government is going to raise taxes.*

   _____

5. *E-commerce is important for the growth of the company.*

   _____

   _____

6. *Our agency is going to launch an advertising campaign for this product.*

   _____

   _____

7. *There is not much money in our savings account.*

_____

8. *The CEO and the consultants have just left.*

_____

9. *The company stays in touch with consumers through social media.*

_____

_____

10. *The chief financial officer is going to draw up a budget.*

_____

_____

6

Reisen, Ferien und Freizeit
Travel, vacation, and leisure

This chapter presents vocabulary related to airplane, train, and car travel, as well as vacation destinations, sports, and leisure activities. You will learn the German words for the days of the week, months, seasons, and cardinal points, and you'll be able to describe—and complain about—the weather!

Many travel expressions using the verb *to take* in English have German equivalents with the verb **machen** *to make*, which takes an accusative object.

We're taking . . .

We're taking a trip.
  a bike ride
  a cruise
  a hike
  a ride
  a walk

Wir machen...

Wir machen eine Reise.
  eine Radtour
  eine Kreuzfahrt
  eine Wanderung
  eine Autofahrt
  einen Spaziergang

Seeing the sights

We're going to go sightseeing.
  to buy a guidebook
  to go all around the region
  to go horseback riding
  to go on an excursion/outing
  to go sightseeing in the city
  to go to the casino
  to see the old city
  to take a guided tour
  to take a riverboat
  to travel around

Sehenswürdigkeiten

Wir werden Sightseeing machen.
  einen Reiseführer kaufen
  die gesamte Region anschauen
  reiten gehen
  einen Ausflug machen
  Sightseeing in der Stadt machen
  in die Spielbank gehen
  die Altstadt anschauen
  eine Führung machen
  mit dem Boot den Fluß entlang fahren
  eine Rundreise machen

The preposition **mit** *with, by* takes a dative object.

Means of transportation

I like to travel by plane.
    by bike
    by boat
    by bus, by coach
    by car
    by taxi
    by train
    on foot

Fortbewegungsmittel

Ich bin gerne mit dem Flugzeug unterwegs. [N.]
    mit dem Fahrrad [N.]
    mit dem Schiff [N.]
    mit dem Bus [M.]
    mit dem Auto [N.]
    mit dem Taxi [N.]
    mit dem Zug [M.]
    zu Fuß [M.]

Traveling by airplane

I prefer an overnight flight.
    a direct flight, a nonstop flight
    a flight with a stopover
    to fly standby
    an aisle seat
    a window seat

Reisen im Flugzeug

Ich bevorzuge einen Nachtflug.
    einen Direktflug
    einen Flug mit Zwischenlandung
    einen Standby-Flug
    einen Platz am Gang
    einen Platz am Fenster

At the airport

Do you have any carry-on luggage?
    any bags to check
    the gate number
    your boarding pass
    your passport

Am Flughafen

Haben Sie Handgepäck? [N.]
    Gepäck zum Einchecken, Gepäck zum Aufgeben
    die Gate-Nummer
    Ihren Boarding-Paß / Boarding-Pass
    Ihren Paß / Pass, Ihren Ausweis

The flight

The plane is taking off now.
    is landing now
    is arriving now
    is late
    is on time

takeoff
landing

Der Flug

Das Flugzeug startet jetzt.
    landet jetzt
    kommt jetzt an
    hat Verspätung
    ist pünktlich

der Start
die Landung

The plane has taken off.	Das Flugzeug ist gestartet.
The plane has landed.	Das Flugzeug ist gelandet.
The flight has been canceled.	Der Flug wurde gestrichen.
The plane is full.	Das Flugzeug ist voll.
You must speak with the flight attendant.	Wenden Sie sich an den Flugbegleiter.
Fasten your seat belts.	Schnallen Sie sich an.

How was the trip?   ### Wie war die Reise?

We had a <u>wonderful</u> trip. — Wir hatten eine <u>wunderbare</u> Reise.

boring	langweilige
fun	lustige
horrible	furchtbare
memorable	unvergeßliche/unvergessliche
terrific	fabelhafte
tiring	ermüdende
very long	sehr lange
very short	sehr kurze

We had an <u>interesting</u> trip. — Wir hatten eine <u>interessante</u> Reise.

enjoyable	lustige
exhausting	anstrengende
impressive	beeindruckende

Taking the train   ### Mit dem Zug unterwegs

You have to <u>look for the platform</u>. — Sie müssen <u>das Gleis suchen</u>.

to check the schedule, to check the timetable	den Fahrplan überprüfen
to wait in line at the ticket window	am Schalter in der Schlange stehen
to buy tickets	Fahrkarten kaufen
to buy a round-trip ticket	eine Hin- und Rückfahrkarte kaufen
to check your luggage	Ihr Gepäck aufgeben
to look at the arrivals/departures board	die Fahrplanauskunft anschauen
to take the high-speed train	den ICE nehmen (ICE = Inter-City Express)
to punch your ticket	die Fahrkarte entwerten
to get on the train	einsteigen
to get off the train	aussteigen
to find the dining car	den Speisewagen finden
to find the sleeping car	den Schlafwagen finden

My car has broken down.

You have to repair the brakes.
  the brake lights
  the carburetor
  the exhaust pipe
  the front axle
  the gas pedal
  the gearshift
  the headlights
  the ignition
  the windshield wiper

I can't manage to open the trunk.
  the car door
  the gas tank
  the glove compartment
  the hood
  the windows

There's a problem with the backup lights.
  the air conditioning
  the back seat
  the front seat
  the high-beam headlights
  the gas gauge
  the horn
  the jack
  the license plate
  the rearview mirror
  the spare tire
  the speedometer
  the tires
  the turn signals

Weather: the forecast

What's the weather like?
It's nice.
It's very nice.
It's bad.

Ich hatte eine Panne.

Sie müssen die Bremsen reparieren. [die Bremse]
  das Bremslicht
  den Vergaser
  das Auspuffrohr
  die Vorderachse
  das Gaspedal
  die Schaltung
  das Vorderlicht, die Scheinwerfer
  die Zündung
  den Scheibenwischer

Ich kriege den Kofferraum nicht auf.
  die Autotür
  den Tank
  das Handschuhfach
  die Haube
  die Fenster [das Fenster]

Es gibt ein Problem mit dem Rückscheinwerfer. [M.]
  der Klimaanlage
  dem Rücksitz [M.]
  dem Vordersitz [M.]
  dem Fernlichtscheinwerfer [M.]
  der Tankanzeige
  der Hupe
  dem Anlasser [M.]
  dem Nummernschild [N.]
  dem Rückspiegel [M.]
  dem Ersatzreifen [M.]
  dem Tachometer [M./N.], dem Tacho [M./N.]
  den Reifen [der Reifen]
  den Blinkern [der Blinker]

Das Wetter: die Vorhersage

Wie ist das Wetter?
Es ist schön.
Es ist sehr schön.
Es ist schlecht.

It's cold.	Es ist kalt.
It's very cold.	Es ist sehr kalt.
It's cool.	Es ist kühl.
It's hot.	Es ist heiß.
It's sunny.	Es ist sonnig.
It's windy.	Es ist windig.
It's clear.	Der Himmel ist klar.
It's very clear.	Der Himmel ist sehr klar.
It's cloudy.	Es ist bewölkt.
It's drizzling.	Es nieselt.
It's hailing.	Es hagelt.
It's raining.	Es regnet.
It's snowing.	Es schneit.
It's thundering.	Es donnert.
There's fog.	Es gibt Nebel.
lightning	Blitze [der Blitz]
rain	Regen [M.]
a shower	einen Schauer
snow	Schnee [M.]
a snowstorm	einen Schneesturm
a storm	einen Sturm
What's the temperature?	Wie ist die Temperatur?
It's 90 degrees (Fahrenheit).	Es sind neunzig Grad (Fahrenheit).
It's 30 degrees (Celsius).	Es sind dreißig Grad (Celsius).

Climate

Das Klima

This region has a cold climate.	Diese Region hat kaltes Klima.
dry	trockenes
hot	warmes
humid	feuchtes
mild, temperate	mildes

The seasons

Die Jahreszeiten

Are you going on vacation in the summer?	Machst du im Sommer Ferien?
in the autumn	im Herbst
in the winter	im Winter
in the spring	im Frühling

Cardinal points on the compass

north
south
east
west
northeast
northwest
southeast
southwest

The months

I'm taking a trip in <u>January</u>.
  February
  March
  April
  May
  June
  July
  August
  September
  October
  November
  December

Sports and games

I love <u>swimming</u>.
  baseball
  basketball
  bike riding
  board games
  cards
  checkers
  chess
  football
  skating
  skiing
  soccer
  sports
  tennis

Die Himmelsrichtungen

Nord
Süd
Ost
West
Nordost
Nordwest
Südost
Südwest

Die Monate

Ich verreise im <u>Januar</u>. [Jänner: AUS.]
  Februar
  März
  April
  Mai
  Juni
  Juli
  August
  September
  Oktober
  November
  Dezember

Sport und Spiel

Ich liebe <u>Schwimmen</u>.
  Baseball [M.]
  Basketball [M.]
  Radsport [M.]
  Gesellschaftsspiele [das Gesellschaftsspiel]
  Kartenspiele [das Kartenspiel]
  Dame [F.]
  Schach [N.]
  American Football [M.]
  Schlittschuhlaufen [N.]
  Skilaufen [N.]
  Fußball [M.]
  Sport [M.]
  Tennis [N.]

>>>

video games	Videospiele [das Videospiel]
volleyball	Volleyball [M.]
weightlifting	Gewichtheben [N.]

I play golf.	Ich spiele Golf. [M.]
basketball	Basketball [M.]
cards	Karten [PL.]
hockey	Hockey [N.]
ice hockey	Eishockey [N.]
marbles	Murmeln [die Murmel]
ping-pong	Tischtennis [N.]
skat (a popular card game in Germany)	Skat [M.]
soccer	Fußball [M.]
video games	Videospiele [das Videospiel]
volleyball	Volleyball [M.]

I'd like to learn to ride a bike.	Ich möchte fahrradfahren lernen.
to box	boxen
to cook	kochen
to dance	tanzen
to dive	tauchen
to ice skate	eislaufen
to ride a horse	reiten
to skate	Schlittschuh laufen
to ski	Ski fahren
to swim	schwimmen
to wrestle	ringen

Other sports

Andere Sportarten

bowling	Bowling [N.]
to go bowling	Bowling spielen gehen
marathon	Marathon [M.]
to run a marathon	einen Marathon laufen
marathon runner	der Marathonläufer / die Marathonläuferin
rock climbing	Klettern [N.]
to go rock climbing	Klettern gehen
rowing	Rudern [N.]
to go rowing	rudern

sailing	Segeln [N.]
to go sailing	segeln gehen
wrestling	Ringen [N.]
to wrestle	ringen
ball (small)	der Ball, die Kugel
ball (large)	der Ball
game	das Spiel
score	der Spielstand
serve (tennis)	der Aufschlag
tennis court	der Tennisplatz
tennis player	der Tennisspieler / die Tennisspielerin
World Cup (soccer)	die Weltmeisterschaft (WM)
to throw the ball to someone	jemandem den Ball zuwerfen

The form **am** (**an** + **dem**) may appear before the name of the day of the week or not: **Wir werden (am) Montag Tennis spielen.**

The days of the week

Die Wochentage

We're going to play tennis <u>on Monday</u>.	Wir werden <u>Montag</u> Tennis spielen.
on Tuesday	Dienstag
on Wednesday	Mittwoch
on Thursday	Donnerstag
on Friday	Freitag
on Saturday	Samstag
on Sunday	Sonntag

Leisure activities

Freizeitaktivitäten

In my free time, I like <u>to read</u>.	In meiner Freizeit mag ich <u>lesen</u>.
to browse on the Web	im Internet surfen
to cook	kochen
to do charity work	für wohltätige Zwecke arbeiten
to go camping	campen gehen
to go dancing	tanzen gehen
to go fishing	angeln
to go for a walk	spazieren gehen
to go to a concert	ins Konzert gehen
to go to a crafts fair	auf einen Kunsthandwerks-Markt gehen

>>>

to go to a nightclub	in einen Nachtclub/Nachtklub gehen
to go to the movies	ins Kino gehen
to go to the theater	ins Theater gehen
to go shopping	shoppen gehen
to go to a café	ins Café gehen
to ice skate	Schlittschuh laufen
to listen to music	Musik hören
to play the piano	Klavier spielen
to putter around the house, to do projects around the house	heimwerken
to sketch, to draw	zeichnen
to ski	Ski laufen
to swim	schwimmen
to take an online class	einen Online-Kurs belegen
to take pictures	Photos/Fotos machen
to visit a museum	ins Museum gehen
to walk my dog	den Hund ausführen
to watch TV	Fernsehen gucken
to work out	trainieren
to write poetry	Gedichte schreiben

On vacation

In den Ferien

I want to spend my vacation <u>at the beach</u>.	Ich will meine Ferien <u>am Strand</u> verbringen.
abroad	im Ausland
at an archaeological dig	an einer Ausgrabungsstätte
at a campground	auf einem Campingplatz
on the coast	an der Küste
in the country	auf dem Land
in the desert	in der Wüste
in the mountains	in den Bergen
at a seaside resort	in einem Seebad
at a five-star hotel	in einem Fünf-Sterne-Hotel
at a youth hostel	in einer Jugendherberge

At the hotel

Im Hotel

Do you have <u>a room for one night</u>?	Haben Sie <u>ein Zimmer für eine Nacht</u>?
adjoining rooms	zwei Zimmer nebeneinander
an air-conditioned room	ein Zimmer mit Klimaanlage

a room for one person	ein Zimmer für eine Person
a room for two nights	ein Zimmer für zwei Nächte
a room that faces the inner courtyard	ein Zimmer zum Innenhof
a room that faces the street	ein Zimmer zur Straße
a room with a balcony	ein Zimmer mit Balkon
a room with a refrigerator	ein Zimmer mit Kühlschrank
a room with a shower	ein Zimmer mit Dusche
a room with an Internet connection	ein Zimmer mit Internetzugang
a room with two beds	ein Zimmer mit zwei Betten
a single room	ein Einzelzimmer

Is there <u>an elevator</u> in the hotel?	Gibt es im Hotel <u>einen Aufzug?</u>
a ballroom	einen Tanzsaal
a bar	eine Bar
a bellhop	einen Hotelboy
a concierge	einen Concierge
a conference room	einen Konferenzraum
a fitness center	einen Fitneßraum / Fitnessraum
a florist	einen Floristen
a hair salon	einen Frisör
an indoor pool	ein Schwimmbad
laundry service	Wäscheservice [M.]
a lobby	eine Empfangshalle
a lounge for guests	eine Gästelounge
an outdoor pool	einen Außenpool
a parking garage	eine Garage
a restaurant	ein Restaurant
room service	Zimmerservice [M.]
a sauna	eine Sauna
a security system	eine Alarmanlage
shoeshine service	Schuhputz-Service [M.]
a shop	einen Laden
a souvenir shop	einen Souvenirladen
a whirlpool	einen Whirlpool

I have <u>to pay the bill</u>.	Ich muß <u>die Rechnung bezahlen</u>.
to pay cash	bar bezahlen
to pay with a credit card	mit Kreditkarte bezahlen
to change money	Geld wechseln
to get a different room	ein anderes Zimmer nehmen

>>>

to turn in my keys	den Schlüssel abgeben
to leave tomorrow	morgen abreisen
to reserve a room	ein Zimmer reservieren

Klingen Sie authentisch!

to pack the suitcases	die Koffer packen
to play a sport	einen Sport ausüben

The fans cheer their team on.	Die Fans feuern ihre Mannschaft an.
This plane has a stopover in Athens.	Dieses Flugzeug landet in Athen zwischen.
The train is in the station.	Der Zug ist im Bahnhof.
Our car broke down.	Unser Auto hat eine Panne.
You have to make preparations for the trip.	Du mußt dich auf die Reise vorbereiten.

Ausdrücke, Sprichwörter und Zitate

to set out in a new direction	zu neuen Ufern aufbrechen

A rolling stone gathers no moss.	Wer rastet, der rostet.
Grass doesn't grow on a busy street.	Auf viel betretenem Fußsteig wächst kein Gras.
All roads lead to Rome.	Alle Wege führen nach Rom.

„Eine Reise von tausend Meilen beginnt mit einem einzigen Schritt."
    LAO-TZE

„Gott sei dank, daß die Menschen noch nicht fliegen können und den Himmel ebenso verschmutzen wie die Erde."
    HENRY DAVID THOREAU

„Reisen veredelt den Geist und räumt mit allen unseren Vorurteilen auf."
    OSCAR WILDE

„Reisen bedeutet entdecken, daß alle unrecht haben mit dem, was sie über andere Länder denken."
    ALDOUS HUXLEY

„Das Reisen führt uns zurück."
    ALBERT CAMUS

„Die meisten reisen nur, um wieder heimzukommen."
    MICHEL DE MONTAIGNE

„Nur wo du zu Fuß warst, bist du auch wirklich gewesen."
    JOHANN WOLFGANG VON GOETHE

Übung 32

Complete each German phrase or sentence so that it expresses the meaning of the English phrase or sentence.

1. *to look at the arrivals/departures board*   die _____ anschauen
2. *to check your luggage*   das _____ aufgeben
3. *to browse the web*   im _____ surfen
4. *to buy tickets*   _____ kaufen
5. *to go sightseeing*   _____ machen
6. *a tiring trip*   eine ermüdende _____
7. *to ice skate*   _____ laufen
8. *to punch your ticket*   die Fahrkarte _____
9. *to go see the old city*   die _____ anschauen
10. *to go to a concert*   ins _____ gehen
11. *I love swimming.*   Ich liebe _____.
12. *a round-trip ticket*   eine _____fahrkarte
13. *to go shopping*   _____ gehen
14. *We're going to play tennis.*   Wir gehen _____.
15. *a mild and dry climate*   ein _____
16. *You must check the suitcase.*   Sie müssen _____.
17. *I took a trip in July.*   Ich bin _____ verreist.
18. *I'm working on Friday.*   Ich arbeite _____.
19. *to walk the dog*   den _____
20. *to go horseback riding*   _____ gehen

Übung 33

In German, use weather and climate expressions to describe each of the following places.

1. Berlin

_____

_____

_____

2. München

_____

_____

_____

3. Moskau

_____

_____

_____

4. Rom, Italien

_____

_____

_____

5. Vancouver

_____

_____

_____

6. Dallas

_____

_____

_____

Übung 34

List ten things you like to do in your leisure time. Begin each sentence with either **Ich mag...** or **Ich liebe...**

1. _____
2. _____
3. _____
4. _____
5. _____
6. _____
7. _____

8. _____

9. _____

10. _____

Übung 35

Describe a trip you took. Tell where and when you went, how you prepared for your trip, how you traveled, with whom you traveled, and what you did there. If you prefer, describe a trip you plan to take.

_____

_____

_____

_____

_____

_____

_____

_____

_____

_____

Übung 36

Select the verb or separable prefix that correctly completes each phrase or sentence.

1. Das Flugzeug _____. (hebt auf / hebt ab)

2. in die Ferien _____ (fahren / besuchen)

3. Schach _____ (spielen / spülen)

4. eine Runde _____ (essen / schwimmen)

5. einen Sport _____ (ausmachen / ausüben)

6. eine Autofahrt _____ (suchen / machen)

7. Es _____ sehr heiß. (ist / macht)

8. Schnallen Sie sich _____. (ab / an)

9. Der ICE _____. (fährt ab / landet)

10. Der Flug _____. (ist gestrichen / ist registriert)

Übung 37

Give the noun phrase (definite article + noun) found in this chapter that is derived from each of the following verbs.

1. landen _____
2. regnen _____
3. fliegen _____
4. reisen _____
5. stürmen _____
6. wandern _____
7. sich verspäten _____
8. blitzen _____
9. spielen _____
10. schneien _____
11. starten _____
12. spazieren gehen _____

Übung 38

Unscramble the letters in each item to create a noun that appears in the chapter.

1. gannsto _____
2. therafakr _____
3. gulf _____
4. belen _____
5. dulnasa _____
6. äkecpg _____
7. aarggespinz _____
8. mihelm _____
9. suumme _____
10. green _____

Übung 39

Translate the following sentences into German.

1. *You (du) ought to pack the suitcases.*

   _____

2. *Here are my boarding pass and my passport.*

   _____

3. The plane has landed, but it is late.

_____

4. We had a wonderful but very long trip.

_____

5. When I am in Hamburg, I like to go sightseeing.

_____

_____

6. The weather is bad today. It's windy and it's hailing.

_____

_____

7. We are going to stand in line at the ticket window and buy a round-trip ticket.

_____

_____

8. They like to play chess.

_____

9. I want to spend my vacation in the mountains or in the country.

_____

_____

10. In my spare time, I like to go camping and fishing.

_____

_____

7

Der Alltag; die Ausbildung
The daily routine; education

In this chapter, you will learn vocabulary related to your daily routine, from waking up in the morning to going to sleep at night. You will learn how to describe your feelings and emotions and how to talk about important life events. The vocabulary related to education will enable you to describe your school experiences, fields of study, and favorite teachers.

The daily routine

One has <u>to get up</u> early.
   to wake up
   to go to bed
   to fall asleep

Der Alltag

Man muß früh <u>aufstehen</u>.
   aufwachen
   ins Bett gehen
   einschlafen

Some German verbs that describe daily routine and personal grooming are reflexive verbs, composed of a verb and a reflexive pronoun like **mich**, **dich**, or **sich**. Examples are **sich anziehen** *to get dressed* and **sich waschen** *to wash (oneself)*.

I have <u>to get dressed</u> early.
   to get ready early
   to get undressed early

Ich muß <u>mich früh anziehen</u>.
   mich früh fertigmachen
   mich früh ausziehen

Personal grooming

You have <u>to floss your teeth</u> every day.
   to bathe, to take a bath
   to shower, to take a shower

You ought <u>to shave</u>.
   to put on makeup
   to wash

Körperpflege

Du mußt jeden Tag <u>Zahnseide benutzen</u>.
   baden
   duschen

Du sollst <u>dich rasieren</u>.
   dich schminken
   dich waschen

When a German reflexive verb has a noun object, the reflexive pronouns **mich** and **dich** are replaced by **mir** and **dir; sich** remains unchanged. In the English equivalents of these expressions, a possessive adjective is used.

I want to wash my hair.	Ich will <u>mir die Haare waschen.</u>
to brush my hair	mir die Haare bürsten
to dry my hair	mir die Haare trocknen
to get a haircut	mir die Haare schneiden lassen
You have to brush your teeth.	Du mußt <u>dir die Zähne putzen.</u>
to comb your hair	dir die Haare kämmen
to put on lipstick	dir die Lippen schminken
to wash your face	dir das Gesicht waschen
to wash your hands	dir die Hände waschen
She wants to file her nails.	Sie will <u>sich die Nägel feilen.</u>
to shave her legs	sich die Beine rasieren

Beauty and personal care products   Körperpflegeprodukte

There is <u>shampoo</u> in the medicine chest.	Im Spiegelschrank ist <u>Shampoo.</u> [N.]
an antiperspirant	ein Antitranspirant [M.]
a comb	ein Kamm [M.]
a conditioner	eine Haarspülung
a deodorant	ein Deodorant [N.]
a depilatory, a hair remover	ein Enthaarungsmittel [N.]
hair coloring	Haarfarbe [F.]
a hairbrush	eine Haarbürste
a lipstick	ein Lippenstift [M.]
makeup	Schminke [F.], Make-up [N.]
a moisturizing cream	eine Feuchtigkeitscreme
a mouthwash	ein Mundwasser [N.]
a nail clippers	ein Nagelknipser [M.], ein Nagelzwicker [M.] [AUS.]
nail polish	Nagellack [M.]
perfume	Parfum/Parfüm [N.]
a razor (electric)	ein Rasierapparat [M.]
shaving cream	Rasiercreme/Rasierkrem [F.]
soap	Seife [F.]
a toothbrush	eine Zahnbürste
toothpaste	Zahncreme/Zahnkrem [F.], Zahnpasta [F.]
a tweezers	eine Pinzette

There are bath oils and bath salts in the medicine chest.	Im Spiegelschrank sind <u>Badeöle und Badesalze</u>. [das Badeöl, das Badesalz]
razor blades	Rasierklingen [die Rasierklinge]

The pronoun **man** is used with a third-person singular verb to express English *people, one, you, they.* This expression often replaces **wir** in everyday speech.

Feelings and emotions

People should <u>be happy</u>.	Man sollte <u>glücklich sein</u>.
be moved, be touched	gerührt sein
calm down	sich beruhigen
cheer up	fröhlich sein
feel happy	sich glücklich fühlen
get excited	sich aufregen
get interested	sich interessieren
have a good time	sich amüsieren
laugh	lachen

They shouldn't <u>get annoyed</u>.	Sie sollten nicht <u>genervt werden</u>.
be disappointed	enttäuscht sein
be surprised	überrascht sein
be worried	besorgt sein
complain about everything	über alles klagen
feel sad	sich traurig fühlen
get angry	sauer werden
get bored	gelangweilt werden
get impatient	ungeduldig werden
get insulted	beleidigt werden
get irritated	gereizt werden
get scared	erschrocken werden
get upset	aufgeregt werden

Health and accidents

to break something (a part of the body)	sich etwas brechen
to burn oneself	sich verbrennen
to catch a cold	sich erkälten
to faint	ohnmächtig werden
to fall down	(hin)fallen, stürzen
to get dizzy	Schwindel empfinden

to get sick	krank werden
to get the flu	die Grippe bekommen
to get tired	müde werden
to hurt one's hand	sich die Hand verletzen
to hurt oneself	sich verletzen
to lie down	sich hinlegen
to relax	sich entspannen
to take care of oneself	auf sich aufpassen
to twist one's ankle	sich den Fuß umknicken

German uses imperative forms to express commands. For most German verbs, you simply omit **-en** at the end of the infinitive: **gehen** > **geh**.

Movement

Please come closer.
- go *away*
- go *for a walk*
- *hurry up*
- *move, budge*
- *move away*
- *move over*
- *sit down*
- *stand up*
- *stay*
- *stop*
- *turn around*

Bewegung

Bitte komm näher.
- geh weg
- geh spazieren
- beeil dich
- beweg dich
- zieh aus
- mach Platz
- setz dich
- steh auf
- bleib
- halt an
- dreh dich um

Life events

They hope to fall in love.
- *to register, to enroll (in the university)*
- *to graduate*
- *to get engaged*
- *to get married (to)*
- *not to get divorced*
- *to move (to their dream home)*

- *to settle in (into a house)*

Lebenserfahrungen

Sie hoffen, sich zu verlieben.
- sich einzuschreiben, sich zu immatrikulieren
- einen Abschluß/Abschluss zu machen
- sich zu verloben
- sich zu verheiraten (mit)
- sich nicht scheiden zu lassen
- umzuziehen (in die Traumwohnung / in das Traumhaus)
- sich einzuleben

Clothing

They're going <u>to put on their coats</u>.	
to button/zip their jackets	
to unbutton/unzip their jackets	
to take off their hats	
to try on their suits	
to tie their shoes	
to untie their shoes	

Kleidung

Sie werden <u>ihre Mäntel anziehen</u>.
   ihre Jacken schließen
   ihre Jacken aufmachen
   ihre Hüte abnehmen
   ihre Anzüge anprobieren
   ihre Schuhe zubinden
   ihre Schuhe aufbinden

The verb **werden** is used to express physical or emotional changes; its English equivalents are *to get* and *to become*. The past-tense conjugation of **werden** is as follows: **ich wurde, du wurdest, er/sie/es wurde, wir wurden, ihr wurdet, sie wurden.**

To become/get

I became an architect.
She became an engineer.
We became friends.
They got rich.
It's getting late.
Did he get angry?
She went mad.

Werden

Ich wurde Architekt.
Sie wurde Ingenieur.
Wir wurden Freunde.
Sie wurden reich.
Es wird spät.
Wurde er böse?
Sie wurde wütend.

The German equivalents for English *student* and *to study* vary on the basis of age:

	Secondary/high school	University
student	der Schüler	der Student
to study	lernen	studieren

Studieren means *to study a subject in depth* (for example, modern history), while **lernen** means *to study details of a subject* (for example, dates of specific events).

Education
What should students do?

They should <u>go to class</u>.
   apply for a scholarship
   do their homework

Die Ausbildung
Was sollten Schüler/Studenten machen?

Sie sollten <u>zum Unterricht gehen</u>.
   sich um ein Stipendium bewerben
   ihre Hausaufgaben machen [die Hausaufgabe]   >>>

>>>

get a high school diploma	Abitur machen [das Abitur], Matura machen [die Matura] [AUS., SWITZ.]
get good grades	gute Noten bekommen [die Note]
graduate	einen Abschluß/Abschluss machen
hand in their reports	ihre Referate einreichen [das Referat]
learn a lot	viel lernen
pass their exams	ihre Prüfungen bestehen [die Prüfung]
pay attention	aufmerksam sein, aufpassen
read their textbooks	ihre Lehrbücher lesen [das Lehrbuch]
study hard	fleißig lernen, fleißig studieren
take courses	Kurse belegen [der Kurs]
take five courses	die Pflichtkurse belegen [der Pflichtkurs]
take exams	Prüfungen ablegen [die Prüfung]
take notes	mitschreiben
write compositions	Kompositionen schreiben [die Komposition]

What should students not do?

Was sollten Schüler/Studenten nicht machen?

They shouldn't fail an exam.	Sie sollten nicht durchfallen.
be absent, skip class	den Unterricht schwänzen
cut class, play hooky	die Schule schwänzen

Education vocabulary

Ausbildungsvokabular

online course	der Online-Kurs
school	die Schule
nursery school	die Vorschule
elementary school	die Grundschule, die Primarschule [SWITZ.]
middle school	die Sekundarstufe [SWITZ.]
high school	die Oberschule, das Gymnasium, die Kantonsschule [SWITZ.]
university	die Universität
school (of a university)	die Fakultät
preschooler	der Vorschüler / die Vorschülerin
pupil	der Schüler / die Schülerin
student	der Student / die Studentin, der Schüler / die Schülerin
teacher	der Lehrer / die Lehrerin
to major in (a subject)	(ein Fach) als Hauptfach studieren
to get a degree (in)	einen Abschluß/Abschluss machen (in)
to teach	lehren, unterrichten

School supplies

The student has a pen.	Der Schüler hat einen Stift.
books	Bücher [das Buch]
a calculator	einen Taschenrechner
a compass	einen Kompaß/Kompass
a computer	einen Rechner, einen Computer
an e-book reader	einen E-Book-Reader
a locker	einen Spind
a marker	einen Marker
a notebook	ein Notizbuch
a notepad	einen Block
a pencil	einen Bleistift
a pencil case	eine Federtasche
a pencil sharpener	einen Anspitzer
a ruler	ein Lineal

Schulutensilien

In school, a teacher is called **Lehrer** _____ or **Herr** _____. In the university, a professor is called **Professor** _____ or **Herr Professor** _____.

Our professor

Professor Apitz is demanding.	Herr Professor Apitz ist anspruchsvoll.
boring	langweilig
brilliant	hervorragend
cranky	reizbar
famous	berühmt
lenient	nachsichtig
pleasant, nice	angenehm
popular	beliebt
respected	angesehen
rigid	unnachgiebig
scholarly	gelehrt
smart	gewandt, schlau
strict	streng
understanding	verständnisvoll
unpleasant	unangenehm

Unser Lehrer

The verbal expression **arbeiten in** *to work in* takes a dative object.

### Working in education	### In der Ausbildung arbeiten

She's working in adult education.   Sie arbeitet in der Erwachsenenbildung.

   in pre-school education   in der Vorschule

   in elementary education   in der Grundstufe

   in secondary education   in der Oberstufe

   in higher education   in der Hochschulbildung

   in distance learning   im Fernunterricht [M.]

My studies
Mein Studium

I'm most interested in chemistry.   Chemie interessiert mich sehr. [F.]

   accounting   Rechnungswesen [N.]

   architecture   Architektur [F.]

   art   Kunst [F.]

   biology   Biologie [F.]

   communications   Nachrichtenwesen [N.]

   computer science   Informatik [F.]

   dentistry   Zahnmedizin [F.]

   economics   Wirtschaft [F.]

   engineering   Ingenieurwissenschaft [F.]

   graphic design   Grafikdesign [F.]

   history   Geschichte [F.]

   hotel management   Hotelmanagement [N.]

   law   Rechtswissenschaft [F.], Jura [NO GENDER]

   mathematics   Mathematik [F.]

   medicine   Medizin [F.]

   music   Musik [F.]

   physics   Physik [F.]

At the university
In der Universität

Where is the law school, please?   Wo ist bitte die juristische Fakultät?

   the business school   die betriebswirtschaftliche Fakultät

   the medical school   die medizinische Fakultät

   the school of continuing education   die pädagogische Fakultät

   the school of dentistry   die zahnmedizinische Fakultät

   the school of engineering   die Ingenieurwissenschaft

   the school of fine arts   die Kunstwissenschaft   >>>

the school of liberal arts	die philosophische Fakultät
the school of political science	die Politikwissenschaft
the school of sciences	die naturwissenschaftliche Fakultät
the school of social sciences	die Soziologie
the school of veterinary medicine	Veterinärmedizin [F.]

Klingen Sie authentisch!

to pull a fast one on somebody	jemanden verschaukeln
to study for the test	für die Prüfung lernen
to be educated	gebildet sein
to learn the hard way	etwas am eigenen Leibe erfahren
He enjoys his schoolwork.	Ihm macht das Lernen Spaß.
Do you regret your decision?	Bereuen Sie Ihre Entscheidung?
He doesn't get along with his sister.	Er verträgt sich nicht mit seiner Schwester.
I refused to be outdone.	Ich weigerte mich, zurückzustecken.
She got into a jam (literally, a dead end).	Sie geriet in eine Sackgasse.
Did you forget her birthday?	Hast du ihren Geburtstag vergessen?
You don't remember anything.	Du erinnerst dich an nichts.
They got lost on the highway.	Sie verfuhren sich auf der Autobahn.
He gets together with his friends.	Er trifft sich mit seinen Freunden.
I took advantage of the opportunity.	Ich habe die Gunst der Stunde genutzt.
She's saying goodbye to her colleagues.	Sie verabschiedet sich von ihren Kollegen.
Functional illiteracy continues to be a huge problem in many countries.	Der funktionelle Analphabetismus ist nach wie vor ein großes Problem in vielen Ländern.

Ausdrücke, Sprichwörter und Zitate

„Es ist die höchste Kunst des Lehrers, die Freude am Schaffen und am Erkennen zu erwecken."
ALBERT EINSTEIN

„Nichtwissen tut niemand weh, mit Ausnahme derer, denen wehgetan werden kann, weil niemand es weiß."
ERICH FRIED

„Das einzige Kriterium der Pädagogik ist die Freiheit, die einzige Methode ist die Erfahrung."
LEO TOLSTOJ

„Vieles hätte ich verstanden, wenn man es mir nicht erklärt hätte."
STANISŁAW JERZY LEC

„Es gibt nichts Gutes, außer: man tut es!"
ERICH KÄSTNER

Übung 40

Complete each German phrase or sentence so that it expresses the meaning of the English phrase or sentence.

1. *toothpaste*   _____creme

2. *law school*   die juristische _____

3. *calculator*   _____rechner

4. *a pencil*   ein _____stift

5. *razor blades*   Rasier_____

6. *notebook*   _____buch

7. *mouthwash*   Mund_____

8. *homework*   Haus_____

9. *textbook*   _____buch

10. *a nail clippers*   ein Nagel_____

11. *a pencil case*   eine Feder_____

12. *to pass an exam*   eine _____ bestehen

13. *One should take care of oneself.*   Man sollte _____.

14. *They're going to move in July.*   Sie werden im Juli _____.

15. *dental floss*   Zahn_____

Übung 41

Match each verb in the first column with its synonym in the second column.

1. _____ sich immatrikulieren   a. erregen

2. _____ sich beruhigen   b. hinfallen

3. _____ stürzen   c. stehen bleiben

4. _____ sich beeilen   d. sauer werden

5. _____ stoppen   e. einschlafen

6. _____ wütend werden   f. sich einschreiben

7. _____ sich erkälten   g. sich verwunden

8. _____ sich aufregen   h. zur Ruhe kommen

9. _____ sich verletzen   i. schnell machen

10. _____ sich hinlegen   j. krank werden

Übung 42

Select the verb that correctly completes each sentence.

1. Sie will sich die Lippen _____. (lackieren / schminken)

2. Du mußt dir die Schuhe _____. (zubinden / abnehmen)

3. Hast du dir die Hände _____? (gewaschen / rasiert)

4. Du solltest den Mantel _____. (anprobieren / verbrennen)

5. Du solltest die Gunst der Stunde _____. (schwänzen / nutzen)

6. Viele Schüler _____ die Prüfungen nicht. (bereuen / bestehen)

7. Sie lieben sich nicht mehr. Sie werden sich _____. (scheiden lassen / immatrikulieren)

8. Alles ist gut, sie sollten nicht so _____. (müde sein / besorgt sein)

9. Sie haben vor, in ihr Traumhaus zu _____. (ziehen / fliegen)

10. Der Schüler _____ unregelmäßige Verben. (studiert / lernt)

Übung 43

Respond in German as specified for each of the following situations.

1. **Der Alltag.** List some of the things you do every day, from waking up to going to bed.

   _____

   _____

   _____

   _____

   _____

2. **Gefühle und Emotionen.** Create five sentences about your emotions or feelings.

   _____

   _____

   _____

   _____

   _____

3. **Lebenserfahrungen.** Create five sentences about what experiences you would like to have.

_____

_____

_____

_____

_____

4. **Schule und Universität.** Describe students, teachers, or courses in a school or university setting.

_____

_____

_____

_____

_____

Übung 44

Unscramble the letters in each item to create a noun that appears in the chapter.

1. ultaftäk   _____
2. luhsec   _____
3. pripeg   _____
4. ickarteht   _____
5. dinsp   _____

6. kusim   _____
7. nahbotau   _____
8. erstübnhaz   _____
9. fesie   _____
10. rahea   _____

Übung 45

Translate the following sentences into German.

1. _They like to go to bed late and wake up early._

_____

2. _She's going to wash her hair with this shampoo._

_____

3. _The students have just registered in the school of fine arts._

_____

4. *The pupils have to go to class every day. They must not skip class.*

_____

_____

5. *He plans* (beabsichtigt) *to get together with his friends.*

_____

_____

6. *I'm very interested in literature. I'm going to apply for a scholarship to study in the school of liberal arts.*

_____

_____

7. *He gets up, brushes his teeth, takes a shower, shaves, and gets dressed.*

_____

_____

8. *Professor Apitz is strict and demanding, and also very nice.*

_____

_____

9. *He studied law and became a lawyer.*

_____

10. *We're going to have a lot of fun at the party.*

_____

11. *You* (du) *should take care of yourself. If not, you're going to get sick.*

_____

_____

12. *When do you* (ihr) *plan to move to your dream home?*

_____

8

Gesundheit
Health

In this chapter, you will learn the German words for illnesses, diseases, parts of the body, and medicines, and you will be able to describe your symptoms to the doctor and dentist. The vocabulary you learn will enable you to express your ideas about how to lead a healthy life.

Where does it hurt?	**Was tut Ihnen weh?**
<u>*My head hurts.*</u> *(I have a headache.)*	Mir tut <u>mein Kopf</u> weh. [M.]
My back	mein Rücken [M.]
My mouth	mein Mund [M.]
My stomach	mein Magen [M.], mein Bauch [M.]
My throat	mein Hals [M.]
<u>*My ears hurt.*</u>	Mir tun <u>meine Ohren</u> weh. [das Ohr]
My eyes	meine Augen [das Auge]
My feet	meine Füße [der Fuß]
My legs	meine Beine [das Bein]

> German reflexive verbs use either the definite article or the possessive adjective with parts of the body and articles of clothing: **Er hat sich den/seinen Finger gebrochen.** *He broke his finger.*

Breaks and sprains	**Brüche und Verstauchungen**
He broke <u>his elbow</u>.	Er hat sich <u>den/seinen Ellbogen</u> gebrochen.
his finger	den/seinen Finger
his knee	das/sein Knie
his neck	den/seinen Nacken
his nose	die/seine Nase
She broke <u>her arm</u>.	Sie hat sich <u>den/ihren Arm</u> gebrochen.
a rib	eine Rippe
her shoulder	die/ihre Schulter

Did you sprain your ankle?	Hast du dir <u>den/deinen Knöchel</u> verstaucht?
your toe	den/deinen Zeh
your wrist	das/dein Handgelenk

I broke a tooth.	Ich habe mir einen Zahn verletzt.
I cut my hand.	Ich habe mir in die Hand geschnitten.
I fractured a bone.	Ich habe mir etwas gebrochen.
I hurt my arm.	Ich habe meinen Arm verletzt.

At the doctor's office

Beim Arzt

The doctor has <u>to examine his patients.</u>	Der Doktor muß <u>seine Patienten untersuchen.</u>
to do a blood test	das Blut untersuchen
to do a throat culture	einen Rachenabstrich machen
to do an examination	eine Untersuchung machen
to do an X-ray	ein Röntgenbild machen
to give an injection	eine Spritze geben
to listen to his patient's chest	die Brust seines Patienten abhören
to listen to his patient's lungs	die Lungen seines Patienten abhören [die Lunge]
to take his patient's blood pressure	den Blutdruck seines Patienten messen
to take his patient's pulse	den Puls seines Patienten messen
to take his patient's temperature	die Temperatur seines Patienten messen
to vaccinate children	Kinder impfen [das Kind]
to write a prescription	ein Rezept verschreiben

What are your symptoms?

Welche Symptome haben Sie?

I don't feel well.	Ich fühle mich nicht gut.
I feel awful.	Ich fühle mich furchtbar.
I feel stressed.	Ich fühle mich gestreßt/gestresst.
I have a backache.	Ich habe Rückenschmerzen. [der Rückenschmerz]
I have a headache.	Ich habe Kopfschmerzen. [der Kopfschmerz]
I have a migraine.	Ich habe Migräne. [F.]
I have a sore throat.	Ich habe Halsschmerzen. [der Halsschmerz]
I have a stomachache.	Ich habe Bauchschmerzen. [der Bauchschmerz]
I have a stuffy nose.	Ich habe eine verstopfte Nase.
I have chapped lips.	Ich habe aufgesprungene Lippen. [die Lippe]
I have diarrhea.	Ich habe Durchfall. [M.]
I have fever.	Ich habe Fieber. [N.]
I have no energy.	Ich habe keine Energie.
I'm constipated.	Ich habe Verstopfung. [F.]

I'm coughing., I have a cough.	Ich habe Husten. [M.]
I'm dehydrated.	Ich bin dehydriert.
I'm gaining weight.	Ich nehme zu.
I'm losing weight.	Ich nehme ab.
I'm nauseous.	Mir ist übel.
I'm sneezing.	Ich niese.

Remedies/medicines

Medikamente

The doctor gave me a prescription.	Der Arzt hat mir ein Rezept gegeben.
an antibiotic	ein Antibiotikum
an antihistamine	ein Antihistamin
some cough drops	Hustentropfen [PL.]
cough syrup	Hustensaft [M.]
a flu shot	eine Grippeimpfung
an injection	eine Spritze
some medicine	Medikamente [das Medikament]
a pain killer	Schmerzmittel [N.]
sleeping pills	Schlaftabletten [die Schlaftablette]
some pills	Tabletten [die Tablette]
a tranquilizer	ein Beruhigungsmittel

What do the patients have?

Was fehlt den Patienten?

He has an illness.	Er hat eine Krankheit.
an ache, a pain	Schmerzen [der Schmerz]
a bruise	ein Hämatom
a burn	eine Verbrennung
a cut	eine Schnittwunde
an infection	eine Infektion, eine Entzündung
an injury	eine Verletzung
a rash	einen Hautausschlag
a virus	ein Virus

The patient has a cold.	Die Patientin hat eine Erkältung.
is in critical condition	befindet sich in einem kritischen Zustand
is dying	stirbt
is pregnant	ist schwanger
is sick	ist krank
has indigestion	hat eine Magenverstimmung
has the flu	hat die Grippe

I have a mosquito bite <u>on my forehead</u>.   Ich habe einen Mückenstich <u>auf der Stirn</u>.

on my cheek   auf der Wange

on my eyelid   auf dem Augenlid [N.]

on my face   in meinem Gesicht [N.]

Medical specialists   Fachärzte

I have an appointment <u>with the doctor</u>.   Ich habe einen Termin <u>beim Arzt</u>.

with the cardiologist   beim Kardiologen

with the dermatologist   beim Hautarzt

with the general practitioner,   beim Hausarzt

    with the family doctor,

    with the primary care physician

with the internist   beim Internisten

with the obstetrician   beim Geburtshelfer

with the ophthalmologist   beim Augenarzt

with the pediatrician   beim Kinderarzt

with the psychiatrist   beim Psychologen

Some parts of the body   Einige Körperteile

bones   Knochen [der Knochen]

brain   das Gehirn

breast   die Brust

chest   der Brustkorb

glands   die Drüsen [die Drüse]

heart   das Herz

hip   die Hüfte

joints   die Gelenke [das Gelenk]

kidney   die Niere

liver   die Leber

lung   die Lunge

muscles   die Muskeln [der Muskel]

spine   die Wirbelsäule

thigh   der Oberschenkel

Illnesses and medical conditions   Krankheiten und Beschwerden
Medical history   Die Krankengeschichte

allergy   die Allergie

arthritis   die Arthritis

asthma   das Asthma

bronchitis	die Bronchitis
cancer	der Krebs
chicken pox	die Windpocken
cold	die Erkältung
cough	der Husten
diabetes	der Diabetes
flu	die Grippe
heart attack	der Herzinfarkt
heart disease	die Herzerkrankung
hypertension	der Bluthochdruck
laryngitis	die Kehlkopfentzündung
mental illness	die Geisteskrankheit
pneumonia	die Lungenentzündung
sinusitis	die Nasennebenhöhlenentzündung
skin disease	die Hautkrankheit
stomach bug	die Magen-Darm-Grippe
strep throat	die Streptokokken-Infektion
urinary infection	die Harnwegsentzündung

The verbal expression **leiden an** *to suffer from* takes a dative object.

What does he have?

He's suffering from a chronic disease.
  a contagious/infectious disease
  a fatal disease
  a hereditary disease
  a serious illness/disease

Was fehlt ihm?

Er leidet an einer chronischen Krankheit.
  einer ansteckenden Krankheit
  einer tödlichen Krankheit
  einer Erbkrankheit
  einer ernsthaften Krankheit

In the dentist's office

The dentist has to fill cavities.
  to clean the teeth
  to pull a wisdom tooth
  to put on braces

crown
dental checkup
dental floss
filling
gums

Beim Zahnarzt

Der Zahnarzt muß Löcher füllen. [das Loch]
  die Zähne säubern [der Zahn]
  einen Weisheitszahn ziehen
  eine Spange einsetzen

die Krone
die Zahnuntersuchung
die Zahnseide
die Füllung
das Zahnfleisch

molar	der Backenzahn
plaque	der Zahnbelag
tongue	die Zunge
toothache	die Zahnschmerzen [der Zahnschmerz]
to brush one's teeth	die Zähne putzen
to rinse the mouth	den Mund ausspülen
to swallow	schlucken

Accidents

Unfälle

The accident victims are in an ambulance.	Die Opfer des Unfalls sind im Krankenwagen. [M.]
in the hospital	im Krankenhaus [N.], im Spital [N.] [AUS., SWITZ.]
in the emergency room	in der Notaufnahme
in intensive care	auf der Intensivstation
bleeding	die Blutung
casualty	das Opfer
first aid	die erste Hilfe
paramedic	der Sanitäter / die Sanitäterin

In the operating room

Im Operationssaal

operation	die Operation, der Eingriff
surgeon	der Chirurg / die Chirurgin
surgery	die Chirurgie
He's going to have heart surgery.	Er wird eine Herzoperation bekommen.
The surgeon is removing the patient's gallbladder.	Die Chirurgin entfernt die Gallenblase des Patienten.

To lead a healthy life

Gesunde Lebensführung

To lead a healthy life, you have to eat well.	Für ein gesundes Leben mußt du gut essen.
to control your weight	auf dein Gewicht achten
to drink a lot of water	viel Wasser trinken
to enjoy life	das Leben genießen
to exercise, to work out	Sport machen
to follow a balanced diet	dich ausgewogen ernähren
to get enough sleep	ausreichend schlafen
to have a positive attitude	eine positive Einstellung haben
to live with purpose	sich Ziele stecken
to reduce stress	Streß / Stress reduzieren >>>

>>>

to stop smoking	das Rauchen aufgeben
to take vitamins	Vitamine nehmen

Klingen Sie authentisch!

alternative medicine	die alternative Medizin, die Naturheilkunde
heartsickness	der Liebeskummer
preventive medicine	die Präventivmedizin
to prevent	vorbeugen
to treat	behandeln

The five senses	Die fünf Sinne
sight	das Sehen
hearing	das Hören
smell	das Riechen
taste	das Schmecken
touch	das Fühlen

He died of natural causes.	Er starb an natürlichen Ursachen.
His leg is in a cast, and he walks with crutches.	Sein Bein ist eingegipst, und er läuft an Krücken.
Her nose is bleeding.	Ihre Nase blutet.
I have a sprained ankle.	Ich habe einen verstauchten Knöchel.
She's having her period.	Sie hat ihre Tage., Sie hat ihre Regel.
Alcohol has damaged his liver.	Der Alkohol hat seine Leber beschädigt.
Get well soon!	Gute Besserung!

Ausdrücke, Sprichwörter und Zitate

to be as close as can be	ganz nahe dran sein
to be very outspoken	direkt sein
to pull someone's leg	jemandem ein Bein stellen
to talk incessantly	ununterbrochen reden

Break a leg!	Hals- und Beinbruch!

A happy heart, a healthy man.	Ein heiteres Herz ist die beste Medizin.
Health is better than wealth.	Lieber arm und gesund als reich und krank.
No use crying over spilt milk.	Über vergossene Milch soll man nicht jammern.
Out of sight, out of mind.	Aus den Augen, aus dem Sinn.
Prevention is better than cure.	Vorsicht ist besser als Nachsicht.

„In der einen Hälfte des Lebens opfern wir unsere Gesundheit, um Geld zu erwerben. In der anderen Hälfte opfern wir Geld, um die Gesundheit wiederzuerlangen."

VOLTAIRE

„Abwechslung ist eine gute Medizin für die meisten Leiden."

CHRISTINA VON SCHWEDEN

„Vernunft, das ist so etwas wie ansteckende Gesundheit."

ALBERTO MORAVIA

Übung 46

Complete each German phrase or sentence so that it expresses the meaning of the English phrase or sentence.

1. *a wisdom tooth*   ein Weisheits_____

2. *first aid*   erste _____

3. *He has a cold.*   Er hat eine _____.

4. *a mosquito bite*   ein _____stich

5. *a backache*   ein _____schmerzen

6. *a sprained wrist*   ein verstauchtes _____

7. *a balanced diet*   eine ausgewogene _____

8. *to talk incessantly*   _____ reden

9. *to live with purpose*   sich _____ stecken

10. *to be very outspoken*   _____ sein

11. *The leg is in a cast.*   Das Bein ist _____.

12. *I feel awful.*   Ich fühle mich _____.

13. *No use crying over spilt milk.*   _____ soll man nicht jammern.

14. *dental plaque*   Zahn_____

15. *Health is better than wealth.*   Lieber arm und gesund als _____.

Übung 47

Select the verb from the following list that correctly completes each phrase.

abhören	schneiden	ausspülen	genießen
messen	untersuchen	brechen	ziehen
aufgeben	putzen	verstauchen	verschreiben

1. sich den Arm _____

2. sich das Handgelenk _____

3. sich in die Hand _____

4. das Blut _____

5. die Lunge _____

6. den Puls _____

7. ein Rezept _____

8. die Zähne _____

9. einen Weisheitszahn _____

10. den Mund _____

11. das Leben _____

12. das Rauchen _____

Übung 48

For which medical problems would you . . .

1. go to a doctor?

_____

_____

_____

_____

2. use medication?

_____

_____

_____

_____

3. do nothing?

_____

_____

_____

_____

Übung 49

Respond in German as specified for each of the following situations.

1. **Ein Arztbesuch.** You go to the doctor because you're not feeling well. Detail your symptoms, what hurts you, what kind of doctor you're seeing, and what he or she prescribes.

_____

_____

_____

_____

_____

_____

_____

_____

2. **Sie sind der Arzt.** You are a family doctor or internist. Describe some of the things you do for your patients.

_____

_____

_____

_____

_____

_____

_____

_____

3. **Die Krankengeschichte.** You are filling out a medical history for your doctor. List the diseases that you and your family members have or have had.

_____

_____

_____

_____

_____

_____

_____

_____

4. **Beim Zahnarzt.** Describe some of the things a dentist does for his patients.

_____

_____

_____

_____

_____

_____

_____

_____

5. **Das gesunde Leben.** List some of the things you can do to lead a healthy life.

_____

_____

_____

_____

_____

_____

_____

_____

Übung 50

Tell what kind of doctor each person needs, using the indefinite article with the noun. There may be more than one correct answer for some items.

1. Franziska ist erkältet. _____

2. Daniel tun die Augen weh. _____

3. Hannah ist schwanger. _____

4. Klaus hat die Windpocken. _____

5. Justus hat eine Herzkrankheit. _____

6. Ingmar hat eine Hautkrankheit. _____

7. Tessa ist geisteskrank. _____

8. Alfred hat Zahnschmerzen. _____

9. Anna braucht eine Routineuntersuchung. _____

10. Martin benötigt eine Operation. _____

11. Oliver hat Hautausschlag. _____

12. Annett braucht eine Zahnspange. _____

Übung 51

Unscramble the letters in each item to create a noun that represents a part of the body.

1. eigscht _____

2. leiregla _____

3. tiehknark _____

4. dahn _____

5. ämengir _____

6. beerl _____

7. eitsprz _____

8. etteblat _____

9. sirvu _____

10. prigep _____

Übung 52

Translate the following sentences into German.

1. *I'm going to the doctor because I have a backache.*

_____

2. *What are your (Sie) symptoms?*

_____

3. I don't feel well. I have a stomachache and I'm nauseous.

_____

_____

4. The doctor gave him an antibiotic because he has an infection.

_____

_____

5. Her gums bleed. She should go to the dentist.

_____

6. How did you (du) break your nose?

_____

7. The paramedics are treating the accident victims in the ambulance.

_____

_____

8. Did you (du) hurt your wrist?

_____

9. Yes, I sprained it.

_____

10. The pediatrician has just vaccinated the child.

_____

11. Henrik is using crutches because he broke his leg.

_____

12. They are very outspoken and talk incessantly.

_____

13. What can one do to lead a healthy life?

_____

14. I try to follow a balanced diet and reduce stress.

_____

Familie und Beziehungen; Menschen beschreiben

Family and relationships; describing people

This chapter presents German terms for members of the family, as well as vocabulary that will enable you to talk about age, civil status, and physical and personality traits. You will learn how to describe your relationships and talk about important stages of life.

The verb **vorstellen** *to introduce* takes both an accusative object and a dative object. The accusative object is the person being introduced, and the dative object is the person to whom he or she is introduced.

Family	**Die Familie**
I'm going to introduce you to my father.	Ich werde dich meinem Vater vorstellen.
to my dad	meinem Papa
to my mother	meiner Mutter
to my mom	meiner Mama
to my parents	meinen Eltern
to my brother	meinem Bruder
to my sister	meiner Schwester
to my older brother	meinem älteren Bruder
to my older sister	meiner älteren Schwester
to my younger brother	meinem jüngeren Bruder
to my kid brother	meinem kleinen Bruder
to my kid sister	meiner kleinen Schwester
to my half brother	meinem Halbbruder
to my half sister	meiner Halbschwester
to my grandfather	meinem Großvater
to my grandmother	meiner Großmutter
to my grandson	meinem Enkel
to my granddaughter	meiner Enkelin

>>>

to my great-grandfather	meinem Urgroßvater
to my great-grandmother	meiner Urgroßmutter
to my son	meinem Sohn
to my daughter	meiner Tochter
to my firstborn (oldest child)	meinem/meiner Erstgeborenen, meinem/meiner Ältesten
to my last born (youngest child)	meinem/meiner Jüngsten
to my adopted son	meinem Adoptivsohn
to my adopted daughter	meiner Adoptivtochter
to my stepson	meinem Stiefsohn
to my stepdaughter	meiner Stieftochter
to my husband	meinem Mann
to my wife	meiner Frau

How to introduce someone

Wie man jemanden vorstellt

I want you to meet my son.	Ich möchte dir meinen Sohn vorstellen.
Glad to meet you.	Sehr erfreut.
The pleasure is mine.	Das Vergnügen ist ganz meinerseits.

The verb **treffen** *to meet* takes an accusative object.

Relatives

Die Verwandten

I met <u>your uncle</u> at a family gathering.	Ich habe <u>deinen Onkel</u> auf einer Familienfeier getroffen.
your aunt	deine Tante
your nephew	deinen Neffen
your niece	deine Nichte
your cousin	deinen Cousin / deine Cousine
your brother-in-law	deinen Schwippschwager
your sister-in-law	deine Schwippschwägerin
your father-in-law	deinen Schwiegervater
your mother-in-law	deine Schwiegermutter
your son-in-law	deinen Schwiegersohn
your daughter-in-law	deine Schwiegertochter
your twin brothers	deine Zwillingsbrüder
your twin sisters	deine Zwillingsschwestern

More relatives

We're going to invite the close relatives.
   the distant relatives
   all the relations, all the relatives

Godparents and godchildren

She loves her godfather a lot.
   her godmother
   her godson
   her goddaughter

What is his/her marital status?

He/She is single.
He/She is engaged.
He/She is married.
He/She is separated.
He/She is divorced.
He is a widower.
She is a widow.

He's a confirmed bachelor.
She's an unmarried woman.

How old is he/she?

How old is the teenager?
   your (male) friend, your boyfriend
   your fiancé
   the little boy
   that man
   that man, that gentleman
   that young man
   your (female) friend, your girlfriend
   your fiancée
   the little girl
   that woman
   that young woman

Mehr Verwandte

Wir werden die engeren Verwandten einladen.
   die entfernten Verwandten
   alle Verwandten

Paten und Patenkinder

Sie liebt ihren Paten sehr.
   ihre Patin
   ihren Patensohn
   ihre Patentochter

Was ist sein/ihr Familienstand?

Er/Sie ist Single.
Er/Sie ist verlobt.
Er/Sie ist verheiratet.
Er/Sie ist getrennt.
Er/Sie ist geschieden.
Er ist Witwer.
Sie ist Witwe.

Er ist ein eingefleischter Junggeselle.
Sie ist eine unverheiratete Frau.

Wie alt ist er/sie?

Wie alt ist der/die Jugendliche?
   dein Freund
   dein Verlobter
   der kleine Junge
   dieser Mann
   dieser Herr
   dieser junge Mann
   deine Freundin
   deine Verlobte
   das kleine Mädchen
   diese Frau
   diese junge Frau

Unlike English numbers, German numbers are written as one word, without spaces or hyphens.

How old are they?

The baby is six months old.
Ms. Hennig is twenty-three years old.
Mr. Mengelberg is fifty-seven years old.
Mrs. Blomberg is thirty-nine years old.
Emil was orphaned at the age of eight.
Ida lost her father when she was twelve.
Ida lost her mother when she was twelve.

Wie alt sind sie?

Das Baby ist sechs Monate alt.
Fräulein Hennig ist dreiundzwanzig Jahre alt.
Herr Mengelberg ist siebenundfünfzig Jahre alt.
Frau Blomberg ist neununddreißig Jahre alt.
Emil wurde mit acht Jahren Waise.
Ida verlor ihren Vater als sie zwölf war.
Ida verlor ihre Mutter als sie zwölf war.

Human relations

They have a close relationship.
  changing
  cold
  complex
  complicated
  confusing
  cordial
  difficult
  distant
  harmonious
  hostile
  intimate
  loving
  professional
  respectful
  serious
  solid
  stormy
  strange

Beziehungen

Sie haben eine enge Beziehung.
  wechselhafte
  kühle
  komplexe
  komplizierte
  verwirrende
  herzliche
  schwierige
  distanzierte
  harmonische
  feindliche
  intime
  liebevolle
  professionelle, kollegiale
  respektvolle
  ernste
  stabile
  stürmische
  merkwürdige

What's the family like?

It's a close family.
  conservative
  happy
  hospitable

Wie ist die Familie?

Es ist eine enge Familie.
  konservative
  glückliche
  gastfreundliche   >>>

large	große
open-minded	offene
poor	arme
religious	religiöse
respected	angesehene
rich	reiche
traditional	traditionelle
warm	warme
welcoming	einladende

Character and personality

Fritz is <u>amusing</u>.

annoying	lästig, sekkant [AUS.]
arrogant	arrogant
boring	langweilig
brave	tapfer
calm	ruhig
capable	kompetent
charming	reizend
compassionate	mitfühlend
competitive	wetteifernd
conceited	eingebildet
cowardly	feige
crazy	verrückt
creative	kreativ
curious	neugierig
dishonest	unehrlich
embittered	verbittert
focused	konzentriert
friendly	freundlich
generous	großzügig
gullible	leichtgläubig
hard-working	fleißig
honest	ehrlich
humble	bescheiden
hypocritical	heuchlerisch
idealistic	idealistisch
insufferable	unerträglich

Charakter und Persönlichkeit

Fritz ist <u>lustig</u>.

intelligent	intelligent
interesting	interessant
kind	lieb
lazy	faul
likeable	sympathisch
loyal	loyal
mean	gemein
naive	naiv
nervous	nervös
nice	sympathisch
optimistic	optimistisch
patient	geduldig
pessimistic	pessimistisch
phony	verlogen
pleasant	angenehm
realistic	realistisch
responsible	verantwortungsvoll
self-assured	selbstbewußt / selbstbewusst
selfish	egoistisch
sensible	vernünftig
sensitive	einfühlsam
shameless	schamlos
shy	schüchtern
silly	albern
sincere	aufrichtig
stingy	geizig
stubborn	stur
stupid	dumm
unpleasant	unangenehm

What does she look like?

Wie sieht sie aus?

My (girl)friend is <u>pretty</u>.	Meine Freundin ist <u>hübsch</u>.
attractive	attraktiv
beautiful	schön
blond	blond
cute	süß, niedlich, herzig [AUS., SWITZ.]
dark-haired	dunkelhaarig
dark(-skinned)	dunkelhäutig

>>>

fat	dick
old	alt
red-headed	rothaarig
short	klein
strong	stark
tall	groß
thin	dünn
ugly	häßlich / hässlich
weak	schwach
young	jung

She has <u>brown</u> eyes.	Sie hat <u>braune</u> Augen.
blue	blaue
gray	graue
green	grüne
hazel	grün-braune

The stages of life   Lebensabschnitte

birth	die Geburt
baptism	die Taufe
first communion	die Erstkommunion
bar mitzvah	die Bar-Mizwa
bat mitzvah	die Bat-Mizwa
school	die Schule
college	die Universität, die Hochschule
graduation	der Abschluß / Abschluss
military service	der Wehrdienst
work	die Arbeit
engagement	die Anstellung
marriage	die Ehe
wedding	die Hochzeit
pregnancy	die Schwangerschaft
children	die Kinder [das Kind]
divorce	die Scheidung
remarriage	die Wiederverheiratung
retirement	der Ruhestand
old age	das Alter
death	der Tod

Klingen Sie authentisch!

Jan and I have a close friendship.	Jan und ich sind eng befreundet.
Henrik is afraid of commitment.	Henrik hat Angst vor Beziehungen.
What a nice couple!	Was für ein schönes Paar!
I'm looking for my soul mate.	Ich suche nach meinem Seelenverwandten.
Marie is looking for a mate/partner online.	Marie sucht einen Partner im Internet.
Pia doesn't like dating websites.	Pia mag keine Dating-Websites.
Karla doesn't go out with Dirk anymore.	Karla trifft sich nicht mehr mit Dirk.
She broke off with him.	Sie hat mit ihm Schluß/Schluss gemacht.
They adopted a war orphan.	Sie haben einen Kriegswaisen adoptiert.

Ausdrücke, Sprichwörter und Zitate

He was born with a silver spoon in his mouth.	Er ist mit dem Silberlöffel im Mund auf die Welt gekommen.
He's a chip off the old block.	Der Apfel fällt nicht weit vom Stamm.
They are like two peas in a pod.	Die beiden gleichen sich wie ein Ei dem anderen.
Blood is thicker than water.	Blut ist dicker als Wasser.
Unlucky in cards, lucky in love.	Pech im Spiel, Glück in der Liebe.
The more the merrier.	Je mehr, desto besser.
It's better to be alone than in bad company.	Besser allein als in schlechter Gesellschaft.
Looks can be deceiving.	Es ist nicht alles Gold, was glänzt.

„Die Kinder von heute sind Tyrannen. Sie widersprechen ihren Eltern, kleckern mit dem Essen und ärgern ihre Lehrer."

SOKRATES

„Viele Kinder haben schwer erziehbare Eltern."

JEAN-JACQUES ROUSSEAU

„Es gibt viele Möglichkeiten, Karriere zu machen, aber der sicherste ist noch immer, in der richtigen Familie geboren zu sein."

DONALD TRUMP

„In den Kindern erlebt man sein eigenes Leben noch einmal, und erst jetzt versteht man es ganz."

SØREN KIERKEGAARD

„Du sollst deinen Vater und deine Mutter ehren."

DAS VIERTE GEBOT

Übung 53

Complete each sentence with the term for the appropriate family member.

1. Die Tochter meiner Tante ist _____.

2. Die Mutter meines Vaters ist _____.

3. Der Ehemann meiner Tochter ist _____.

4. Die Eltern meines Großvaters sind _____.

5. Der Sohn meiner Frau aus erster Ehe ist _____.

6. Die Frau meines Bruders ist _____.

7. Zwei Babys, die gleichzeitig von derselben Mutter geboren werden, sind

   _____.

8. Der Mann, der die Schwester meines Vaters geheiratet hat, ist

   _____.

9. Die Eltern meines Ehemannes sind _____.

10. Die Schwester meiner Mutter ist _____.

11. Ich bin genauso alt wie meine Schwester. Ich bin _____.

12. Die Kinder meiner Kinder sind _____.

Übung 54

Complete each German phrase or sentence so that it expresses the meaning of the English phrase or sentence.

1. *our distant relatives*   unsere entfernten _____

2. *his marital status*   sein Familien_____

3. *my soul mate*   meine _____verwandte

4. *How old is he?*   Wie _____ ist er?

5. *a large family*   eine _____ Familie

6. *They're like two peas in a pod.*   Die beiden gleichen sich wie _____.

7. *all the relatives*   alle _____

8. *She's conceited and selfish.*   Sie ist _____ und

   _____.

9. *their strange relationship*   ihre _____ Beziehung

10. *our close friendship*   unsere _____ Freundschaft

11. *my brother-in-law*   mein _____

12. *He's tall, dark, and handsome.*   Er ist _____,

_____ und

_____ .

13. *Blood is thicker than water.*   _____ ist dicker als

_____ .

14. *your half brother*   dein _____bruder

15. *She has hazel eyes.*   Sie hat _____ Augen.

Übung 55

Select the word from the following list that correctly completes each sentence.

Paar	feige	Gold	Waise	Augen
Junggeselle	Hochzeit	merkwürdige	reiche	

1. Er ist ein eingefleischter _____ .

2. Er wurde mit sechs Jahren _____ .

3. Sie haben eine _____ Beziehung.

4. Es ist eine _____ Familie.

5. Fritz ist _____ .

6. Tessa hat braune _____ .

7. Die _____ war sehr nett.

8. Was für ein schönes _____!

9. Es ist nicht alles _____, was glänzt.

Übung 56

Describe three members of your family. Tell who they are, their ages, what they look like, and their character and personality traits.

_____

_____

_____

_____

_____

_____
_____
_____
_____
_____
_____

Übung 57

Describe what you look like and list your character and personality traits.

_____
_____
_____
_____
_____
_____
_____
_____
_____
_____
_____

Übung 58

Unscramble the letters in each item to find out who will attend the family party.

1. insouc   _____
2. durreb   _____
3. ertva   _____
4. ertumt   _____
5. tape   _____

6. rotumgerßt   _____
7. lahrebbrud   _____
8. hosn   _____
9. klene   _____
10. hotterc   _____

Übung 59

Match each word in the first column with its antonym in the second column.

1. _____ intelligent   a. interessant
2. _____ dünn   b. angenehm
3. _____ schüchtern   c. dumm
4. _____ langweilig   d. nervös
5. _____ großzügig   e. häßlich
6. _____ schön   f. klein
7. _____ arrogant   g. dick
8. _____ reich   h. arm
9. _____ unangenehm   i. alt
10. _____ lieb   j. geizig
11. _____ jung   k. unehrlich
12. _____ ruhig   l. gemein
13. _____ tapfer   m. schamlos
14. _____ groß   n. optimistisch
15. _____ ehrlich   o. bescheiden
16. _____ pessimistisch   p. feige

Übung 60

Translate the following sentences into German.

1. *I want to introduce you* (du) *to my parents.*

   _____

2. *You* (du) *are going to meet my uncle and aunt at the party.*

   _____

   _____

3. *The godparents love their godson and goddaughter a lot.*

   _____

   _____

4. *Richard and Erika Schmidt have a close and warm family.*

_____

_____

5. *Their daughter Franziska and son-in-law Moritz have a two-month-old baby.*

_____

_____

6. *Their son Emil is engaged.*

_____

7. *Their younger son Arno is twenty-two years old.*

_____

8. *Anna is hardworking, generous, and charming. Her twin brother is lazy, selfish, and annoying.*

_____

_____

9. *Rita broke off with her boyfriend because he's afraid of commitment.*

_____

_____

10. *What does your* (deine) *(female) cousin look like?*

_____

11. *She's dark-haired, short, thin, and very pretty.*

_____

12. *My brother, my sister, and I have blue eyes.*

_____

Musik, Theater, Film und bildende Kunst

Music, theater, film, and the visual arts

This chapter presents vocabulary that will enable you to describe a concert, a play, a film, and a visit to the art museum. You will learn how to express time in German so that you can tell at what time the concert starts. You will also be able to talk about your experiences playing an instrument, making a film, and painting a picture.

Music for all tastes	**Musik für jeden Geschmack**
I love classical music.	Ich liebe klassische Musik. [F.]
ballet music	Ballettmusik [F.]
chamber music	Kammermusik [F.]
disco music	Discomusik [F.]
electronic music	elektronische Musik [F.]
folk music	Folk [M.], Volksmusik [F.]
German pop music, schlager music	Schlager [M.]
musical theater	Musicals [das Musical]
opera	Oper [F.]
rock 'n' roll	Rockmusik [F.], Rock 'n' roll [M.]
techno music	Techno [M./N.]
vocal music	Vokalmusik [F.]
world music	Weltmusik [F.]

Schlager is a particular style of popular music that is sung in German and has little in common with traditional folklore. Schlager songs are usually light pop tunes or romantic or sentimental ballads with simple, catchy melodies. The performers typically dress in traditional costumes and include "folksy" instruments like accordions and zithers.

Musical instruments

Do you know how to play *the piano*?
   the bassoon
   the cello
   the clarinet
   the drum
   the English horn
   the flute
   the French horn
   the guitar
   the harp
   the harpsichord
   the oboe
   the organ
   percussion
   the piccolo
   the recorder
   the saxophone
   the trombone
   the trumpet
   the tuba
   the viola
   the violin

Musikinstrumente

Kannst du Klavier spielen? [N.]
   Fagott [N.]
   Cello [N.]
   Klarinette [F.]
   Trommel [F.]
   Englischhorn [N.]
   Flöte [F.]
   Waldhorn [N.]
   Gitarre [F.]
   Harfe [F.]
   Cembalo [N.]
   Oboe [F.]
   Orgel [F.]
   Schlagzeug [N.]
   Piccoloflöte [F.]
   Blockflöte [F.]
   Saxophon / Saxofon [N.]
   Posaune [F.]
   Trompete [F.]
   Tuba [F.]
   Viola [F.]
   Violine [F.]

Germany and Austria are often referred to as the homeland of classical music. They are the birthplace of some of the world's greatest composers: Bach, Beethoven, Mozart, Schubert, Schumann, and Brahms. While Italian composers focused mainly on operas, German and Austrian composers initiated a long tradition of orchestral and chamber music. It is not surprising, therefore, that there are so many world-class orchestras in Germany and Austria today.

Artists

band
choir, chorus
conductor
dancer
ensemble, music group
instrumentalist

Künstler

die Band
der Chor
der Dirigent / die Dirigentin
der Tänzer / die Tänzerin
die Gruppe, das Ensemble
der Instrumentalist

musician	der Musiker / die Musikerin
performer	der Interpret / die Interpretin
singer	der Sänger / die Sängerin
street musician, busker	der Straßenmusiker / die Straßenmusikerin

She likes to dance.	Sie mag <u>tanzen</u>.
to compose	komponieren
to conduct	dirigieren
to sing	singen

Symphonic music has a long tradition in Germany and Austria, and many world-class orchestras were founded there. The two most famous are **die Berliner Philharmoniker** and **die Wiener Philharmoniker**. Among their chief conductors have been Wilhelm Furtwängler, Karl Böhm, Claudio Abbado, and Sir Simon Rattle. In fact, most major cities in these two countries have more than one elite symphony orchestra. In Berlin alone, there are four: **die Philharmoniker, das Deutsche Symphonie-Orchester, das Konzerthausorchester,** and **das Radiosymphonieorchester.**

The symphony orchestra — Das Symphonieorchester

There are four sections in the orchestra.	Es gibt vier Instrumentengruppen im Orchester. [die Instrumentengruppe]
woodwinds	Holzbläser
brass	Blechbläser
strings	Streicher
percussion	Schlaginstrumente [das Schlaginstrument]

The concert hall — Der Konzertsaal

Beethoven was a great composer.	Beethoven war ein großer Komponist.
The audience applauded a lot.	Das Publikum applaudierte begeistert.
The dancers received a lot of applause.	Die Tänzer erhielten viel Applaus.
They called for an encore.	Sie forderten eine Zugabe.
We loved his performance of the sonata.	Uns gefiel seine Interpretation der Sonate.
We attended the world premiere of the symphony.	Wir wohnten der Uraufführung der Symphonie bei.
The song has a beautiful melody and lyrics.	Das Lied hat eine schöne Melodie und einen schönen Text.

acoustics	die Akustik
baton	der Taktstock
microphone	das Mikrophon / Mikrofon
recording/sound engineer	der Tonmeister
rehearsal	die Probe
dress rehearsal	die Kostümprobe
score	die Partitur
stand	das Notenpult

Telling time and expressions of time

Zeit und Zeitausdrücke

What time is it?	Wie spät ist es?
It's one o'clock.	Es ist eins.
It's two o'clock.	Es ist zwei.
It's 4:15.	Es ist vier Uhr fünfzehn., Es ist viertel nach vier., Es ist viertel fünf.
It's 7:30.	Es ist halb acht.
It's ten to nine.	Es ist zehn vor neun.
It's 10:45.	Es ist zehn Uhr fünfundvierzig., Es ist viertel vor elf., Es ist dreiviertel elf.
It's noon.	Es ist Mittag.
It's midnight.	Es ist Mitternacht.

There are three methods of telling time in German. The first is the "official" form, used for show listings, train schedules, and so on. It's a 24-hour-system, in which 8:15 p.m. is expressed as 20:15, **zwanzig Uhr fünfzehn**. In informal German, it's more common to express 20:15 as **viertel nach acht** *a quarter past eight*. Speakers from southwest and east Germany say **viertel neun** for 20:15, meaning that the first quarter of the ninth hour has passed. The spoken-German equivalents of a.m. and p.m. are **morgens** *in the morning*, **nachmittags** *in the afternoon*, **abends** *in the evening*, and **nachts** *at night*.

At what time is the concert?

Wann ist das Konzert?

The concert is at 11 a.m.	Das Konzert ist um elf Uhr vormittags.
at 3 p.m.	um drei Uhr nachmittags
at 8 p.m.	um acht Uhr abends

We'll get to the theater <u>about seven o'clock</u>.	Wir werden <u>gegen sieben</u> am Theater sein.
a little after five o'clock	kurz nach fünf
at exactly six o'clock	genau um sechs
early	früh
on time	pünktlich
late	spät
in the morning	morgens
in the afternoon	nachmittags
in the evening	abends

To talk about time

Von der Zeit sprechen

I'm going to take a flute lesson <u>today</u>.	Ich werde <u>heute</u> eine Flötenstunde haben.
tomorrow	morgen
tomorrow morning	morgen früh
tomorrow afternoon	morgen nachmittag
tomorrow evening	morgen abend
the day after tomorrow	übermorgen
on Wednesday	(am) Mittwoch
this week	diese Woche
during the week	unter der Woche
next week	nächste Woche
next month	nächsten Monat
around the beginning of the month	Anfang des Monats
around the middle of the month	Mitte des Monats
around the end of the month	Ende des Monats

The theater

Das Theater

We're going to see <u>a show</u> tonight.	Wir werden uns heute abend <u>eine Vorstellung</u> anschauen.
a comedy	eine Komödie
a drama	ein Drama
a musical	ein Musical
a musical revue	eine Revue
a play	ein Theaterstück
a tragedy	eine Tragödie

German abounds with compound nouns. The gender of a compound noun is the gender of the final noun in the sequence.

die Kunst + der Film   > der Kunstfilm *art film*
der Abend + die Kasse > die Abendkasse *box office*
die Bühne + das Bild   > das Bühnenbild *scenery*

There is the stage.	Dort ist die Bühne.
the balcony	der Rang
the box office	die Abendkasse
the curtain	der Vorhang
the scenery, the set	das Bühnenbild
There are the costumes.	Dort sind die Kostüme. [das Kostüm]
the rows	die Reihen [die Reihe]
the seats	die Plätze [der Platz]

The play

Das Theaterstück

act	der Akt
actor	der Schauspieler
actress	die Schauspielerin
audition	das Vorsprechen
cast	die Besetzung
character	die Person
dialogue	der Dialog
intermission	die Pause
monologue	der Monolog
playwright, dramatist	der Dramaturg
plot	die Handlung
protagonist	die Hauptperson
scene	die Bühne
script (film)	das Drehbuch
script (play)	das Regebuch
smash hit	der Riesenerfolg
understudy	die Zweitbesetzung
to act	spielen
to come on stage, to go on stage	auf die Bühne gehen
to play the part, to play the role	die Rolle spielen

to stage	inszenieren
to go on tour, to go on the road	auf Tournee gehen
Everyone on stage!	Alle auf die Bühne!
The box office opens at 10 a.m.	Die Abendkasse öffnet um zehn Uhr morgens.
There are some tickets available.	Es gibt noch einige Eintrittskarten.
The tickets are sold out.	Die Eintrittskarten sind ausverkauft.
The play ran for two years.	Das Stück lief zwei Jahre lang.

Germany has a long tradition of filmmaking. In fact, the German Universum Film AG (UFA), founded in 1917, was for many years, along with Paramount and Metro-Goldwyn-Mayer, one of the global players of the film industry. Some German silent movies and talkies from the 1920s and 1930s are world famous: Friedrich Murnau's *Faust* and Fritz Lang's *Metropolis* and *M* are timeless masterpieces. German actors such as Emil Jannings (who won the very first Oscar), Marlene Dietrich, and Klaus Kinski enjoyed international careers. The best-known German movies of the modern era include *Das Boot*, *Das Leben der Anderen*, and *Der Untergang*, each dealing with a different period of German history.

Film　　Der Film

action film	der Actionfilm
adventure film	der Abenteuerfilm
art film	der Kunstfilm
blockbuster	der Kassenschlager
cartoons	Zeichentrickfilme [der Zeichentrickfilm]
censorship	die Zensur
cinematography	die Kinematographie / Kinematografie
documentary	der Dokumentarfilm
ending	das Ende
film noir	der Film Noir
filmmaker	der Filmemacher
foreign film	der ausländische Film
historical film	der historische Film
horror film	der Horrorfilm
movie buff	der Cineast / die Cineastin
movie fan	der Kinofan
movie star	der Filmstar
mystery	der Krimi
photography	die Fotografie

premiere	die Erstaufführung
producer	der Produzent / die Produzentin
review	die Kritik
science fiction film	der Science-Fiction-Film
screen	die Leinwand
silent film	der Stummfilm
shooting (of a film)	die Dreharbeiten
television film	der Fernsehfilm
thriller	der Thriller
war film	der Kriegsfilm
western	der Western
to dub	synchronisieren
to film, to shoot a film	filmen, einen Film drehen
to premiere	erstaufführen
to show a film	einen Film zeigen
to win the Oscar	den Oscar gewinnen
What film is showing this week?	Welcher Film wird diese Woche gezeigt?
Where is that film playing?	Wo wird der Film gezeigt?
The film was well received.	Der Film ist gut angenommen worden.
One can consult the film schedules in the movie listings.	Die Vorführzeiten stehen in der Liste der gezeigten Filme.
Casablanca won the Oscar for best film in 1944.	„Casablanca" gewann 1944 den Oscar für den besten Film.
The 30s and 40s: "The Golden Age of Hollywood"	Die 30er und 40er: „Hollywoods goldenes Zeitalter"

Radio and television

Rundfunk und Fernsehen

announcer (radio, TV)	der Sprecher / die Sprecherin
channel (TV)	der Sender
commercial	die Werbung
educational television	das Bildungsfernsehen
music program	das Musikprogramm
news (radio, TV)	die Nachrichten [die Nachricht *piece of news*]
quiz show	die Quiz-Show
radio (broadcasting)	der Rundfunk
radio (set)	das Rundfunkgerät, das Radio
reality show	die Reality-Show
recorded program	die aufgezeichnete Sendung
serial	die Serie

station (radio)	der Kanal
talk show	die Talk-Show
television show	die Fernseh-Show
TV	das Fernsehen
TV set	das Fernsehgerät

Visual arts / Bildende Kunst

architecture	die Architektur
arts and crafts	das Kunsthandwerk
digital art	die digitale Kunst
drawing	das Zeichnen
fine arts	die schönen Künste
graphic arts	die Graphik / Grafik
installation	die Installation
painting	die Malerei
performance art	die Performance-Kunst
photography	die Fotografie
plastic arts	die plastische Kunst
pottery, ceramics	das Töpfern
printmaking	die Druckgraphik / Druckgrafik
sculpture	die Skulptur

At the art museum / Im Kunstmuseum

art gallery	die Kunstgalerie
curator	der Kurator / die Kuratorin
exhibition, exhibit	die Ausstellung, das Ausstellungsstück
landscape	die Landschaft
museum piece	das Museumsstück
oil painting	die Ölmalerei
painting (process)	die Malerei
painting (on a wall)	das Gemälde
portrait	das Portrait / Porträt
poster	das Poster
print	der Druck
room (in a museum), hall	der Saal
sculpture	die Skulptur
self-portrait	das Selbstportrait / Selbstporträt
sketch	die Zeichnung
still life	das Stilleben / Stillleben

In the painter's studio	Im Atelier
There is a canvas.	Dort ist eine Leinwand.
an easel	eine Staffelei
a model	ein Modell [N.]
a palette	eine Palette
a palette knife	ein Palettmesser [N.]
There are brushes.	Dort sind Pinsel. [der Pinsel]
frames	Rahmen [der Rahmen]
paints	Farben [die Farbe]
oil paints	Ölfarben [die Ölfarbe]
watercolors	Wasserfarben [die Wasserfarbe]
He loves to paint.	Er liebt es, zu malen.
to draw	zu zeichnen
to sculpt	zu bildhauern
to sketch	zu zeichnen, zu entwerfen
to take photos	Photos / Fotos zu machen

Artists and art experts
Künstler und Kunstexperten

He's a craftsman.	Er ist ein Kunsthandwerker.
a landscape painter	ein Landschaftsmaler / eine Landschaftsmalerin
a photographer	ein Fotograf / eine Fotografin
a portrait painter, a portraitist	ein Portraitmaler / Porträtmaler / eine Portraitmalerin / Porträtmalerin
a sculptor	ein Bildhauer / eine Bildhauerin
He's an antique dealer.	Er ist Antiquar.
an art connoisseur	Kunstkenner
an art dealer	Kunsthändler
an art expert	Kunstexperte

Describing artists and their works
Künstler und ihre Arbeit beschreiben

abstract	abstrakt
accessible (of music)	zugänglich, eingängig
aesthetic	ästhetisch
artistic	künstlerisch
avant-garde	avantgardistisch
creative	kreativ
evocative	sinnträchtig

imaginative	phantasievoll / fantasievoll
innovative	innovativ
inspiring	inspirierend
minimalist	minimalistisch
naturalist	naturalistisch
picturesque	malerisch
prolific	produktiv
realist	realistisch
romantic	romantisch
sensitive	einfühlsam
stylized	stilisiert
surrealist	surrealistisch
talented	begabt

Klingen Sie authentisch!

The child prodigy plays by ear.	Das Wunderkind spielt nach Gehör.
Listen. Music is playing.	Hör zu. Dort ist Musik.
The piano is a keyboard instrument.	Das Klavier ist ein Tasteninstrument.
The Gemäldegalerie has one of the most complete collections in the world.	Die Gemäldegalerie hat eine der größten Sammlungen der Welt.
Zwei Liebespaare (Two lovers) is one of Gerhard Richter's many masterpieces.	„Zwei Liebespaare" ist eines der vielen Meisterwerke von Gerhard Richter.
Emil Nolde was a member of the artist group "Die Brücke."	Emil Nolde war Mitglied der Künstlergruppe „Die Brücke".
Kreidefelsen auf Rügen is a romantic painting by Caspar David Friedrich.	„Kreidefelsen auf Rügen" ist ein romantisches Gemälde von Caspar David Friedrich.

Berlin's **Gemäldegalerie** houses one of the world's greatest collections of European paintings. The museum's collection is especially strong in German and Italian paintings, as well as in the art of the Low Countries. Masterpieces by Dürer, Van Eyck, Rembrandt, Caravaggio, and Botticelli can be viewed by visitors to the museum's galleries.

Ausdrücke, Sprichwörter und Zitate

to be in the spotlight	im Rampenlicht stehen
to go off without a hitch	reibungslos über die Bühne gehen
to paint the town red	auf die Pauke hauen

I can't get this song out of my head.	Dieses Lied ist für mich ein Ohrwurm.
This is music to my ears!	Das ist Musik in meinen Ohren!
Don't talk bilge!	Quatsch keine Opern!
There's nothing to it.	Das ist keine Kunst.
Take your nonsense elsewhere., Get lost.	Nimm deinen Kram und verschwinde.

Life is folly, and for good or bad, we have to live it.	Das Leben ist ein Zirkus. Wir müssen mitspielen, ob wir wollen oder nicht.

„Musik ist eine höhere Offenbarung als alle Weisheit und Philosophie."
  LUDWIG VAN BEETHOVEN

„Ohne Musik wäre das Leben ein Irrtum."
  FRIEDRICH NIETZSCHE

„Wer Musik nicht liebt, verdient nicht ein Mensch genannt zu werden. Wer sie liebt, ist ein halber Mensch; wer sie aber treibt, ein ganzer Mensch."
  JOHANN WOLFGANG VON GOETHE

„Das Drama soll keine neuen Geschichten bringen, sondern neue Verhältnisse."
  CHRISTIAN FRIEDRICH HEBBEL

„Es gibt eine alte, aber sehr moderne Definition von Theater: *eine Bühne, zwei Menschen und eine Leidenschaft*. Eine Malerei ist nur eine Leinwand mit Farbe drauf. Das Originalmanuskript von *Romeo und Julia* hat nicht mehr als wenige Pfennig an Papier und Tinte gekostet. Den Rest kann man nicht mit Hilfe von Geld, Lautsprechern und Lichtanlagen machen. Früher nannte man dieses etwas *Geist*."
  JENS BJØRNEBOE

„Künstler sind die Fühlhörner der Menschheit."
  EZRA POUND

„Ich nutze Würde statt Make-up."
  AKI KAURISMÄKI

Übung 61

Complete each German phrase or sentence so that it expresses the meaning of the English phrase or sentence.

1. *woodwinds* — Holz_____

2. *a masterpiece* — ein _____werk

3. *at exactly eight o'clock* — genau um _____

4. *available tickets* — verfügbare _____

5. *avant-garde art* — _____ Kunst

6. *sound engineer* — Ton_____

7. *Everyone on stage!* — Alle auf die _____!

8. *the world premiere* — Ur_____

9. *an oil painting* — ein Öl_____

10. *brass* — _____bläser

11. *fine arts* — die _____ Künste

12. *the chief conductor* — der Chef-_____

13. *these movie stars* — diese _____

14. *It's 11:00 p.m.* — Es ist _____ Uhr _____.

15. *the landscape* — die Land_____

16. *some foreign films* — einige _____ Filme

17. *a play* — ein Theater_____

18. *a blockbuster* — ein Kassen_____

19. *the box office* — die _____kasse

20. *"The Golden Age of Hollywood"* — Hollywoods _____

Übung 62

Select the verb from the following list that correctly completes each sentence.

beginnen   dirigieren   anschauen   malen
öffnen   synchronisieren   drehen   gewinnen
spielen   singen   können   uraufführen

1. Er liebt es, Klavier zu _____.

2. Der Dirigent bevorzugt es, das Orchester ohne Taktstock zu _____.

3. Der Tenor kann keine hohen Cs _____.

4. Wollen wir uns diesen Film im Kino _____?

5. Die Schauspieler werden die Probe um fünf Uhr _____.

6. Dieser Film sollte den Oscar _____.

7. Die Produzenten wollen den Film in Hamburg _____.

8. Sollte man fremdsprachige Filme _____ oder nicht?

9. Das Orchester wird die neue Symphonie im Juli _____.

10. Erik möchte am liebsten nur mit Ölfarben _____.

11. Die Abendkasse wird um sieben Uhr _____.

12. Ich würde so gerne ein Instrument spielen _____!

Übung 63

Unscramble the letters in each item to find out which musical instruments are played in an orchestra.

1. lolec   _____
2. erfah   _____
3. artitekeln   _____
4. booe   _____
5. neupaso   _____

6. oilvein   _____
7. baut   _____
8. petetorm   _____
9. oliva   _____
10. rohadlwn   _____

Übung 64

Give the noun phrase (definite article + noun) that appears in this chapter and is related to each of the following verbs.

1. filmen _____
2. aufführen _____
3. komponieren _____
4. applaudieren _____
5. spielen _____
6. interpretieren _____
7. zeichnen _____
8. malen _____
9. dirigieren _____
10. bildhauern _____

Übung 65

Use the vocabulary in this chapter to discuss the following topics.

1. **Die Musik.** Tell about your musical interests: what kind of music you like and your favorite instrumental and vocal performers. Talk about the musical instrument you play and your experience playing in an orchestra or band.

   _____
   _____
   _____
   _____
   _____

2. **Das Theater.** Describe a play you attended, the actors who performed, and what roles they played. What did you like or not like about the play?

   _____
   _____
   _____
   _____
   _____

3. **Der Film.** Tell about a film you saw and why you liked or didn't like it. What are your favorite films? Who are your favorite actors and directors?

_____

_____

_____

_____

_____

4. **Die Kunst.** Describe the paintings and sculpture you see as you walk around the art museum. Who are your favorite artists? Describe some of their works. If you paint or create other types of art, discuss your work.

_____

_____

_____

_____

_____

Übung 66

Give the noun phrase (definite article + noun) that appears in this chapter and is a German cognate for each of the following English words.

1. orchestra _____
2. gallery _____
3. clarinet _____
4. acoustics _____
5. comedy _____
6. tragedy _____
7. melody _____
8. musician _____
9. concert _____
10. guitar _____
11. theater _____
12. dialogue _____

13. *curator* _____

14. *palette* _____

15. *photographer* _____

Übung 67

Match each noun or noun phrase in the first column with the item in the second column that is related to it.

1. _____ die Klarinette   a. der Vorhang fällt

2. _____ Sänger   b. ein Saiteninstrument

3. _____ das Ende der Vorstellung c. die Abendkasse

4. _____ die Pause   d. der Chor

5. _____ die Viola   e. ein Blechblasinstrument

6. _____ Eintrittskarten   f. Ölfarben

7. _____ die Schauspieler   g. ein Holzblasinstrument

8. _____ das Drehbuch   h. der Dirigent

9. _____ die Posaune   i. zwischen den Akten

10. _____ der Cineast   j. der Dramaturg

11. _____ Malerei   k. Hollywood

12. _____ die Partitur   l. die Besetzung

Übung 68

Translate the following sentences into German.

1. *Do you* (du) *know how to play the piano?*

   _____

2. *The audience applauded and called for an encore.*

   _____

3. *The actors are going to begin the rehearsal at 1:30.*

   _____

4. *We're going to see the play tomorrow evening.*

   _____

5. *At what time does the box office close?*

_____

6. *Are there tickets available for the nine o'clock show?*

_____

7. *The show is a blockbuster; it has been running for three years.*

_____

_____

8. *The art connoisseurs like these abstract paintings.*

_____

9. *They're shooting a film in our city.*

_____

10. *The orchestra premiered the symphony last night. It's innovative, but accessible.*

_____

_____

11. *I like to paint landscapes, portraits, and still lifes.*

_____

12. *There's an exhibition of my paintings at the Klemm's Gallery.*

_____

_____

11

Berufe, Länder, Nationalitäten und Sprachen

Professions, countries, nationalities, and languages

In this chapter, you will learn the German terms for professions and vocabulary related to the workplace. You will learn the German names of countries, nationalities, and languages, and you'll be able to talk about your nationality and background, as well as ask others where they are from.

For additional lists of professions, see Chapters 5, 7, 8, 10, 13, 14, and 15.

The feminine form of nouns of profession is created by adding the suffix **-in** to the masculine form; examples are **der Buchhalter** > <u>die</u> **Buchhalterin** and **der Ökonom** > <u>die</u> **Ökonomin**). If the masculine form ends in unstressed **-e**, the **-e** is omitted before **-in** is added; an example is **der Archäologe** > <u>die</u> **Archäologin**. Exceptions to these rules are noted in the list below.

What's your profession?	**Was ist dein Beruf?**
accountant	der Buchhalter
actor	der Schauspieler
actress	die Schauspielerin
analyst	der Analyst
anthropologist	der Anthropologe
archaeologist	der Archäologe
architect	der Architekt
artist	der Künstler
astronaut	der Astronaut
babysitter	der Babysitter
baker	der Bäcker
bank clerk	der/die Bankangestellte
barber	der Friseur
bookseller	der Buchverkäufer
business manager	der Geschäftsführer
businessman	der Geschäftsmann

businesswoman	die Geschäftsfrau
butcher	der Schlachter, der Fleischer, der Metzger
carpenter	der Tischler
chef	der Koch / die Köchin
chemist	der Chemiker
composer	der Komponist
computer engineer	der Computertechniker, der Computeringenieur
conductor	der Zugbegleiter
consultant	der Berater
contractor	der Leiharbeiter
craftsman	der Handwerker
dean (university)	der Dekan
dentist	der Zahnarzt / die Zahnärztin
designer	der Designer
dietician	der Ernährungswissenschaftler
diplomat	der Diplomat
doctor	der Arzt / die Ärztin
domestic worker	der/die Hausangestellte
driver	der Fahrer
economist	der Ökonom
electrician	der Elektriker
engineer	der Ingenieur
farmer	der Bauer / die Bäuerin
fashion designer	der Modedesigner
financial advisor	der Finanzberater
firefighter	der Feuerwehrmann / die Feuerwehrfrau
fisherman	der Fischer
flight attendant	der Flugbegleiter
foreman	der Aufseher
forewoman	die Aufseherin
gardener	der Gärtner
government employee	der Beamte
graphic designer	der Grafikdesigner
hairdresser	der Friseur
hotel manager	der Hotelmanager
housekeeper	der Haushälter
househusband	der Hausmann
housewife	die Hausfrau
information technology (IT) director	der Informationschef
jeweler	der Juwelier

journalist	der Journalist
judge	der Richter
lawyer	der Richter, der Advokat [SWITZ.]
linguist	der Linguist
mail carrier	der Briefträger
manager	der Manager
massage therapist	der Masseur
mechanic	der Mechaniker
medical examiner	der Vertrauensarzt / die Vertrauensärztin
miner	der Grubenarbeiter
model (male or female)	das Modell
musician	der Musiker
nanny	das Kindermädchen
nurse	der Krankenpfleger
office worker (male or female)	die Bürokraft
orchestra conductor	der Dirigent
painter	der Maler
pastry chef	der Konditor
performer	der Künstler
pharmacist	der Apotheker
physical therapist	der Physiotherapeut
physicist	der Physiker
pilot	der Pilot
plumber	der Klempner
police officer	der Polizist
politician	der Politiker
programmer	der Programmierer
project manager	der Projektmanager
proprietor	der Betriebsinhaber
psychiatrist	der Psychiater
psychologist	der Psychologe
psychotherapist	der Psychotherapeut
public servant	der Beamte
real estate agent	der Immobilienmakler
receptionist	der Empfangsmitarbeiter
reporter	der Reporter
sailor	der Matrose
sales clerk	der Verkäufer
sales representative	der Vertreter
salesperson	der Händler

scientist	der Wissenschaftler
secretary	der Sekretär
security engineer	der/die Sicherheitsbeauftragte
service engineer	der Wartungstechniker
shoemaker	der Schuster
social worker	der Sozialarbeiter
soldier	der Soldat
sound engineer	der Tonmeister
stockbroker	der Börsenmakler
surgeon	der Chirurg
tailor	der Schneider
taxi driver	der Taxifahrer
teacher	der Lehrer
technician	der Techniker
tour guide	der Touristenführer
translator	der Übersetzer
truck driver	der Lastwagenfahrer
TV news anchor	der Fernsehmoderator
veterinarian	der Tierarzt / die Tierärztin
waiter	der Kellner
waitress	die Kellnerin, die Serviertochter [SWITZ.]
watchmaker	der Uhrmacher
web designer	der Webdesigner
worker, laborer	der Arbeiter
writer	der Schriftsteller

Where do you work?

Wo arbeitest du?

I work <u>at a firm</u>.

Ich arbeite <u>bei einer Firma</u>.

at the airport	am Flughafen
in an art gallery	in einer Kunstgalerie
in a conservatory	an einem Konservatorium
in a courtroom	in einem Gerichtssaal
in a department store	in einem Kaufhaus
in a factory	in einer Fabrik
on a farm	auf einem Bauernhof
in a government department	in einem Ministerium, in einem Departement [SWITZ.]
at home	zu Hause

>>>

in a hospital	in einem Krankenhaus, in einem Spital [AUS., SWITZ.]
at an international company	in einem internationalen Unternehmen
in an Internet café	in einem Internetcafé
in a laboratory	in einem Labor
in a law office/firm	in einer Kanzlei
in a medical office	in einer Arztpraxis
at a military facility	in einer Militäreinrichtung
in a museum	in einem Museum
at a navy yard, at a naval base	auf einem Marinestützpunkt
in an office	in einem Büro
in a private clinic	in einer Privatklinik
in a production and recording studio	in einem Tonstudio
at a resort	in einem Kurort
in a restaurant	in einem Restaurant
in a school	an einer Schule
at a state agency	bei einem Amt
at the stock exchange	an der Börse
in a store, in a shop	in einem Laden, in einem Geschäft
in a studio	in einem Studio
in a theater	in einem Theater
at a university	an einer Universität

Unlike English, German omits the indefinite article **ein/eine** with a profession after forms of **sein** *to be*: **Ich bin Architekt.** *I am an architect.*

Oswald's job

Oswalds Arbeit

Oswald *is a consultant.*	Oswald ist Berater.
works in a multinational company	arbeitet in einem internationalen Unternehmen
earns a good salary	hat ein gutes Einkommen
earns a living	verdient seinen Lebensunterhalt
gets a pension	bekommt Rente
gets a raise	bekommt eine Gehaltserhöhung
has a full-time job	hat eine Vollzeitstelle
has a part-time job	hat eine Teilzeitstelle
has many benefits	erhält viele Leistungen
is fluent in English	spricht fließend Englisch
is overqualified	ist überqualifiziert
is retired	ist im Ruhestand

is underemployed	ist unterbeschäftigt
is unemployed	ist arbeitslos
knows/speaks three languages	spricht drei Sprachen
wants to work in the Berlin branch	will in der Berliner Filiale arbeiten

The firm and the employees

Die Firma und die Arbeitnehmer

The firm is going <u>to hire</u> 500 employees.	Die Firma wird fünfhundert Arbeitnehmer <u>einstellen</u>.
to fire	entlassen
to relocate	versetzen
to train	einlernen

Working conditions

Arbeitsbedingungen

The workers plan <u>to form a union</u>.	Die Arbeiter planen, <u>eine Gewerkschaft zu gründen</u>.
to demand paid vacations	bezahlten Urlaub zu fordern
to demand a bonus	Bonuszahlungen zu verlangen
to go on strike	zu streiken
to retire	in den Ruhestand zu gehen
to sign a collective bargaining agreement	einen Tarifvertrag zu unterschreiben, einen Gesamtarbeitsvertrag zu unterschreiben [SWITZ.]
Christmas (year-end) bonus	das Weihnachtsgeld
disability insurance	die Berufsunfähigkeitsversicherung
health insurance	die Krankenversicherung
life insurance	die Lebensversicherung
minimum wage	der Tarif, der gesetzliche Mindestlohn
pension plan	die Betriebsrente
salary	das Gehalt
daily	täglich
weekly	wöchentlich
biweekly	zweiwöchentlich
monthly	monatlich
yearly	jährlich
strikebreaker, scab	der Streikbrecher
unemployment insurance	die Arbeitslosenversicherung
They're paid by the week.	Sie werden jede Woche ausgezahlt.

To identify people's nationalities in German, nouns are used, not adjectives: **Er ist Amerikaner.** *He is American.* **Sie ist Amerikanerin.** *She is American.* Note that no article, definite or indefinite, is used with a noun of nationality after a form of **sein.** Most masculine nouns of nationality end in **-er**, while most feminine nouns of nationality end in **-erin**. Some masculine nouns of nationality, however, end in **-e**. The **-e** is omitted before the feminine suffix **-in** is added; examples are **Chilene/ Chilenin, Franzose/Französin,** and **Russe/Russin.**

German-speaking countries   Deutschsprachige Länder

| *Where are you from?* | Woher kommst du? |
| *I'm German.* | Ich bin Deutscher/Deutsche. |

Country	Land	*Nationality*	Nationalität
Germany	Deutschland	*German*	Deutscher/Deutsche
Austria	Österreich	*Austrian*	Österreicher(in)
Switzerland	Schweiz	*Swiss*	Schweizer(in)
Luxembourg	Luxemburg	*Luxembourgian*	Luxemburger(in)
Liechtenstein	Liechtenstein	*Liechtensteiner*	Liechtensteiner(in)

In German, the names of some countries have obligatory definite articles, for example, **die Schweiz** *Switzerland.* In a prepositional phrase with **in** to express location, the dative case of the article is used: **in der Schweiz.**

What country were you born in?   In welchem Land bist du geboren?

| *I was born in Germany.* | Ich wurde in Deutschland geboren. |
| *I'm German.* | Ich bin Deutscher/Deutsche. |

Country	Land	*Nationality*	Nationalität
Afghanistan	Afghanistan	*Afghan*	Afghaner(in)
Albania	Albanien	*Albanian*	Albaner(in)
Algeria	Algerien	*Algerian*	Algerier(in)
Andorra	Andorra	*Andorran*	Andorraner(in)
Argentina	Argentinien	*Argentinean*	Argentinier(in)
Armenia	Armenien	*Armenian*	Armenier(in)
Australia	Australien	*Australian*	Australier(in)
Bahrain	Bahrain	*Bahraini*	Bahrainer(in)
Belarus	die Republik Belarus	*Belarusian*	Belarusse/Belarussin

Country	Land	Nationality	Nationalität
Belgium	Belgien	Belgian	Belgier(in)
Bolivia	Bolivien	Bolivian	Bolivianer(in)
Bosnia	Bosnien	Bosnian	Bosnier(in)
Brazil	Brasilien	Brazilian	Brasilianer(in)
Bulgaria	Bulgarien	Bulgarian	Bulgare/Bulgarin
Cambodia	Kambodscha	Cambodian	Kambodschaner(in)
Canada	Kanada	Canadian	Kanadier(in)
Chile	Chile	Chilean	Chilene/Chilenin
China	China	Chinese	Chinese/Chinesin
Colombia	Kolumbien	Colombian	Kolumbianer(in)
Costa Rica	Costa Rica	Costa Rican	Costa Ricaner(in)
Croatia	Kroatien	Croatian	Kroate/Kroatin
Cuba	Kuba	Cuban	Kubaner(in)
Cyprus	Zypern	Cypriot	Zypriote/Zypriotin
Czech Republic	Tschechien	Czech	Tscheche/Tschechin
Denmark	Dänemark	Danish	Däne/Dänin
Dominican Republic	die Dominikanische Republik	Dominican	Dominikaner(in)
Ecuador	Ecuador	Ecuadorian	Ecuadorianer(in)
Egypt	Ägypten	Egyptian	Ägypter(in)
El Salvador	El Salvador	Salvadoran	Salvadorianer(in)
England	England	English	Engländer(in)
Equatorial Guinea	Äquatorialguinea	Equatorial Guinean	Äquatorialguineer(in)
Estonia	Estland	Estonian	Este/Estin
Ethiopia	Äthiopien	Ethiopian	Äthiopier(in)
Finland	Finnland	Finnish	Finne/Finnin
France	Frankreich	French	Franzose/Französin
Gibraltar	Gibraltar	Gibraltarian	Gibraltarer(in)
Great Britain	Großbritannien	British	Brite/Britin
Greece	Griechenland	Greek	Grieche/Griechin
Guatemala	Guatemala	Guatemalan	Guatemalteke/Guatemaltekin
Haiti	Haiti	Haitian	Haitianer(in)
Holland	Holland, Niederlande	Dutch	Holländer(in), Niederländer(in)
Honduras	Honduras	Honduran	Honduraner(in)
Hungary	Ungarn	Hungarian	Ungar(in)
Iceland	Island	Icelandic	Isländer(in)
India	Indien	Indian	Inder(in)

Country	Land	Nationality	Nationalität
Indonesia	Indonesien	*Indonesian*	Indonesier(in)
Iran	der Iran	*Iranian*	Iraner(in)
Iraq	der Irak	*Iraqi*	Iraker(in)
Ireland	Irland	*Irish*	Ire/Irin
Israel	Israel	*Israeli*	Israeli
Italy	Italien	*Italian*	Italiener(in)
Jamaica	Jamaika	*Jamaican*	Jamaikaner(in)
Japan	Japan	*Japanese*	Japaner(in)
Jordan	Jordanien	*Jordanian*	Jordanier(in)
Korea	Korea	*Korean*	Koreaner(in)
Kuwait	Kuwait	*Kuwaiti*	Kuwaiter(in)
Laos	Laos	*Laotian*	Laote/Laotin
Latvia (Letonia)	Lettland	*Latvian (Letonian)*	Lette/Lettin
Lebanon	der Libanon	*Lebanese*	Libanese/Libanesin
Libya	Libyen	*Libyan*	Libyer(in)
Lithuania	Litauen	*Lithuanian*	Litauer(in)
Luxembourg	Luxemburg	*Luxembourger*	Luxemburger(in)
Madagascar	die Republik Madagaskar	*Malagasy*	Madagasse/Madagassin
Malaysia	Malaysia	*Malaysian*	Malaysier(in)
Mexico	Mexiko	*Mexican*	Mexikaner(in)
Moldova (Moldavia)	die Republik Moldau	*Moldavian*	Moldauer(in)
Monaco	Monaco	*Monégasque*	Monegasse/Monegassin
Morocco	Marokko	*Moroccan*	Marokkaner(in)
Netherlands	Niederlande	*Dutch*	Niederländer(in)
New Zealand	Neuseeland	*New Zealand*	Neuseeländer(in)
Nicaragua	Nicaragua	*Nicaraguan*	Nicaraguaner(in)
North Korea	Nordkorea	*North Korean*	Nordkoreaner(in)
Norway	Norwegen	*Norwegian*	Norweger(in)
Oman	das Sultanat Oman	*Omani*	Omaner(in)
Pakistan	Pakistan	*Pakistani*	Pakistaner(in)
Panama	Panama	*Panamanian*	Panamaer(in)
Paraguay	Paraguay	*Paraguayan*	Paraguayer(in)
Peru	Peru	*Peruvian*	Peruaner(in)
Philippines	die Philippinen	*Philippine*	Philippiner(in)
Poland	Polen	*Polish*	Pole/Polin
Portugal	Portugal	*Portuguese*	Portugiese/Portugiesin
Puerto Rico	Puerto Rico	*Puerto Rican*	Puerto Ricaner(in)
Qatar	Katar	*Qatari*	Katarer(in)

Country	Land	Nationality	Nationalität
Rumania	Rumänien	Rumanian	Rumäne/Rumänin
Russia	Rußland / Russland	Russian	Russe/Russin
Saudi Arabia	Saudi-Arabien	Saudi	Saudi-Araber(in)
Scotland	Schottland	Scottish	Schotte/Schottin
Serbia	Serbien	Serbian	Serbe/Serbin
Slovakia	Slowakei	Slovak	Slowake/Slowakin
Slovenia	Slowenien	Slovenian	Slowene/Slowenin
Somalia	die Bundesrepublik Somalia	Somali	Somalier(in)
South Africa	die Republik Südafrika	South African	Südafrikaner(in)
South Korea	Südkorea	South Korean	Südkoreaner(in)
Spain	Spanien	Spaniard	Spanier(in)
Sudan	die Republik Sudan	Sudanese	Sudanese/Sudanesin
Sweden	Schweden	Swedish	Schwede/Schwedin
Switzerland	die Schweiz	Swiss	Schweizer(in)
Syria	Syrien	Syrian	Syrier(in)
Thailand	Thailand	Thai	Thailänder(in)
Tunisia	Tunesien	Tunisian	Tunesier(in)
Turkey	die Türkei	Turkish	Türke/Türkin
Uganda	Uganda	Ugandan	Ugander(in)
Ukraine	die Ukraine	Ukrainian	Ukrainer(in)
United Arab Emirates	die Vereinigten Arabischen Emirate	Emirati	Emirater(in)
United States	die Vereinigten Staaten	American	Amerikaner(in)
Uruguay	Uruguay	Uruguayan	Uruguayer(in)
Venezuela	Venezuela	Venezuelan	Venezolaner(in)
Vietnam	Vietnam	Vietnamese	Vietnamese/Vietnamesin
Wales	Wales	Welsh	Waliser(in)
Yemen	der Jemen	Yemeni	Jemenit(in)

Continents

Kontinente

Africa	Afrika [N.]
Antarctica	die Antarktis
Asia	Asien [N.]
Australia	Australien [N.]
Europe	Europa [N.]
North America	Nordamerika [N.]
South America	Südamerika [N.]

What's your background?

I'm of English descent.
   Arabic
   Chinese
   Indian
   Japanese
   Portuguese
   Russian
   Scottish

Wo kommst du her?

Ich bin englischer Abstammung.
   arabischer
   chinesischer
   indischer
   japanischer
   portugiesischer
   russischer
   schottischer

Languages

English	German
Afrikaans	Afrikaans
Albanian	Albanisch
Arabic	Arabisch
Armenian	Armenisch
Basque	Baskisch
Belarusian (White Russian)	Weißrussisch
Bulgarian	Bulgarisch
Burmese	Burmesisch
Catalan	Katalanisch
Chinese	Chinesisch
Croatian	Kroatisch
Czech	Tschechisch
Danish	Dänisch
Dutch	Niederländisch, Holländisch
English	Englisch
Estonian	Estnisch
Filipino	Philippinisch
Finnish	Finnisch
Flemish	Flämisch
French	Französisch
Galician	Galizisch
German	Deutsch
(Classical) Greek	Altgriechisch
(Modern) Greek	Neugriechisch
Hebrew	Hebräisch
Hindi	Hindi
Hungarian	Ungarisch
Icelandic	Isländisch

Indonesian	Indonesisch
Irish (Gaelic)	Irisch
Italian	Italienisch
Japanese	Japanisch
Khmer, Cambodian	Khmer, Kambodschanisch
Korean	Koreanisch
Kurdish	Kurdisch
Latin	Lateinisch
Latvian	Lettisch
Lithuanian	Litauisch
Malagasy	Malaiisch
Norwegian	Norwegisch
Pashto	Paschtunisch
Persian, Farsi	Persisch, Farsi
Polish	Polnisch
Portuguese	Portugiesisch
Romansh	Rumantsch
Rumanian	Rumänisch
Russian	Russisch
Sanskrit	Sanskrit
Sardinian	Sardisch
Serbian	Serbisch
Sicilian	Sizilianisch
Slovak	Slowakisch
Slovene	Slowenisch
Swahili	Suaheli
Swedish	Schwedisch
Tagalog	Tagalog
Tamil	Tamil
Thai	Thailändisch
Tibetan	Tibetisch
Turkish	Türkisch
Ukrainian	Ukrainisch
Urdu	Urdu
Vietnamese	Vietnamesisch
Welsh	Walisisch
White Russian (Belarusian)	Weißrussisch
Yiddish	Jiddisch

What's his name?	Wie heißt er?

What's the American astronaut's name?	Wie heißt der amerikanische Astronaut?
the Finnish composer's	der finnische Komponist
the French pastry chef's	der französische Konditor
the Russian diplomat's	der russische Diplomat
the Swiss watchmaker's	der Schweizer Uhrmacher
the Welsh linguist's	der walisische Linguist

Klingen Sie authentisch!

the Far East	der Ferne Osten
the Middle East	der Mittlere Osten
German is spoken here.	Hier spricht man Deutsch.
They speak English fluently.	Sie sprechen fließendes Englisch.
They are proficient in Russian., They have a good command of Russian.	Sie beherrschen die russische Sprache.
He has good linguistic skills.	Er hat gute sprachliche Fähigkeiten.
What's the capital of Germany?	Wie heißt die deutsche Hauptstadt?
What town are they from?	Aus welcher Stadt kommen sie?
He became an American citizen.	Er wurde amerikanischer Staatsbürger.
The demographic data include the number of inhabitants.	Die demografischen Daten beinhalten die Anzahl der Staatsangehörigen.
The world population is more than seven billion.	Die Weltbevölkerung ist größer als sieben Milliarden.
Austria is a German-speaking country.	Österreich ist ein deutschsprachiges Land.
What's your name?	Wie heißt du?, Wie heißen Sie?
My name is Franz Völker.	Ich heiße Franz Völker.

Ausdrücke, Sprichwörter und Zitate

Silence is golden.	Reden ist Silber, schweigen ist Gold.
Things turn out differently than you expect.	Erstens kommt es anders, zweitens als man denkt.

„Wer fremde Sprachen nicht kennt, weiß nichts von seiner eigenen."
  JOHANN WOLFGANG VON GOETHE

„Die Entwicklung der Wortsprache führt etwas ganz Entscheidendes herbei: die Emanzipation des Verstehens vom Empfinden."
  OSWALD SPENGLER

„Die Grenzen meiner Sprache bedeuten die Grenzen meiner Welt."
  LUDWIG WITTGENSTEIN

„Eine Sprache mit vielen Konsonanten ist wie ein Kartoffelacker. Eine Sprache mit vielen Vokalen aber ist wie ein Blumenbeet."
  ENRICO CARUSO

„Ich könnte nicht an Projekten arbeiten, die nur deshalb für einige nützlich sind, weil sie anderen schaden."
  RENÉ DESCARTES

Übung 69

Complete each German phrase or sentence so that it expresses the meaning of the English phrase or sentence.

1. *I'm of English descent.* — Ich bin _____.

2. *a TV news anchor* — ein Fernseh_____

3. *Silence is golden.* — Reden ist Silber, _____.

4. *the bimonthly salary* — das _____ Gehalt

5. *life insurance* — Lebens_____

6. *some government employees* — einige _____

7. *the Middle East* — der Mittlere _____

8. *a full-time job* — eine _____stelle

9. *a German-speaking country* — ein _____ Land

10. *She is proficient in German.* — Sie _____ die deutsche Sprache.

11. *What is the capital of Switzerland?* — _____ der Schweiz?

12. *I'm an economist.* — Ich bin _____.

13. *the collective bargaining agreement* — der _____

14. *He's retired.* — Er ist im _____.

15. *What city are you from?* — Aus welcher _____ kommst du?

Übung 70

Give the noun of nationality that corresponds to the country of origin for each of the following people.

1. Richard kommt aus Deutschland, richtig? Ja, er ist _____.
2. Urs kommt aus der Schweiz, richtig? Ja, er ist _____.
3. Seine Eltern kommen aus Japan, richtig? Ja, sie sind _____.
4. Dino und Cecilia kommen aus Italien, richtig? Ja, sie sind _____.
5. Jacques kommt aus Belgien, richtig? Ja, er ist _____.
6. Deine Großeltern kommen aus Polen, richtig? Ja, sie sind _____.
7. Dein Verlobter kommt aus Thailand, richtig? Ja, er ist _____.
8. Deine Frau kommt aus Indien, richtig? Ja, sie ist _____.
9. Sein Adoptivsohn kommt aus dem Iran, richtig? Ja, er ist _____.
10. Deine Freundin kommt aus Schweden, richtig? Ja, sie ist _____.
11. Teresa und Rosa kommen aus Spanien, richtig? Ja, sie sind _____.
12. Albert kommt aus Monaco, richtig? Ja, er ist _____.
13. Ihr seid aus den Vereinigten Staaten, richtig? Ja, wir sind _____.
14. Du kommst aus Vietnam, richtig? Ja, ich bin _____.
15. Dein Schwiegersohn kommt aus England, richtig? Ja, er ist _____.

Übung 71

Give the country in which each of the following people works.

1. Der englische Beamte arbeitet in _____.
2. Die dänische Zahnärztin arbeitet in _____.
3. Der nordamerikanische Chirurg arbeitet in _____.
4. Der norwegische Touristenführer arbeitet in _____.
5. Die ungarische Schauspielerin arbeitet in _____.
6. Der südafrikanische Hotelier arbeitet in _____.
7. Der argentinische Programmierer arbeitet in _____.
8. Der österreichische Übersetzer arbeitet in _____.
9. Die französische Sängerin arbeitet in _____.
10. Der südkoreanische Bankangestellte arbeitet in _____.

Übung 72

Give the official language(s) spoken in each of the following countries.

1. Uruguay   _____
2. Iran   _____
3. Saudi-Arabien   _____
4. Tschechien   _____
5. Österreich   _____
6. Afghanistan   _____
7. Thailand   _____
8. Brasilien   _____
9. Kanada   _____
10. Schweiz   _____

Übung 73

Select the verb from the following list that correctly completes each sentence.

| unterschreiben | gehen | arbeiten | beherrschen | sprechen |
| streiken | entlassen | auszahlen | versetzen | gründen |

1. Wilhelm will am liebsten zu Hause _____.
2. Er soll fließend Englisch _____ können.
3. Die Manager wollen die Arbeiter _____.
4. Die Arbeiter werden eine Gewerkschaft _____.
5. Wir können nicht fahren, die Zugführer _____.
6. Sie findet es zu früh, mit 65 in den Ruhestand zu _____.
7. Wann wird die Firma endlich die Gehälter _____?
8. Die Journalisten _____ gut Russisch.
9. Die Firma will meine Frau nach Rom _____!
10. Hoffentlich werden die Chefs den Tarifvertrag _____.

Übung 74

Match each professional in the first column with his or her probable place of work in the second column.

1.	_____ Schauspieler	a.	Börse
2.	_____ Soldat	b.	Fabrik
3.	_____ Krankenpfleger	c.	Militäreinrichtung
4.	_____ Arbeiter	d.	Labor
5.	_____ Hausangestellter	e.	Restaurant
6.	_____ Börsenmakler	f.	Theater
7.	_____ Verkäufer	g.	Atelier
8.	_____ Künstler	h.	Haus
9.	_____ Koch	i.	Ministerium
10.	_____ Beamte	j.	Bauernhof
11.	_____ Bauer	k.	Laden
12.	_____ Chemiker	l.	Krankenhaus

Übung 75

1. Tell about yourself. Tell where you are from, your family background, what language(s) you speak, what your profession is, and where you work.

_____

_____

_____

_____

_____

2. Describe a foreign friend or a member of your family who was born abroad. Tell where he or she is from, what his or her profession is, what language(s) he or she speaks, and where he or she works.

_____

_____

_____

_____

_____

3. Describe your professional life: what you do, where you work and with whom, working conditions, hours, salary, etc.

_____

_____

_____

_____

_____

Übung 76

Translate the following sentences into German.

1. *The manager plans to hire two accountants.*

_____

2. *The workers are demanding paid vacations and disability insurance.*

_____

_____

3. *If the firm doesn't sign the collective bargaining agreement, the union is going to strike.*

_____

_____

4. *The company fired two hundred employees and relocated another three hundred.*

_____

_____

5. *The physicists and chemists are working together in the laboratory.*

_____

_____

6. *Roland is a judge and his wife is a journalist.*

_____

7. *She is French, of English and Spanish background.*

_____

8. *Daniel is from Switzerland. He speaks German, French, Italian, and Romansh.*

_____

_____

9. *What is that Finnish actress's name?*

_____

10. *What German-speaking country are they from?*

_____

11. *They want to become American citizens.*

_____

12. *Are you (Sie) proficient in Chinese?*

_____

12

Feier- und Festtage
Holidays and celebrations

This chapter presents vocabulary for talking about important secular and religious holidays in the United States and German-speaking countries. You will learn about important celebrations and be able to describe a birthday party or wedding you attended.

> Most German holidays have a religious background; exceptions are German Unity Day, Labor Day, and New Year's Day. Since the strength of each of Germany's religious denominations differs from region to region, many holidays are not celebrated nationwide. The following list includes only those holidays that are celebrated nationally in Germany, Austria, or Switzerland.

National holidays

Today we're celebrating Christmas.

New Year's Day (January 1)
Good Friday
Easter Monday
Labor Day (May 1)
Ascension Day, Father's Day
Whit Monday, Pentecost Monday
Swiss National Day (August 1)
German Unity Day (October 3)
Austrian National Day (October 26)
Christmas Day (December 25)
Boxing Day, St. Stephen's Day
  (December 26)

Überregionale Feiertage

Heute feiern wir Weihnachten.

Neujahrstag
Karfreitag
Ostermontag
Tag der Arbeit, Staatsfeiertag [AUS.]
Christi Himmelfahrt, Auffahrt [SWITZ.], Vatertag
Pfingstmontag
Bundesfeiertag
Tag der Deutschen Einheit
Nationalfeiertag
Ersten Weihnachtstag, Christtag [AUS.]
Stephanitag, Zweiten Weihnachtstag,
  Stephanstag [SWITZ.]

> The two Germanys signed a unification contract on October 3, 1990, about one year after the fall of the Berlin Wall. It was immediately decided to make this day a national holiday.

Mother's Day and Father's Day are not holidays in Germany. However, Ascension Day (the Thursday closest to the thirty-ninth day after Easter) is also celebrated as **Männertag, Herrentag,** and **Vatertag**. On Ascension Day in Germany, men traditionally drink all day long. The Friday following Ascension Day is also a day off and is called **Brückentag** ("bridge day") because it creates a four-day weekend.

Other holidays and celebrations

Sonstige Feier- und Festtage

Halloween (October 31)	das Halloween
Christmas Eve (December 24)	der Heiligabend
New Year's Eve (December 31)	der/das Silvester

Religious holidays
Christian holidays

Religiöse Feiertage
Christliche Feiertage

Epiphany, Three Kings Day (January 6)	Heilige Drei Könige [REGIONAL]
Holy Thursday	der Gründonnerstag [REGIONAL]
Good Friday	der Karfreitag
Easter	das Ostern
Easter Sunday	der Ostersonntag
Pentecost	der Pfingstsonntag [REGIONAL]
Corpus Christi	Fronleichnam [REGIONAL]
Assumption Day (August 15)	Mariä Himmelfahrt [REGIONAL]
Reformation Day (October 31)	der Reformationstag [REGIONAL]
All Saints Day (November 1)	Allerheiligen [REGIONAL]
All Souls Day, Day of the Dead (November 2)	Allerseelen [AUS.]
Penance Day	der Buß- und Bettag [REGIONAL]
Christmas (December 25)	das Weihnachten

Reformationstag is a religious holiday celebrated on October 31 in remembrance of the Lutheran Reformation. In the United States, this holiday is usually moved to a Sunday.

Jewish holidays

Jüdische Festtage

Rosh Hashanah	Rosch ha-Schana
Yom Kippur	Jom Kippur, der Versöhnungstag
Hanukkah (Festival of Lights)	die Chanukka, das Lichterfest

Purim	das Purimfest
Passover	das Passah
Holocaust Remembrance Day	der Internationale Tag des Gedenkens an die Opfer
(Yom HaShoah)	des Holocaust

An Islamic holiday   **Ein islamischer Festtag**

Ramadan	der Ramadan

Christmas and Hanukkah   **Weihnachten und Chanukka**

Christmas carol	das Weihnachtslied
Christmas Eve (midnight) mass	die Christmesse
Christmas tree	der Weihnachtsbaum
holly	der Christdorn
menorah	die Menora
mistletoe	der Mistelzweig
Merry Christmas!	Fröhliche Weihnachten!

German, Swiss, and Austrian holidays and festivals   **Deutsche, Schweizer und österreichische Feiertage und Volksfeste**

New Year's Eve (December 31)	der/das Silvester

The following four holidays are huge events in which a beer or wine festival and a traveling carnival are usually combined. Attractions include amusement rides, games of chance and skill, and stands selling food and merchandise.

Oktoberfest	Oktoberfest, Wiesn (MÜNCHEN)
Danube Island Music Festival	das Donauinselfest
Bremen Free Fair	der Freimarkt
Zurich City Festival	Züri Fäscht

Rites and rituals   **Riten und Rituale**

baptism	die Taufe, die Kindstaufe [AUS., SWITZ.]
bar mitzvah	die Bar-Mizwa
bat mitzvah	die Bat-Mizwa
birthday	der Geburtstag
bris, brit (Covenant of Circumcision)	die Beschneidung
first communion	die Erstkommunion
mass	die Messe

Sabbath, Shabbat (Saturday)	der Sabbat
saint's day	der Namenstag
wedding	die Hochzeit

The verbal expression **teilnehmen an** *to attend* takes a dative object.

Parties and get-togethers

Partys und andere gesellige Treffen

They want us to attend the party.	Sie wollen, daß wir an der Party teilnehmen.
the baby shower	der Geschenkparty
the bachelor party	dem Junggesellenabschied [M.]
the bachelorette party	dem Junggesellinnenabschied [M.]
the banquet	dem Bankett [N.]
the birthday party	der Geburtstagsfeier
the business dinner	dem Geschäftsessen [N.]
the charity event	der Benefizgala
the closing celebration	der Abschlußfeier / Abschlussfeier
the cocktail party	der Cocktailparty
the corporate event	der Betriebsfeier
the costume ball, the masquerade ball	dem Kostümfest [N.], dem Maskenball [M.]
the family gathering	dem Familientreffen [N.]
the fancy dress ball	dem Ball [M.]
the food festival	dem Foodfestival [N.]
the fundraising event	der Benefizveranstaltung
the gala dinner	dem Festbankett [N.]
the golden wedding anniversary celebration	der Goldenen Hochzeit
the housewarming party	der Einzugsparty
the music festival	dem Musikfestival [N.]
the opening celebration	der Eröffnungsfeier
the pre-game party	dem Vorspiel [N.]
the retirement party	der Verabschiedung in den Ruhestand
the street festival	dem Straßenfest [N.]
the wedding party/celebration	der Hochzeitsfeier
the wedding reception	dem Hochzeitsfest [N.]
the welcome home party, the homecoming celebration	dem Willkommensfest [N.]
the working dinner	dem Arbeitsessen [N.]

Party activities

gift giving

to blow out the candles
to celebrate
to clink glasses
to dance
to entertain, to fête, to receive guests
   warmly
to give a gift
to have a drink
to have a good time
to invite
to make a toast
to make a wish
to raise your glass
to sing
to throw a party
to toast someone
to wish someone well

The birthday party

balloon
birthday celebrant (boy or girl)
cake
candle
celebration
champagne
drinks
food
gift
hors d'oeuvres
party
party favor (gift given to guests)
surprise birthday party
wet blanket, party pooper

Cheers!
Happy Birthday!

Auf der Party

das Schenken

die Kerzen ausblasen
feiern
anstoßen
tanzen
unterhalten

ein Geschenk überreichen
einen trinken
sich amüsieren, Spaß haben
einladen
einen Trinkspruch aussprechen
sich etwas wünschen
das Glas erheben
singen
eine Party geben
auf jemanden trinken
jemandem Glück wünschen

Die Geburtstagsparty

der Ballon
das Geburtstagskind
der Kuchen
die Kerze
die Feier
der Champagner
die Getränke
das Essen
das Geschenk
die Vorspeisen [PL.]
die Party
das Gastgeschenk
die Überraschungs-Geburtstagsparty
der Spielverderber

Prost!
Herzlichen Glückwunsch!

to celebrate	feiern
to give something as a gift	etwas schenken
to turn 32 years old	zweiunddreißig werden

The wedding

Die Hochzeit

best man	der Trauzeuge
bridal bouquet	der Brautstrauß
bride	die Braut
bridesmaid	die Brautjungfer
church	die Kirche
civil ceremony	die standesamtliche Hochzeit
couple	das Ehepaar
engagement	die Verlobung
engagement ring	der Verlobungsring
fiancé	der Verlobte
fiancée	die Verlobte
groom	der Bräutigam
guest	der Gast
honeymoon	die Flitterwochen
husband	der Ehemann
kiss	der Kuß / Kuss
love	die Liebe
maid of honor	die Trauzeugin
marriage	die Heirat
marriage certificate	die Heiratsurkunde
marriage proposal	der Heiratsantrag
marriage vows	die Ehegelübde [PL.]
newlyweds	die Frischvermählten [PL.]
priest	der Geistliche
rabbi	der Rabbi
synagogue	die Synagoge
toast	der Trinkspruch
wedding anniversary	der Hochzeitstag
wedding announcement	die Hochzeitsanzeige
wedding ceremony	die Vermählung
wedding day	der Hochzeitstag
wedding favor (gift given to guests)	das Gastgeschenk
wedding gift	das Hochzeitsgeschenk
wedding gown	das Hochzeitskleid

wedding party	die Hochzeitsgesellschaft
wedding planner	der Hochzeitsplaner
wedding reception	das Hochzeitsfest, die Hochzeitsfeier
wedding (gift) registry	der Hochzeitstisch
wedding ring	der Ehering
wife	die Ehefrau
to court	umwerben
to fall in love (with)	sich verlieben (in)
to get engaged (to)	sich verloben (mit)
to get married to someone	jemanden heiraten
to kiss	küssen
to love	lieben
to love each other	einander lieben
to marry into (a family), to become part of (a family)	sich einheiraten
to toss the bridal bouquet	den Brautstrauß hinter sich werfen
I do.	Ich will.

Joyful and sad events | ## Fröhliche und traurige Ereignisse

custom	der Brauch
funeral	die Beerdigung
happiness	das Glück
in honor of someone	jemandem zu Ehren
joy	die Freude
memory	die Erinnerung
in memory/remembrance of	in Erinnerung an
nostalgia	die Nostalgie, das Heimweh
patriotism	der Patriotismus
sadness	die Traurigkeit
tradition	die Tradition
to be in mourning	in Trauer sein
to cry, to mourn	weinen, beweinen
to express one's condolences	sein Beileid aussprechen
My deepest sympathy.	Mein aufrichtiges Beileid.
to laugh	lachen
to burst out laughing	in Lachen ausbrechen
to lay a wreath on someone's grave	einen Kranz an jemandes Grab niederlegen
to put flowers on the grave	Blumen auf das Grab legen

Klingen Sie authentisch!

Let's try to get along.	Laß uns versuchen, miteinander auszukommen.
The Gregorian calendar is used in the West.	Im Westen wird der gregorianische Kalender verwendet.
His birthday falls on Saturday.	Sein Geburtstag fällt auf einen Samstag.
It's an early birthday present.	Das ist ein verfrühtes Geburtstagsgeschenk.
It's a belated birthday present.	Das ist ein verspätetes Geburtstagsgeschenk.
We gave our host and hostess a bottle of wine.	Wir schenkten unseren Gastgebern eine Flasche Wein.
There were floats in the parade.	Es gab Umzugswagen in der Parade.
The celebration ended with fireworks.	Die Feier endete mit einem Feuerwerk.
He crashed the party.	Er ist uneingeladen auf der Party erschienen.
They're out partying as usual.	Die machen wie immer Party.
What a crazy party!	Was für eine geile Party!
What a party animal!	Was für ein Partylöwe!
Happy New Year!	Gutes Neues Jahr!

Ausdrücke, Sprichwörter und Zitate

Look before you leap.	Erst wägen, dann wagen.
When the cat's away, the mice will play.	Wenn die Katze aus dem Haus ist, tanzen die Mäuse auf dem Dach.

„Andere mögen Kriege führen—du, glückliches Österreich, heiratest."
  MATTHIAS CORVINUS

„Der Ring macht Ehen—und Ringe sind's, die eine Kette machen."
  FRIEDRICH SCHILLER

„Die Ware Weihnacht ist nicht die wahre Weihnacht."
  KURT MARTI

„Ein Junggeselle ist ein Mann, der jeden Morgen aus einer anderen Richtung pfeifend zur Arbeit geht."
  WILLY BREINHOLST

Übung 77

Complete each German phrase or sentence so that it expresses the meaning of the English phrase or sentence.

1. *German Unity Day*   Tag der _____
2. *a birthday party*   eine Geburtstags_____

3. *Labor Day* Tag der _____

4. *gift giving* das _____

5. *a business dinner* ein _____essen

6. *They fell in love.* Sie _____.

7. *the bachelor party* der Junggesellen_____

8. *Three Kings Day* Heilige _____

9. *her wedding ring* ihr _____ring

10. *midnight mass* die _____

11. *Christmas Eve* _____abend

12. *the charity event* die _____gala

13. *saint's day* _____tag

14. *a bridal bouquet* ein Braut_____

15. *to raise your glass* das Glas _____

16. *honeymoon* _____wochen

17. *Good Friday* _____freitag

18. *fireworks* Feuer_____

19. *Whit Monday* _____montag

20. *the newlyweds* die Frisch_____

Übung 78

Match each item in the first column with the item in the second column that is related to it.

1. _____ Tag der Deutschen Einheit a. München

2. _____ Heiligabend b. Ostern

3. _____ Silvester c. Nationalfeiertag

4. _____ Oktoberfest d. Junggesellenabschied

5. _____ Züri Fäscht e. Lichterfest

6. _____ Karfreitag f. Neujahr

7. _____ Hochzeit g. Christi Himmelfahrt

8. _____ sich amüsieren h. Weihnachten

9. _____ Chanukka i. Zürich

10. _____ Vatertag j. Spaß haben

Übung 79

Select the verb that correctly completes each sentence.

1. Ich muß an dem Geschäftsessen _____. (teilnehmen / weggehen)

2. Wir _____ auf das Geburtstagskind. (trinken / essen)

3. Wir _____ eine Party. (werfen / geben)

4. Wollen wir „O Tannenbaum" _____? (singen / schenken)

5. Die Braut _____ den Brautstrauß. (ißt / wirft)

6. Ihr Geburtstag _____ auf einen Montag. (fällt / ist)

7. Hannah _____ in Jakob. (verliebt sich / verheiratet sich)

8. Robert _____ nächstes Jahr fünfzig. (füllt / wird)

9. Wir _____ ein Familienfest. (hören / organisieren)

10. Er ist uneingeladen auf der Party _____. (gegangen / erschienen)

Übung 80

Give the name of the month in which each of these German, Austrian, or Swiss holidays is celebrated. Some holidays may be celebrated in more than one month.

1. Oktoberfest _____

2. Heilige Drei Könige _____

3. Ostern _____

4. Allerseelen _____

5. Mariä Himmelfahrt _____

6. Reformationstag _____

7. Vatertag _____

8. Erster Weihnachtstag _____

Übung 81

Give the noun phrase (definite article + noun) that appears in this chapter and is related, by form or meaning, to each of the following verbs. There may be more than one noun phrase for some verbs.

1. sich verlieben _____
2. schenken _____
3. küssen _____
4. anstoßen _____
5. sich einheiraten _____
6. feiern _____
7. sich verabschieden _____
8. trinken _____
9. essen _____
10. sich verloben _____
11. singen _____
12. versprechen _____
13. sich erinnern _____
14. heiraten _____
15. werfen _____

Übung 82

Respond in German as specified for each of the following situations.

1. **Wie ich meinen Geburtstag feiere.** Tell how and with whom you like to celebrate your birthday.

_____
_____
_____
_____
_____
_____
_____
_____

2. **Eine Hochzeit.** Describe a wedding you attended as a guest.

_____

_____

_____

_____

_____

_____

_____

_____

3. **Meine Lieblingsfeiertage.** Talk about your favorite holidays. Tell how you celebrate these holidays and why you like them.

_____

_____

_____

_____

_____

_____

_____

_____

_____

4. **Mein Fest.** Describe an event you organized—a business or charitable event, a bachelor/ bachelorette party, or another type of party.

_____

_____

_____

_____

_____

_____

_____

Übung 83

Translate the following sentences into German.

1. *Erika turned 23 on Saturday.*

   _____

2. *We threw a surprise birthday party for her.*

   _____

3. *The birthday girl made a wish and blew out the candles on the cake.*

   _____

   _____

4. *We all sang "Happy Birthday" to her, clinked glasses, and made a toast to her* (auf sie).

   _____

   _____

5. *Maja and Sebastian fell in love, got engaged, and got married.*

   _____

   _____

6. *The bride tossed the bridal bouquet.*

   _____

7. *Our German friends want us to spend October with them in Munich.*

   _____

   _____

8. *They plan to spend Christmas in Berlin.*

   _____

9. *Did you* (du) *have a good time at the New Year's Eve party?*

   _____

   _____

10. *The festivities* (Feierlichkeiten) *on German Unity Day ended with a parade and fireworks.*

    _____

    _____

13

Regierung, Politik und Gesellschaft
Government, politics, and society

This chapter presents vocabulary for talking about types of government, political systems, ideologies, and leaders. You will be able to discuss the political process, having learned vocabulary relevant to political parties, elections, and public opinion. You will also acquire the necessary vocabulary to talk about social problems.

Many of the German words in the following sections are similar to their English equivalents. They are international terms shared by most European languages.

Kinds of government

It's a democratic country.
  capitalist
  communist
  fascist
  progressive
  secular
  socialist
  totalitarian

It's an authoritarian country.
  autocratic

Political systems

That country is a democracy.
  an absolute monarchy
  a constitutional monarchy
  a dictatorship
  a kingdom
  a military dictatorship
  a monarchy
  an oligarchy

Verschiedene Regierungsformen

Das ist ein demokratisches Land.
  kapitalistisches
  kommunistisches
  faschistisches
  fortschrittliches
  säkulares
  sozialistisches
  totalitäres

Das ist ein autoritäres Land.
  autokratisches

Politische Systeme

Dieses Land ist eine Demokratie.
  eine absolute Monarchie
  eine konstitutionelle Monarchie
  eine Diktatur
  ein Königreich [N.]
  eine Militärdiktatur
  eine Monarchie
  eine Oligarchie

>>>

a republic	eine Republik
a theocracy	eine Theokratie
a welfare state	ein Wohlfahrtsstaat [M.]

Rulers/leaders — **Herrscher/Führer**

czar	der Zar
dictator	der Diktator
emperor	der Kaiser
empress	die Kaiserin
head of government, chancellor (Germany)	der Bundeskanzler
head of state	das Staatsoberhaupt, der Präsident
king	der König
leader, strongman	der Führer
monarch	der Monarch
prince	der Prinz
princess	die Prinzessin
queen	die Königin
tyrant	der Tyrann

Ideologies — **Ideologien**

anarchism	der Anarchismus
capitalism	der Kapitalismus
colonialism	der Kolonialismus
communism	der Kommunismus
conservatism	der Konservativismus
despotism	der Despotismus
fascism	der Faschismus
imperialism	der Imperialismus
jihadism	der Dschihadismus
liberalism	der Liberalismus
libertarianism	der Libertarismus
Marxism	der Marxismus
militarism	der Militarismus
nationalism	der Nationalismus
objectivism	der Objektivismus
populism	der Populismus
progressivism	der Progressivismus

racism	der Rassismus
radicalism	der Radikalismus
socialism	der Sozialismus
totalitarianism	der Totalitarismus
Zionism	der Zionismus

The Constitution of the United States — Die Verfassung der USA

The first ten amendments of the Constitution of the United States make up the Bill of Rights.	Die ersten zehn Ergänzungsartikel der Verfassung der USA stammen aus der Bill of Rights.

freedom of assembly	die Versammlungsfreiheit
freedom of opinion	die Meinungsfreiheit
freedom of the press	die Pressefreiheit
freedom of religion	die Religionsfreiheit
freedom of speech	die Redefreiheit
right to keep and bear arms	das Recht auf den Besitz und das Tragen von Waffen
right to petition the government for redress of grievances	das Recht zur Beseitigung von Mißständen/Missständen aufzufordern, die Regierung zur Beseitigung von Mißständen/Missständen aufzufordern

federal government (Germany)	die Bundesregierung
independence	die Unabhängigkeit
nation	die Nation
power	die Macht
separation of church and state	die Trennung von Kirche und Staat
sovereignty	die Staatshoheit

The feminine form of nouns of profession is created by adding the suffix **-in** to the masculine form; examples are **der Präsident** > <u>die</u> **Präsident<u>in</u>** and **der Richter** > <u>die</u> **Richter<u>in</u>**.

The government — Die Regierung

separation of powers	die Gewaltenteilung
head of state	das Staatsoberhaupt
president	der Präsident
vice president	der Vizepräsident
prime minister	der Ministerpräsident

legislature	die Legislative
bicameral legislature	die Zweikammernlegislative
legislator	der Gesetzgeber
Senate (U.S.)	der Senat
senator	der Senator
House of Representatives (U.S.)	das Repräsentantenhaus
congress	der Kongreß/Kongress
congressman	der Kongreßabgeordnete/Kongressabgeordnete
congresswoman	die Kongreßabgeordnete/Kongressabgeordnete
representative	der Repräsentant
parliament	das Parlament
member of parliament	das Parlamentsmitglied
judiciary	die Judikative
court	das Gericht
Supreme Court (Germany)	das Oberste Bundesgericht
judge	der Richter
executive, executive branch	die Exekutive
president's cabinet	das Kabinett des Präsidenten
department of government	das Ministerium
secretary of a government department	der Minister
ambassador	der Botschafter
Department of Agriculture	das Landwirtschaftsministerium
Department of Commerce	das Wirtschaftsministerium
Department of Defense	das Verteidigungsministerium
Department of Education	das Bildungsministerium
Department of Energy	das Energieministerium
Department of Health and Human Services	das Gesundheitsministerium
Department of Homeland Security	das Ministerium für nationale Sicherheit
Department of Housing and Urban Development	das Verkehrsministerium
Department of the Interior	das Innenministerium
Department of Justice	das Justizministerium
Department of Labor	das Arbeitsministerium
State Department	das Außenministerium, das Auswärtige Amt
Department of the Treasury	das Finanzministerium
Department of Veterans Affairs	das Kriegsveteranenministerium

Germany has a central federal government and 16 states. The basic law (**Grundgesetz**), promulgated in 1945, is binding in all the states. Major decisions are made by the central government, while local issues are handled by the states: schooling and tertiary education, internal security and policing, as well as the organization of local self-government.

In the congress

There are <u>debates</u>.
  agreements
  bills
  coalitions
  committees
  deals
  disagreements

  motions
  speeches
  votes (in favor of and opposed to)

obstruction of justice
perjury

to amend the constitution
to come to a decision
to deliberate
to filibuster
to pass a bill
to present a motion
to table a motion

National defense

He did his military service.
He served <u>in the Army</u>.
  in the Navy
  in the Air Force
  in the Marine Corps
  in the Coast Guard
  in the National Guard
  on an aircraft carrier
  on a nuclear submarine

Im Kongreß/Kongress

Es gibt <u>Debatte</u>. [die Debatte]
  Abkommen [das Abkommen]
  Gesetzesvorschläge [der Gesetzesvorschlag]
  Koalitionen [die Koalition]
  Ausschüsse [der Ausschuß/Ausschuss]
  Abmachungen [die Abmachung]
  Meinungsverschiedenheiten
    [die Meinungsverschiedenheit]
  Anträge [der Antrag]
  Reden [die Rede]
  Abstimmungen (für und gegen) [die Abstimmung]

die Behinderung der Justiz
der Meineid

die Verfassung abändern
eine Entscheidung treffen
sich beraten
filibustern
einen Gesetzesvorschlag annehmen
einen Antrag stellen
einen Mißtrauensantrag/Misstrauensantrag stellen

Landesverteidigung

Er hat seinen Militärdienst abgeleistet.
Er hat <u>in der Armee</u> gedient.
  in der Marine
  in der Luftwaffe
  in der Marineinfanterie
  in der Küstenwache
  in der Nationalgarde
  auf einem Flugzeugträger
  auf einem Atom-U-Boot

They served the country.	Sie haben dem Vaterland gedient.
armed forces	die Streitkräfte
bombing	das Bombardement
military service, tour of duty	der Militärdienst
troops	die Truppen [die Truppe]

He was a private.	Er war Soldat.
an admiral	Admiral
a bomber pilot	Bomberpilot
a captain	Kapitän
a colonel	Oberst
a general	General
a lieutenant	Leutnant
a major	Major
an officer	Offizier
a sailor	Matrose

to defend the border	die Grenzen verteidigen
to enlist in the army	in die Armee eintreten

The most important election in Germany is held to elect representatives to the **Bundestag** (parliament). Every four years, the majority in the Bundestag elects the **Bundeskanzler** (head of the federal government, or chancellor), who has political power. The **Bundespräsident** has predominantly representative functions and duties.

The most influential political parties of the right/conservative wing are the CDU (**Christlich Demokratische Union**) and the CSU (**Christlich Soziale Union**). On the left/liberal wing are the SPD (**Sozialdemokratische Partei Deutschlands**), **die Grünen** (the Green Party), and **die Linke** (the Left). Usually, parties form coalitions with like-minded parties so that Germany is normally ruled by either a pure left- or right-wing government. A model called **Große Koalition** (grand coalition), which is a coalition of the two major parties, CDU and SPD, may occur, but it is unpopular because most people associate such a coalition with legislative inertia rather than consensus.

Political parties

Are you going to vote for the socialist party?	**Politische Parteien** Wirst du die sozialistische Partei wählen?
the center-left party	die Mitte-Links-Partei
the center-right party	die Mitte-Rechts-Partei
the communist party	die Kommunistische Partei

>>>

the conservative party	die Konservativen
the Democratic Party (U.S.)	die Demokraten
the green party	die Grünen
the left-wing party	die Linken
the liberal party	die Liberalen
the nationalist party	die Nationalistische Partei
the Republican Party (U.S.)	die Republikaner
the right-wing party	die Rechten

Elections   Wahlen

The candidate is running for the office.	Der Kandidat bewirbt sich um das Amt.
He's running for president.	Er bewirbt sich um die Präsidentschaft.
He's running in the local elections.	Er kandidiert in der Kommunalwahl.
The candidates study the results of the poll.	Die Kandidaten analysieren die Ergebnisse der Abstimmung.
These politicians are running the campaign.	Diese Politiker machen den Wahlkampf.
There will be a referendum on the ballot.	Auf dem Stimmzettel ist ein Referendum.
This issue will be decided at the polls.	Diese Angelegenheit wird sich an den Wahlurnen entscheiden.
Please register to vote.	Bitte registrieren Sie sich vor der Wahl.
The voters go to the polls.	Die Wähler gehen an die Urnen.
We vote by secret ballot.	Wir wählen mittels geheimer Wahl.
Each voter submits a ballot or pulls the lever.	Jeder Wähler gibt einen Stimmzettel ab oder benutzt den Wahlcomputer.
The votes are counted.	Die Stimmen werden gezählt.
absentee voter	der Briefwähler
ballot box	die Wahlurne
caucus	der Parteienausschuß / Parteienausschuss
census	die Volkszählung
citizens over eighteen	Bürger über achtzehn [der Bürger]
electronic voting	elektronisches Wahlverfahren
eligible voter	der Wahlberechtigter, der Stimmbürger [SWITZ.]
paper ballot	der Stimmzettel
primary	die Vorwahl
registered voter	der eingetragene Wähler
electoral register, voter roll	das Wählerverzeichnis

right to vote	das Stimmrecht
slate	die Kandidatenliste
universal suffrage	allgemeines Wahlrecht
to be of voting age	das Wahlalter erreicht haben
to put on the ballot	zur Abstimmung freigeben

Political and legal problems

This year there was a scandal.	Dieses Jahr gab es einen Skandal.
a breach of the constitution	einen Verfassungsbruch
rampant corruption	zügellose Korruption
a coup (d'état)	einen Staatsstreich
government overreach	Amtsmißbrauch/Amtsmissbrauch [M.]
a major economic crisis	eine schwere Wirtschaftskrise
a repeal of tax loopholes	ein Stopfen von Steuerschlupflöchern
a slew of regulations	eine Menge Bestimmungen
slow economic growth	langsames Wirtschaftswachstum
a spate of resignations	eine Flut von Rücktritten

Politische und rechtliche Probleme

This year there were demonstrations.	Dieses Jahr gab es Demonstrationen. [die Demonstration]
diplomatic disasters	diplomatische Katastrophen [die Katastrophe]
new laws	neue Gesetze [das Gesetz]
new taxes	neue Steuern [das Steuer]
street riots	Straßenkämpfe [der Straßenkampf]

Public opinion

Die öffentliche Meinung

Would you vote for the legalization of drugs?	Würdest du für die Legalisierung von Drogen stimmen?
against	gegen
Many people are in favor of an affordable health care system.	Viele sind für ein günstiges Gesundheitssystem.
opposed to	gegen
A majority of American citizens support repeal of the law.	Eine Mehrheit der US-Bürger unterstützt eine Aufhebung des Gesetzes.
A minority	Eine Minderheit
Polls not only reflect public opinion, but can also influence it.	Umfragen spiegeln nicht nur die öffentliche Meinung wider, sondern können sie auch beeinflussen.

attitude	die Gesinnung
political campaign	der Wahlkampf, die politische Kampagne
to conduct a poll	eine Umfrage durchführen
to exert influence	Einfluß / Einfluss ausüben
to influence	beeinflussen
to oppose	sich entgegensetzen, ablehnen
to support	unterstützen

In the 1960s, West Germany became an immigration country when the federal government hired **Gastarbeiter** (guest workers) from Italy and Turkey to relieve the labor shortage and help build up the country. Many of these immigrants decided to stay, and that's why there are many families of Italian and Turkish descent in Germany. Today, Germany is a popular immigration country, mainly for immigrants from Eastern Europe. Germany's major cities offer an exciting multicultural panorama where the integration of immigrants has been successful. Social exclusion and ghettoization are drawbacks in those places where the integration of immigrants has failed.

A complex society

Eine komplexe Gesellschaft

Our society has an ethnically diverse population.	Unsere Gesellschaft besteht aus einer ethnisch gemischten Bevölkerung.
Immigration has had a profound influence on our society.	Einwanderung hat einen tiefgreifenden Einfluß / Einfluss auf unsere Gesellschaft.
Immigration is a very contentious political issue.	Einwanderung ist eine sehr kontroverse politische Frage.
The differences between the social classes are more and more striking.	Die Unterschiede zwischen den sozialen Schichten sind immer deutlicher.
There are many minority groups.	Es gibt viele Minoritäten.

Society's problems

Gesellschaftsprobleme

Citizens are worried about <u>the economy</u>.	Bürger sorgen sich um <u>die Wirtschaft</u>.
air pollution	die Luftverschmutzung
the availability of firearms	die Verfügbarkeit von Feuerwaffen
climate change	den Klimawandel
the corrupt political class	die korrupte Politik
crime	die Kriminalität
the deficit	die Staatsschulden [die Staatsschuld]
drug trafficking	den Drogenhandel

>>>

drug use	den Drogenkonsum
environmental pollution	die Umweltverschmutzung
government intrusion into private life	die staatliche Verletzung der Privatsphäre
human trafficking	den Menschenhandel
the loss of their constitutional rights	den Verlust ihrer Bürgerrechte
the national debt	die Staatsschulden [die Staatsschuld]
their security at home and abroad	die innere und äußere Sicherheit
social security	die soziale Absicherung
terrorism	den Terrorismus
unemployment	die Arbeitslosigkeit
unfair law enforcement	die ungerechte Strafverfolgung
war	den Krieg
water pollution	die Wasserverschmutzung

Crime

Kriminalität

There are many kidnappings.	Es gibt viele Entführungen. [die Entführung]
armed robberies	Raubüberfälle [der Raubüberfall]
burglaries	Einbrüche [der Einbruch]
crimes	Verbrechen [das Verbrechen]
muggings	Überfälle [der Überfall]
murders	Morde [der Mord]
rapes	Vergewaltigungen [die Vergewaltigung]
robberies, thefts	Diebstähle [der Diebstahl]
shoot-outs	Schießereien [die Schießerei]

Those criminals committed many crimes.	Diese Kriminellen haben viele Verbrechen begangen.
The police arrested all the thugs in the gang.	Die Polizei hat alle Mitglieder der Bande festgenommen.

blackmail	die Erpressung
to blackmail	erpressen
bribe	die Bestechung
to bribe	bestechen
crime rate	die Kriminalitätsrate
death sentence	die Todesstrafe
jail, prison	das Gefängnis
to jail, to imprison	einsperren
murderer	der Mörder
to murder	ermorden
thief	der Dieb

Social values

Members of society share certain core values and beliefs.

accountability	die Verantwortung
charity	die Nächstenliebe
community	die Gemeinschaft
compassion	das Mitleid
courage	der Mut
diversity of opinion	die Meinungsvielfalt
empathy	die Empathie
enterprising spirit	der Unternehmergeist
equal opportunity	die Chancengleichheit
equality	die Gleichheit
ethical conduct	der Verhaltenskodex
freedom	die Freiheit
generosity	die Großzügigkeit
gratitude	die Dankbarkeit
honesty	die Ehrlichkeit
humility	die Bescheidenheit
justice	die Gerechtigkeit
kindness	die Güte
loyalty	die Loyalität
moderation	die Mäßigung
open-mindedness	die Offenheit
perseverance	die Beharrlichkeit
purpose in life	das Lebensziel
reason, rational thought	die Vernunft
responsibility	die Verantwortlichkeit
rule of law	die Rechtsstaatlichkeit
self-knowledge	die Selbsterkenntnis
self-reliance	das Selbstvertrauen
self-respect	der Selbstrespekt
sense of duty	das Pflichtbewußtsein
social responsibility	die soziale Verantwortung
solidarity	die Solidarität
stability	die Stabilität
tolerance	die Toleranz
truth	die Wahrheit
wisdom	die Weisheit

Gesellschaftliche Werte

Mitglieder einer Gesellschaft teilen bestimmte Werte und Ansichten.

The preposition **von** *of* takes a dative object.

The state, my city, and the people who live there	**Der Bundesstaat, meine Stadt und ihre Bewohner**
Here's a photo of city hall.	Hier ist ein Photo/Foto von dem Rathaus. [N.]
capital	der Hauptstadt
capitol	dem Kapitol [N.]
county	dem Landkreis [M.]
the governor	dem Gouverneur [M.]
the mayor	dem Bürgermeister [M.]
the municipality	der Stadtverwaltung

The genitive case is sometimes used instead of **von** + the dative case.

| *Here's a photo of the town council.* | Hier ist ein Photo/Foto des Stadtrates. |
| of the town/city councilmen/ councilwomen | der Stadträte |

city administration	die Stadtverwaltung
downtown	das Zentrum
fire department	die Brandwache
firefighter	der Feuerwehrmann / die Feuerwehrfrau
garbage collection	die Müllabfuhr
gentrification	die Gentrifizierung
hustle and bustle	der Trubel
infrastructure	die Infrastruktur
metropolitan area	das Ballungsgebiet
neighborhood	die Nachbarschaft
police department	die Polizeidienststelle
policeman	der Polizist
policewoman	die Polizistin
red tape	der Amtsschimmel
sewer system	das Kanalisationssystem
state government	die Landesregierung
traffic	der Verkehr
traffic jam	der Stau
urban planning	die Stadtplanung

Klingen Sie authentisch!

Education improves one's chances of social mobility.	Bildung begünstigt den sozialen Aufstieg.
The term of the American president is four years.	Die Legislaturperiode des US-Präsidenten beträgt vier Jahre.
He is elected indirectly by the electoral college.	Er wird indirekt vom Wahlmännergremium gewählt.
The German chancellor is elected for a four-year term.	Der deutsche Kanzler wird für eine Legislaturperiode von vier Jahren gewählt.
He resigned from the position of advisor.	Er trat von seiner Position als Berater zurück.
He occupied the office of president for eight years.	Er bekleidete das Präsidentenamt für acht Jahre.
He was proclaimed president for life.	Er wurde zum Präsidenten auf Lebenszeit ernannt.

Ausdrücke, Sprichwörter und Zitate

„Wir halten diese Wahrheiten für ausgemacht, daß alle Menschen gleich erschaffen worden, daß sie von ihrem Schöpfer mit gewissen unveräußerlichen Rechten begabt worden, worunter sind Leben, Freiheit und das Bestreben nach Glückseligkeit. Daß zur Versicherung dieser Rechte Regierungen unter den Menschen eingeführt worden sind, welche ihre gerechte Gewalt von der Einwilligung der Regierten herleiten."

UNABHÄNGIGKEITSERKLÄRUNG DER VEREINIGTEN STAATEN

„Die hauptsächlichen Grundlagen, die alle Staaten brauchen, sind gute Gesetze und ein gutes Heer."

NICCOLÒ MACHIAVELLI

„Der Krieg ist die bloße Fortsetzung der Politik mit anderen Mitteln."

CARL VON CLAUSEWITZ

„Keine Strafe ohne Gesetz."

ANSELM VON FEUERBACH

„Der Faschismus verneint die Gleichsetzung von Wohlstand und Glück, die die Menschen in Tiere verwandelt, weil sie nur noch einen einzigen Gedanken haben, nämlich den, wohlgenährt und gemästet zu sein, wodurch sie auf ein rein vegetatives Leben herabgedrückt werden."

BENITO MUSSOLINI

„Die größte Strafe für alle, die sich nicht für Politik interessieren, ist, daß sie von Leuten regiert werden, die sich für Politik interessieren."

ARNOLD TOYNBEE

„Das Problem ist nicht rechts oder links, sondern die richtige Mischung. Ich wäre ja dafür, an Stelle der Wahlkabinen Duschkabinen aufzustellen, die mit zwei Wasserhähnen ausgestattet sein müßten, einer für kaltes Wasser mit der Aufschrift ‚Egoismus‘, der andere für heißes Wasser mit der Aufschrift ‚Solidarität‘. Die Wähler müßten an beiden Hähnen drehen und solange probieren, bis schließlich angenehmes warmes Wasser zum Duschen aus der Leitung kommt.“

LUCIANO DE CRESCENZO

„Wenn man keine Beschäftigung hat, beginnt man, sich mit Politik zu befassen.“

JÜDISCHES SPRICHWORT

Übung 84

Complete each German phrase or sentence so that it expresses the meaning of the English phrase or sentence.

1. *separation of powers*   die _____teilung

2. *the first ten amendments*   die ersten zehn _____

3. *a bill*   ein Gesetzes_____

4. *the mayor of this city*   der _____ dieser Stadt

5. *the department of the treasury*   das _____ministerium

6. *the poll results*   die Ergebnisse der _____

7. *He served in the Navy.*   Er diente in der _____.

8. *a four-year term*   eine _____ von vier Jahren

9. *an eligible voter*   ein Stimm_____

10. *She resigned from the position.*   Sie trat vom _____ zurück.

11. *the local election*   die _____wahlen

12. *the center-right party*   die _____-Partei

13. *red tape*   Amts_____

14. *certain unalienable rights*   gewisse _____ Rechte

15. *the rule of law*   die _____

16. *a contentious issue*   eine _____ Frage

17. *freedom of the press*   die _____freiheit

18. *He is president for life.*   Er ist Präsident auf _____.

19. *the pursuit of happiness*   das _____ nach Glückseligkeit

20. *all American citizens*   alle amerikanischen _____

Übung 85

Form logical verb phrases by matching each verb in the first column with an appropriate phrase in the second column.

1. _____ abändern   a. eine Entscheidung
2. _____ ableisten   b. die Wahl
3. _____ treffen   c. im Gefängnis
4. _____ stellen   d. der Militärdienst
5. _____ durchführen   e. das Amt
6. _____ sich registrieren für f. eine Umfrage
7. _____ dienen   g. ein Verbrechen
8. _____ begehen   h. die Verfassung
9. _____ bewerben   i. in der Marine
10. _____ einsperren   j. ein Antrag

Übung 86

Select the verb that correctly completes each sentence.

1. Die Bürger _____ grundlegende Werte. (teilen / sammeln)
2. _____ sie bereits die Stimmen? (Zählen / Fälschen)
3. Der Verbrecher _____ den Richter. (trifft / besticht)
4. Sie wollte nicht von dem Amt _____. (wählen / zurücktreten)
5. Es ist notwendig, daß die Armee das Land _____. (verteidigt / bewirbt)
6. Sie _____ den Wahlkampf. (organisieren / abändern)
7. Sollen wir den Antrag _____? (beeinflussen / stellen)
8. Der Stadtrat _____ sich mit den Abgeordneten. (berät / betrinkt)
9. Die Verbrecher _____ einen Raubüberfall. (begehen / schießen)
10. Ich _____ die Gesetzesänderung. (unterstütze / erpresse)

Übung 87

Choose the word that does not belong in each group.

1. a. Land   b. Staat   c. Gesetz   d. Stadt

2. a. Marine   b. Armee   c. Luftwaffe   d. Ministerium

3. a. Minister   b. Präsident   c. Führer   d. Abgeordneter

4. a. Staatshoheit   b. Nächstenliebe   c. Empathie   d. Loyalität

5. a. Oberst   b. Bomberpilot   c. Admiral   d. Soldat

6. a. Königin   b. Kaiser   c. Richter   d. Diktator

7. a. Verbrechen   b. Trubel   c. Überfall   d. Raub

8. a. Republik   b. Monarchie   c. Oligarchie   d. Legislaturperiode

9. a. Umfrage   b. Stimme   c. Stimmzettel   d. Wahlcomputer

10. a. Gouverneur   b. Bürgermeister   c. Tyrann   d. Stadtrat

Übung 88

Describe the type of government in your country. What are the different branches of government? What does each one do? What parties are there? What are elections like?

_____

_____

_____

_____

_____

_____

_____

_____

_____

Übung 89

Discuss the problems in society that worry you most. What should be done to solve them? What departments of government should be called upon in each case?

_____

_____

_____

_____

_____

_____

_____

_____

Übung 90

Describe the rights and freedoms that you enjoy as a citizen of your country. What are your civic responsibilities? What are the core values and beliefs of your society?

_____

_____

_____

_____

_____

_____

_____

_____

Übung 91

Translate the following sentences into German.

1. *In the congress, there are the Senate and the House of Representatives.*

_____

_____

2. The president is elected for a four-year term.

_____

3. Konrad Adenauer occupied the office of chancellor for 14 years.

_____

_____

4. The Constitution guarantees freedom of speech, freedom of religion, and freedom of the press.

_____

_____

5. He was a general in the army and served his country for many years.

_____

_____

6. The representatives tabled a motion and passed a bill.

_____

_____

7. The dictator took power in a coup d'état.

_____

8. The citizens are against government intrusion into private life.

_____

_____

9. They oppose not only new taxes but also the repeal of tax loopholes.

_____

_____

10. There are scandals and rampant corruption in city government.

_____

_____

11. The election will be on Tuesday. Please register (Sie) to vote!

_____

_____

12. The political parties conducted polls that influenced the results of the election.

_____

_____

14

Geistiges und geistliches Leben

Intellectual life and spiritual life

This chapter presents vocabulary for talking about your intellectual pursuits, philosophy, religion, and the relationship between thought and language. You will be able to discuss your favorite books, as well as important existential questions.

Reading	Das Lesen
I like to read fiction.	Ich lese gerne Schönliteratur. [F.]
adventure novels	Abenteuerromane [der Abenteuerroman]
children's literature	Kinderliteratur [F.]
comics, comic strips	Comics [der Comic]
detective novels	Kriminalromane [der Kriminalroman]
e-zines	E-Journale [das E-Journal]
fairy tales	Märchen [das Märchen]
the great works of world literature	große Werke der Weltliteratur [das Werk]
historical novels	historische Romane [der Roman]
horror novels	Schauerromane [der Schauerroman]
humorous books	humoristische Literatur [F.]
masterpieces	Klassiker [der Klassiker]
mystery novels	Kriminalgeschichten [die Kriminalgeschichte]
mythology	Mythologie [F.]
plays	Theaterstücke [das Theaterstück]
poems	Gedichte [das Gedicht]
satire	Satire [F.]
science fiction	Science-Fiction-Literatur [F.]
short stories	Kurzgeschichten [die Kurzgeschichte]
I prefer to read nonfiction.	Ich bevorzuge Fachliteratur. [F.]
articles about current events	Artikel zur Zeitgeschichte [der Artikel]
autobiographies	Autobiographien [die Autobiographie]/ Autobiografien [die Autobiografie]
biographies	Biographien [die Biographie]/Biografien [die Biografie]

⟩⟩⟩

cookbooks	Kochbücher [das Kochbuch]
editorials	Leitartikel [der Leitartikel]
essays	Essays [der/das Essay]
history books	Geschichtsbücher [das Geschichtsbuch]
literary criticism	Literaturkritik [F.]
magazines	Zeitschriften [die Zeitschrift]
newspapers	Zeitungen [die Zeitung]
the op-ed page	Glossen [die Glosse *op-ed article*]
professional journals	Fachzeitschriften [die Fachzeitschrift]
reference books	Nachschlagewerke [das Nachschlagewerk]
textbooks	Lehrbücher [das Lehrbuch]
travel books	Reiseführer [der Reiseführer]

The preposition **in** *into* takes an accusative object when it expresses direction.

I advise you to look at <u>the atlas</u>.	Ich empfehle dir, in <u>den Atlas</u> zu schauen.
the almanac	den Almanach
the anthology	die Anthologie
the catalogue	den Katalog
the dictionary	das Wörterbuch
the dissertation	die Dissertation
the encyclopedia	die Enzyklopädie
the guidebook	den Führer
the manual	die Gebrauchsanweisung
the report	den Bericht
the thesaurus	das Lexikon
the thesis	die Diplomarbeit
the treatise	die Abhandlung

Literary genres and forms

Literarische Genres und Formen

comedy	die Komödie
drama	das Drama
myth	die Sage
novel	der Roman
novella	die Novelle
poem	das Gedicht
poetry	die Dichtung, die Poesie
romance	der Liebesroman

satire	die Satire
short story	die Kurzgeschichte
tragedy	die Tragödie
tragicomedy	die Tragikomödie

Elements of a literary work / Elemente eines literarischen Werkes

I love the dialogue.	Ich liebe den Dialog.
the antagonist	den Gegenspieler
the characters	die Personen
the description	die Beschreibung
the ending, the outcome	das Ende
the figures of speech	die Redewendungen [die Redewendung]
the imagery	die Metaphorik
the ironic tone	den ironischen Ton
the irony	die Ironie
the literary/rhetorical devices	die sprachlichen/rhetorischen Mittel [das Mittel]
the metaphors	die Metaphern [die Metapher]
the narrative frame	den Erzählrahmen
the narrator	den Erzähler
the plot	den Inhalt
the point of view	die Erzählperspektive
the protagonist, the main character	die Hauptperson
the similes	die Gleichnisse [das Gleichnis]
the story	die Geschichte
the structure	die Struktur
the style	den Stil
the theme	das Thema
the tropes	die bildlichen Ausdrücke [der Ausdruck]

Some masculine nouns referring to people (for example, **der Biograf**) and nouns ending in **-ist** (for example, **der Essayist**) add **-en** in all forms except the nominative singular.

Men and women of letters / Schriftsteller

What do you think of the novelist?	Was hältst du von dem Romancier?
the author, the writer	der Autor / der Autorin
the biographer	dem Biografen / der Biografin
the essayist	dem Essayisten / der Essayistin
the journalist	dem Journalisten / der Journalistin

⟩⟩⟩

the man of letters	dem Schriftsteller
the woman of letters	der Schriftstellerin
the playwright	dem Dramatiker / der Dramatikerin
the poet	dem Dichter / der Dichterin

Intellectual pursuits | ## Intellektuelle Beschäftigungen

We love <u>to read</u>.	Wir lieben es, <u>zu lesen</u>.
to attend lectures	Vorlesungen anzuhören
to deliver a speech at a conference	auf Konferenzen zu sprechen
to join a reading group/club	beim Lesekreis mitzumachen
to listen to music	Musik zu hören
to participate in a playwriting workshop	an einem Workshop zum Schreiben von Theaterstücken teilzunehmen
to do research on unfamiliar topics	unbekannte Themen zu erforschen
to study languages abroad	Sprachen im Ausland zu lernen
to take classes at the university	Universitäts-Kurse zu belegen
to take classes online	Online-Kurse zu belegen
to teach classes in continuing/adult education	Fortbildungskurse zu geben
to visit museums	Museen zu besuchen
to write poetry	Gedichte zu schreiben

German nouns ending in **-ismus** are masculine. German nouns ending in **-ik** are feminine; these usually have English equivalents ending in **-ics**.

Philosophy | ## Philosophie

abstraction	die Abstraktion
aesthetics	die Ästhetik
Aristotelianism	der Aristotelismus
causality	die Kausalität
cynicism	der Zynismus
determinism	der Determinismus
dialectic	die Dialektik
empiricism	der Empirismus
epistemology	die Epistemologie
ethics	die Ethik
existentialism	der Existenzialismus

hedonism	der Hedonismus
idealism	der Idealismus
irrationalism	der Irrationalismus
knowledge	das Wissen
logic	die Logik
metaphysics	die Metaphysik
morality	die Moral
nihilism	der Nihilismus
Platonism	der Platonismus
positivism	der Positivismus
pragmatism	der Pragmatismus
skepticism	der Skeptizismus
solipsism	der Solipsismus
spiritualism	der Spiritualismus
stoicism	der Stoizismus
transcendentalism	der Transzendentalismus
utilitarianism	der Utilitarismus
cynical	zynisch
ethical	ethisch
idealistic	idealistisch
logical	logisch
metaphysical	metaphysisch
philosophical	philosophisch
pragmatic	pragmatisch
skeptical	skeptisch
stoical	stoisch
utilitarian	utilitaristisch

The verbal expression **denken an** *to think of* takes an accusative object.

Our existential questions
What do we think about?

Unsere grundlegenden Fragen
Woran denken wir?

We think about <u>*life*</u>.	Wir denken an <u>das Leben</u>.
beauty	die Schönheit
concepts	Begriffe [der Begriff]
death	den Tod
evil	das Böse
fate	das Schicksal >>>

>>>

free will	den freien Willen
good	das Gute
human existence	das menschliche Dasein
ideas	Ideen [die Idee]
immortality	die Unsterblichkeit
the knowable	das Intelligible
knowledge	das Wissen
the mind	den Geist
mortality	die Sterblichkeit
the mystery of life	das Geheimnis des Lebens
reality	die Wirklichkeit
reason	die Vernunft
truth	die Wahrheit

to be, to exist	sein, existieren
to intuit	durch Intuition erkennen
to perceive	begründen
to reflect on something, to think about something, to ponder something	über etwas nachdenken

What is reality?	Was ist die Wirklichkeit?
For what purpose are we here?	Zu welchem Zweck sind wir hier?
What's the purpose of life?	Was ist der Sinn des Lebens?
We human beings try to understand the meaning of life.	Wir Menschen versuchen, den Sinn des Lebens zu verstehen.
We seek rational understanding of the objective world.	Wir streben nach dem rationalen Verstehen der objektiven Welt.

How do we express our thoughts? | Wie drücken wir unsere Gedanken aus?

argument	das Argument
clause	der Satz
communication	die Kommunikation
expression	der Ausdruck
grammar	die Grammatik
letter	der Buchstabe
lexicon	das Lexikon
meaning	die Bedeutung
phrase	die Phrase
semantics	die Semantik

semiotics	die Semiotik
sentence	der Satz
vocabulary	das Vokabular
word	das Wort

It's important that the language be clear.	Es ist wichtig, daß die Sprache klar ist.
comprehensible	verständlich
correct	fehlerfrei
direct	deutlich
eloquent	wortgewandt
evocative	sinnträchtig
expressive	ausdrucksstark
intelligible	begreiflich
precise	präzise

It's bad when the language is unclear.	Es ist schlecht, wenn die Sprache unklar ist.
ambiguous	undeutlich
cryptic	dunkel
incomprehensible	unverständlich
unintelligible	unbegreiflich

We communicate by means of sounds, symbols, signs, and gestures.	Wir kommunizieren durch Laute, Symbole, Zeichen und Gesten.
The meaning of the message is conveyed through context.	Die Bedeutung der Botschaft wird durch den Zusammenhang übermittelt.
We try to grasp the subtleties of the language.	Wir versuchen, die Feinheiten der Sprache zu erfassen.
The English writing system uses the letters of the Latin alphabet.	Das englische Schriftsystem verwendet die Buchstaben des lateinischen Alphabets.

illiteracy	der Analphabetismus
literacy rate	die Alphabetisierungsrate

German nouns ending in **-tum** are neuter. The English equivalent of **-tum** is -*dom*; compare **das Christentum** with English *Christendom*. These cognates have slightly different meanings, however: *Christendom* in German is **die Christenheit**.

Religions and doctrines
Religionen und Doktrinen

agnosticism	der Agnostizismus
Anglicanism	der Anglikanismus
anti-Semitism	der Antisemitismus

asceticism	der Asketismus
atheism	der Atheismus
Bahai	das Bahaitum
Buddhism	der Buddhismus
Catholicism	der Katholizismus
Christianity	das Christentum
Confucianism	der Konfuzianismus
creationism	der Kreationismus
deism	der Deismus
ecumenism	der Ökumenismus
Episcopalianism	der Episkopalismus
fundamentalism	der Fundamentalismus
Hinduism	der Hinduismus
humanism	der Humanismus
Islam	der Islam
Judaism	der Judaismus
Lutheranism	das Luthertum
Methodism	der Methodismus
monasticism	das Mönchswesen
monotheism	der Monotheismus
Mormonism	das Mormonentum
mysticism	der Mystizismus
orthodoxy	die Orthodoxie
paganism	das Heidentum
pantheism	der Pantheismus
polytheism	der Polytheismus
Protestantism	der Protestantismus
Quakerism	das Quäkertum
Shinto	der Shintoismus
Taoism	der Taoismus
theism	der Theismus
Unitarianism	der Unitarismus

People and religion

Menschen und Religion

archbishop	der Erzbischof
atheist	der Atheist / die Atheistin
Baptist	der Baptist
bishop	der Bischof
Buddhist	der Buddhist

Catholic	der Katholik / die Katholikin
Roman Catholic	Römisch katholisch
Christian	der Christ / die Christin
Christian	christlich
clergy	die Geistlichkeit
congregation	die Gemeinde
denomination	die Konfession
heretic	der Ketzer / die Ketzerin
Hindu	der Hindu
imam	der Imam
Jesus Christ	Jesus Christus
Jew	der Jude / die Jüdin
Jewish	jüdisch
minister	der Pfarrer
missionary	der Missionar / die Missionarin
Mohammed	Mohammed
monk	der Mönch
Moses	Moses
muezzin	der Muezzin
mullah	der Mullah
Muslim	der Muslim, der Moslem
nun	die Nonne
pastor	der Pastor
pope	der Papst
preacher	der Prediger / die Predigerin
priest	der Priester
Protestant	der Protestant / die Protestantin
rabbi	der Rabbi
saint	der/die Heilige
sect	die Sekte

See Chapter 12 for religious holidays and rituals.

Religion: faith and practice   Religion: Glaube und Praxis

angel	der Engel
baptism	der Baptismus
belief	die Überzeugung, der Glaube
believer	der/die Gläubige
the Bible	die Bibel

cathedral	die Kathedrale, der Dom, der/das Münster
chapel	die Kapelle
charity	die Nächstenliebe
church	die Kirche
communion	die Kommunion
confession	die Beichte
conscience	das Gewissen
crescent moon and star (symbol of Islam)	Stern und Halbmond (Hilal)
cross	das Kreuz
destiny	das Schicksal
divine	göttlich
dogma	das Dogma
faith	der Glaube
forgiveness	die Vergebung
God	Gott
the Gospel	das Evangelium
hagiography	die Hagiographie / Hagiografie
heaven	der Himmel
the Hebrew Bible	die Hebräische Bibel
hell	die Hölle
the hereafter	das Jenseits
heresy	die Ketzerei
holy, sacred	heilig
the Holy Land	das Heilige Land
the Holy Spirit	der Heilige Geist
the Koran	der Koran
mass	die Messe
miracle	das Wunder
mosque	die Moschee
the New Testament	das Neue Testament
the Old Testament	das Alte Testament
piety	die Frömmigkeit
practicing	praktizierend
prayer	das Gebet
prayer book	das Gebetbuch
psalm	der Psalm
redemption	die Erlösung
repentance	die Buße
rosary	der Rosenkranz
sacrilege	das Sakrileg

sermon	die Predigt
sin	die Sünde
soul	die Seele
stained glass window	das Fenster mit bemaltem Glas
star of David	der Davidstern
synagogue	die Synagoge
the Talmud	der Talmud
temple	der Tempel
the Ten Commandments	die Zehn Gebote
theology	die Theologie
Torah	die Thora
the Tree of Knowledge	der Baum der Erkenntnis
the Trinity	die Dreifaltigkeit
to baptize, to christen	taufen
to believe	glauben
to commit a sin	eine Sünde begehen
to confess	beichten
to forgive	vergeben
to practice (a religion)	(eine Religion) ausüben
to pray	beten
to repent	büßen
to sin	sündigen
to take communion	die Kommunion empfangen
to worship	anbeten
to worship God	Gott anbeten

I wonder, why do bad things happen to good people?	Ich frage mich, warum guten Menschen schlechte Dinge passieren.
Judaism, Christianity, and Islam are monotheistic religions.	Das Judentum, das Christentum und der Islam sind monotheistische Religionen.
They are known as Abrahamic religions because they trace their origin to the patriarch Abraham.	Sie sind bekannt als die Religionen Abrahams, da sich ihr Ursprung auf den Patriarchen Abraham zurückverfolgen läßt.

Klingen Sie authentisch!

Philosophy and religion deal with existential questions—existence, God, good and evil.	Philosophie und Religion beschäftigen sich mit existenziellen Fragen: Dasein, Gott, Gut und Böse.

Aristotle developed the theory of God as the Unmoved Mover (the Prime Mover).	Aristoteles entwickelte die Theorie von Gott als unbewegter Beweger (der erste Beweger).
St. Thomas Aquinas, a Catholic theologian and philosopher, showed the compatibility of the philosophy of Aristotle with the Catholic faith.	Der Heilige Thomas von Aquin, ein katholischer Theologe und Philosoph, zeigte die Vereinbarkeit von Aristoteles' Philosophie und dem katholischen Glauben.
Martin Luther was a German monk, Catholic priest, professor of theology, and seminal figure of a reform movement in sixteenth-century Christianity subsequently known as the Protestant Reformation.	Martin Luther war ein deutscher Mönch, katholischer Priester, Professor der Theologie und wegweisende Figur in einer Reformbewegung im Christentum des 16. Jahrhundert, die in Folge als Reformation bekannt wurde.
The Hebrew Bible was written in Hebrew and Aramaic.	Die Hebräische Bibel wurde auf Hebräisch und Aramäisch geschrieben.
Dante's Divine Comedy has three parts: Hell, Purgatory, and Heaven.	Dantes *Göttliche Komödie* hat drei Teile: Hölle, Purgatorium und Himmel.
Some creationists believe in intelligent design.	Einige Kreationisten glauben an intelligentes Design.

Ausdrücke, Sprichwörter und Zitate

May God bless you.	Gott segne dich.

„Ich denke, also bin ich."
DESCARTES

„Irren ist menschlich, vergeben göttlich."
ALEXANDER POPE

„Sein oder nicht sein. Das ist die Frage."
WILLIAM SHAKESPEARE

„Sogar das Denken kann unter Umständen für die Gesundheit schädlich sein."
ARISTOTELES

„Da es sehr förderlich für die Gesundheit ist, habe ich beschlossen, glücklich zu sein."
VOLTAIRE

„Die Absicht, daß der Mensch ‚glücklich' sei, ist im Plan der ‚Schöpfung' nicht enthalten."
SIGMUND FREUD

„Die Welt ist meine Vorstellung. Dies ist die Wahrheit, welche in Beziehung auf jedes lebende und erkennende Wesen gilt."
ARTHUR SCHOPENHAUER

„Für jene die glauben, daß ‚haben' eine höchst natürliche Kategorie innerhalb der menschlichen Existenz ist, mag es überraschend sein, wenn sie erfahren, daß es in vielen Sprachen gar kein Wort für ‚haben' gibt."

    ERICH FROMM

„Ich habe das, was ich gegeben habe."

    GABRIELE D'ANNUNZIO

„Freiheit ist nur ein anderes Wort dafür, daß man nichts mehr zu verlieren hat."

    JANIS JOPLIN

„Das Leben ist eine Anstrengung, die einer besseren Sache würdig wäre."

    KARL KRAUS

„Es gibt nichts Gutes, außer: man tut es."

    ERICH KÄSTNER

Übung 92

Complete each German phrase or sentence so that it expresses the meaning of the English phrase or sentence.

1. *the Catholic faith*   der katholische _____

2. *the reference book*   das _____werk

3. *the romance*   der _____roman

4. *a playwriting workshop*   ein Workshop zum Schreiben von

                                      _____

5. *the meaning of life*   der _____ des Lebens

6. *the subtleties of the language*   die _____ der Sprache

7. *the Latin alphabet*   das lateinische _____

8. *the literary devices*   die sprachlichen _____

9. *this prayer book*   dieses _____buch

10. *the Holy Land*   das _____ Land

11. *Buddhist monasticism*   Buddhistisches _____

12. *the monotheistic religions*   die _____ Religionen

13. *free will*   der freie _____

14. *To err is human, to forgive, divine.*   Irren ist menschlich, _____.

15. *good and evil*   Gut und _____

16. *the Prime Mover*   der Erste _____

17. *May God bless you.*   Gott _____ .

18. *this writing system*   dieses _____ system

19. *his point of view*   seine _____ perspektive

20. *the Tree of Knowledge* der Baum der _____

Übung 93

Match each item in the first column with the item in the second column that is related to it.

1. _____ Maimonides	a. die Philosophie von Aristoteles
2. _____ Muezzin	b. der Bischof von Rom
3. _____ Hagiographie	c. der Glaube an einen einzigen Gott
4. _____ die Dreifaltigkeit	d. die Thora
5. _____ der Papst	e. das Leben der Heiligen
6. _____ Islam	f. Protestantismus
7. _____ Thomas von Aquin	g. Patriarchat
8. _____ Monotheismus	h. der Heilige Geist
9. _____ Lutheranismus	i. Imam
10. _____ Abraham	j. Aufruf zum Gebet

Übung 94

Choose the word that does not belong in each group.

1. a. Roman   b. Märchen   c. Nachschlagewerk   d. Gedicht   e. Theaterstück

2. a. Kirche   b. Synagoge   c. Moschee   d. Kathedrale   e. Schaufenster

3. a. Deismus   b. Analphabetismus c. Polytheismus   d. Theismus   e. Monotheismus

4. a. Pfarrer   b. Bischof   c. Autor   d. Rabbi   e. Priester

5. a. philosophisch b. jüdisch   c. katholisch   d. hinduistisch   e. protestantisch

6. a. Geschichte   b. Inhalt   c. Personen   d. Handlung   e. Sünde

7. a. Himmel   b. Wunder   c. Hölle   d. Transzendenz   e. Purgatorium

8. a. Metaphysik   b. Logik   c. Epistemologie   d. Dramaturgie   e. Ästhetik

Übung 95

Select the verb that correctly completes each sentence.

1. *Faust* _____ ein Theaterstück von Goethe. (ist / schreibt)

2. Der Autor _____ alle sprachlichen Mittel. (benutzt / verliert)

3. Gott _____ euch, meine Kinder! (segne / stärke)

4. Es ist nötig, daß du über den Inhalt _____. (überlegst / nachdenkst)

5. Das Gemeindemitglied _____ zu Gott. (betet / sündigt)

6. Der Bußfertige _____ dem Priester seine Sünden. (beichtet / hört)

7. Welche Religionen werden in deinem Land _____?
   (verboten / ausgeübt)

8. Ich _____ eine Rede über den Platonismus. (kaufe / halte)

9. Die Mönche _____ die Messe. (lesen / sehen)

10. Ich empfehle dir, an dem Workshop _____. (einzuschreiben /
    teilnehmen)

Übung 96

Give the noun phrase (definite article + noun) that appears in this chapter and is related to each of the following verbs.

1. begreifen _____

2. vergeben _____

3. bedeuten _____

4. beten _____

5. argumentieren _____

6. beichten _____

7. sündigen _____

8. taufen _____

9. glauben _____

10. existieren _____

11. philosophieren _____

12. da sein _____

13. erzählen _____

14. dichten _____

15. denken _____

Übung 97

Unscramble the letters in each item to create a word found in this chapter.

1. sewisn _____
2. estig _____
3. unnerftv _____
4. eblagu _____
5. zenixest _____

6. malis _____
7. totg _____
8. uralbaovk _____
9. zeerkt _____
10. oennn _____

Übung 98

Respond in German as specified for each of the following situations.

1. Analyze a book you have read, identifying its genre and talking about the author and the literary elements in the work. Tell why you liked the book.

_____
_____
_____
_____
_____

2. Describe one of the philosophies mentioned in the chapter, and tell why it interests you.

_____
_____
_____
_____
_____

3. Explain one of the quotations in the **Ausdrücke, Sprichwörter und Zitate** section.

_____
_____
_____
_____
_____

4. Discuss your religion, how you practice it, and its significance in your life. If you do not practice a religion, explain why you choose not to.

_____

_____

_____

_____

_____

Übung 99

Translate the following sentences into German.

1. *The members of the reading club like to read historical novels and short stories.*

_____

_____

2. *We participated in a poetry workshop and attended lectures by famous poets.*

_____

_____

3. *This author's language is ambiguous and incomprehensible.*

_____

_____

4. *He has a pragmatic and cynical point of view.*

_____

5. *Many human beings think about the mystery of life and try to understand the purpose of life.*

_____

_____

6. *I hope they'll get the subtleties of the speech.*

_____

7. *The great majority of Germans are Christian, but Germany doesn't have an official religion.*

_____

_____

8. *The Cologne Cathedral, a Gothic church, is one of the ten largest churches in the world.*

_____

_____

9. *The rabbi and his congregation are praying in the synagogue.*

_____

_____

10. *Lutheranism and Methodism are denominations of Protestantism.*

_____

_____

15

Wie wir die Welt verstehen: Natur und Wissenschaft

How we understand the world: nature and science

In this chapter, you will learn the German terms for the sciences and mathematics, the innovators and the scientists. You will also be introduced to the natural world through the names of animals and plants. The vocabulary you learn will enable you to talk about the greatest discoveries and inventions of humankind.

English and German share much scientific vocabulary. These cognates are international words borrowed either from Greek and Latin or from French.

The gender of most of the names of the sciences is feminine, including all those that end in -ie or -ik.

Physical sciences	**Naturwissenschaften**
We should study astronomy.	Wir sollten Astronomie studieren.
chemistry	Chemie
geography	Geographie / Geografie
geology	Geologie
meteorology	Meteorologie
physics	Physik
I'm majoring in biology.	Ich studiere Biologie im Hauptfach.
anatomy	Anatomie
biochemistry	Biochemie
botany	Botanik
medicine	Medizin [F.]
paleontology	Paläontologie
physiology	Physiologie
psychology	Psychologie
zoology	Zoologie

The verb **interessieren** *to interest* takes an accusative object—the person who is interested. The thing in which the person is interested is the subject of the sentence and is therefore nominative: **Ihn interessiert die Biotechnologie.** *Biotechnology interests him.*

Engineering and technical sciences	**Ingenieurswesen und technische Wissenschaften**
He's interested in <u>biotechnology</u>.	Ihn interessiert <u>die Biotechnologie</u>.
aeronautics	die Luftfahrt
astronautics	die Raumfahrt
biological engineering	die Biotechnik
chemical engineering	die Chemietechnik
chronometry	die Zeitmessung
cognitive science	die Erkenntnistheorie
computer science	die Informatik
ecology	die Ökologie
electrical engineering	das Elektroingenieurswesen
mechanical engineering	der Maschinenbau
microscopy	die Mikroskopie
radiology	die Radiologie
robotics	die Robotertechnik
systems	die Systemwissenschaft

Interest can also be expressed by the verbal idiom **interessieren sich für etwas** *to be interested in something.*

He's interested in <u>Earth sciences</u>.	Er interessiert sich für <u>Geowissenschaften</u>.
environmental sciences	Umweltwissenschaften

Scientific research	**Wissenschaftliche Forschung**
analysis	die Analyse
classification	die Klassifizierung
conclusion	die Schlußfolgerung/Schlussfolgerung
control	die Kontrolle
data	die Daten
discovery	die Entdeckung
empirical-analytical method	die empirisch-analytische Methode
experiment	das Experiment

formula	die Formel
hypothesis	die Hypothese
laboratory	das Labor(atorium)
observation	die Beobachtung
proof	der Beweis
quantification	die Quantifizierung
result	das Resultat
scientific method	die wissenschaftliche Methode
test	der Test
theory	die Theorie
to analyze	analysieren
to classify	klassifizieren
to conclude	schlußfolgern / schlussfolgern
to control	kontrollieren
to discover	entdecken
to experience	experimentieren
to experiment, to test	experimentieren
to formulate	formulieren
to hypothesize	annehmen
to observe	beobachten
to prove	beweisen
to quantify	quantifizieren
to test, to perform a test	testen, einen Test durchführen

Mathematics / Mathematiken

accounting	die Buchführung
addition	die Addition
algebra	die Algebra
angle	der Winkel
area	die Fläche
arithmetic	die Arithmetik
calculus	die Analysis
digit	die Ziffer
dimension	die Dimension
division	die Division
econometrics	die Ökonometrie
equation	die Gleichung
Euclidean geometry	die Euklidische Geometrie
even number	die gerade Zahl

form, shape	die Form
fraction	der Bruch
function	die Funktion
geometry	die Geometrie
hypotenuse	die Hypotenuse
infinity	die Unendlichkeit
logic	die Logik
minus sign (−)	das Minuszeichen
multiplication	die Multiplikation
multiplication table	die Multiplikationstabelle
negative number	die negative Zahl
number	die Nummer, die Zahl
odd number	die ungerade Zahl
operation	die Operation
percentage	das Prozent
plus sign (+)	das Pluszeichen
probability	die Wahrscheinlichkeit
problem	das Problem
proof	der Beweis
ratio	das Verhältnis
shape	die Form
solution	die Lösung
statistics	die Statistik
subtraction	die Subtraktion
symbol	das Symbol
theorem	das Theorem
trigonometry	die Trigonometrie
zero	die Null
to add	addieren
to calculate, to work out	ausrechnen, errechnen
to count	zählen
to divide (by)	dividieren (durch), teilen (durch)
to measure	messen
to multiply (by)	multiplizieren (mit)
to reason	erörtern
to solve	lösen
to subtract	subtrahieren, abziehen

Two plus two equals four.

Eight minus five equals three.

Ten multiplied by ten equals one hundred.

Ten times ten equals one hundred.

Six divided by two equals three.

Zwei plus zwei gleich vier.

Acht minus fünf gleich drei.

Zehn multipliziert mit zehn ist hundert.

Zehn mal zehn gleich hundert.

Sechs geteilt durch zwei ist drei., Sechs dividiert mit zwei ist drei., Sechs durch zwei gleich drei.

Shapes

circle

helix, spiral

rectangle

sphere

spiral

square

triangle

Formen

der Kreis

die Schraublinie

das Rechteck

die Sphäre

die Spirale

das Quadrat

das Dreieck

Physics, chemistry, and biology

acid

atom

base

catalyst

cell

chemical equation

compound

condensation

element

energy

gas

germ

law of conservation of energy

law of conservation of matter

law of gravity

liquid

mass

matter

microorganism

molecule

nucleus

organism

Physik, Chemie und Biologie

die Säure

das Atom

die Base

der Katalysator

die Zelle

die Reaktionsgleichung

der Stoff

die Kondensierung

das Element

die Energie

das Gas

der Erreger

das Energieerhaltungsgesetz

das Gesetz von der Erhaltung der Materie

das Schwerkraftgesetz

die Flüssigkeit

die Masse

die Materie

der Mikroorganismus

das Molekül

der Kern

der Organismus

periodic table of the elements	das Periodensystem
solid	der Feststoff
symbol	das Symbol
water	das Wasser
H_2O (two atoms of hydrogen + one atom of oxygen)	H_2O (zwei Atome Wasserstoff + ein Atom Sauerstoff)

Inventions and discoveries

Erfindungen und Entdeckungen

abacus	der Abakus
analgesics	das Analgetikum
anesthesia	die Anästhesie
aspirin	das Aspirin
atomic bomb	die Atombombe
battery	die Batterie
calendar	der Kalender
cast iron	das Gußeisen / Gusseisen
clock	die Uhr
compass	der Kompaß / Kompass
computer	der Computer, der Rechner
dynamite	das Dynamit
electric motor	der elektrische Motor
electricity	die Elektrizität
eyeglasses	die Brille
fiber optics	die Glasfaser
genetics	die Genetik
germ theory	die Keimtheorie
germs	Erreger [der Erreger], Keime [der Keim], Bakterien [die Bakterie]
internal combustion engine	der Explosionsmotor
lightbulb	die Glühbirne
lightning rod	der Blitzableiter
microscope	das Mikroskop
natural gas (fuel)	das Erdgas
nuclear fission (splitting of the atom)	die Kernspaltung
paper	das Papier
pasteurization	die Pasteurisierung
penicillin	das Penizillin
phonograph	der Phonograph
printing press	die Druckerpresse
pulley	der Flaschenzug

radiography	die Radiographie/Radiografie
radium (element)	das Radium
sewing machine	die Nähmaschine
steam engine	die Dampfmaschine
steamboat	das Dampfschiff
stethoscope	das Stetoskop
telegraph	der Telegraf
telephone	das Telefon
telescope	das Teleskop
theory of electromagnetism	die Theorie des Elektromagnetismus
theory of relativity	die Relativitätstheorie
thermometer	das Thermometer
toilet	die Toilette
vaccines (against smallpox, polio, etc.)	Impfstoffe (gegen Pocken, Kinderlähmung usw.) [der Impfstoff]
wheel	das Rad
writing (alphabet)	die Schrift (das Alphabet)
zero	die Null

The feminine form of nouns of profession is created by adding the suffix **-in** to the masculine form; examples are **der Chemiker** > **die Chemikerin** and **der Erfinder** > **die Erfinderin**). If the masculine form ends in unstressed -e, the -e is omitted before -**in** is added; an example is **der Mikrobiologe** > **die Mikrobiologin**.

Innovators and scientists / Erfinder und Wissenschaftler

archaeologist	der Archäologe
biochemist	der Biochemiker
biologist	der Biologe
botanist	der Botaniker
chemical engineer	der Chemotechniker
chemist	der Chemiker
computer scientist	der Informatiker
discoverer	der Entdecker
geneticist	der Genetiker
inventor	der Erfinder
mathemetician	der Mathematiker
microbiologist	der Mikrobiologe
naturalist	der Naturforscher
nuclear physicist	der Kernphysiker

paleontologist	der Paläontologe
pathologist	der Pathologe
philosopher	der Philosoph
physicist	der Physiker
researcher	der Forscher
thinker	der Denker

A few German nouns vary in meaning, depending on whether they are used with a masculine or feminine article. For example, **der See** means *lake*, while **die See** means *sea*.

Geography and topography — Geografie und Topografie

altitude	die Höhe
archipelago	der Archipel
area	das Gebiet
cape	das Kap
climate	das Klima
desert	die Wüste
elevation	die Erhebung
forest	der Wald
grass	das Gras
gulf	der Golf
hill	der Hügel
island	die Insel
jungle	der Dschungel
lake	der See
land, ground	das Land
latitude	der Breitengrad
longitude	der Längengrad
mesa	der Tafelberg
mountain	der Berg
mountain range	die Bergkette
nature	die Natur
ocean	der Ozean
peak	der Gipfel
peninsula	die Halbinsel
plateau	die Hochebene
rainforest	der Regenwald
river	der Fluß / Fluss

sea	das Meer, die See
terrain	das Gelände
valley	das Tal
waterfall	der Wasserfall

The solar system

Das Sonnensystem

asteroid	der Asteroid
center of gravity	das Schwerkraftzentrum
comet	der Komet
Earth	die Erde
eclipse	die Sonnenfinsternis
galaxy	die Galaxie
meteorite	der Meteorit
Milky Way	die Milchstraße
moon	der Mond
orbit	die Umlaufbahn
planet	der Planet
planets (*from closest to the Sun*)	Planeten
Mercury	Merkur
Venus	Venus
Earth	die Erde
Mars	Mars
Jupiter	Jupiter
Saturn	Saturn
Uranus	Uranus
Neptune	Neptun
satellite	der Satellit
star	der Stern
sun	die Sonne
universe	das Universum

The Earth revolves around the sun.	Die Erde dreht sich um die Sonne.
The Earth rotates on its axis.	Die Erde dreht sich um ihre Achse.
Pluto is a dwarf planet.	Pluto ist ein Zwergplanet.

Social sciences

Sozialwissenschaften

We hope they studied <u>economics</u>.	Wir hoffen, sie haben <u>Ökonomie</u> studiert.
anthropology	Anthropologie
history	Geschichte [F.]
linguistics	Linguistik

>>>

political science	Politikwissenschaft [F.]
sociology	Soziologie

Trees, plants, and flowers

Bäume, Pflanzen und Blumen

acorn	die Eichel
almond tree	der Mandelbaum
apple tree	der Apfelbaum
azalea	die Azalee
bark	die Rinde
birch tree	die Birke
bougainvillea	die Bougainvillea
branch	der Zweig
bud	die Knospe
bulb	die Blumenzwiebel
bush	der Busch
carnation	die Nelke
cedar tree	der Wacholder, die Zeder
cherry tree	der Kirschbaum
chestnut tree	die Kastanie
cypress tree	die Zypresse
daffodil	die Narzisse
dahlia	die Dahlie
daisy	das Gänseblümchen
dandelion	der Löwenzahn
date palm tree	die Dattelpalme
elm tree	die Ulme
eucalyptus	der Eukalyptus
fern	der Farn
fig tree	der Feigenbaum
garden	der Garten
geranium	die Geranie
gladiolus	die Gladiole
grass	das Gras
hyacinth	die Hyazinthe
hydrangea	die Hortensie
iris	die Schwertlilie
jasmine	der Jasmin
leaf	das Blatt

lemon tree	der Zitronenbaum
lilac	der Flieder
lily	die Lilie
lily of the valley	das Maiglöckchen
magnolia	die Magnolie
maple tree	der Ahornbaum
mushroom	der Pilz
oak tree	die Eiche
olive tree	der Olivenbaum
orchid	die Orchidee
palm tree	die Palme
peach tree	der Pfirsichbaum
pear tree	der Birnenbaum
petal	das Kronblatt
pine cone	der Tannenzapfen
pine tree	die Kiefer
poplar	die Pappel
root	die Wurzel
rose	die Rose
sequoia	der Mammutbaum
stem	der Stamm, der Stiel
sunflower	die Sonnenblume
thorn	der Dorn
treetop	die Baumkrone
trunk	der Baumstamm
tulip	die Tulpe
vegetable garden	der Gemüsegarten
vegetation	die Vegetation
violet	das Veilchen
weeds	das Unkraut
weeping willow	die Trauerweide
withered	verwelkt

Animals

Domestic and farm animals

Tiere

Haus- und Nutztiere

bull	der Stier
cat	die Katze
chicken	das Huhn
cow	die Kuh

dog	der Hund
donkey	der Esel
duck	die Ente
goat	die Ziege
goose	die Gans
hare	der Hase
hen	die Henne
horse	das Pferd
lamb	das Lamm
pig	das Schwein
rabbit	das Kaninchen
rooster	der Hahn
sheep	das Schaf
turkey	der Truthahn

Insects

Insekten

ant	die Ameise
bee	die Biene
beetle	der Käfer
bumblebee	die Hummel
butterfly	der Schmetterling
cockroach	die Kakerlake
cricket	die Grille
dragonfly	die Libelle
firefly	das Glühwürmchen
fly	die Fliege
grasshopper	der Grashüpfer
lice	Läuse [die Laus *louse*]
mosquito	die Mücke
spider	die Spinne
tick	der Holzbock

Wild animals

Wilde Tiere

alpaca	das Alpaka
anteater	der Ameisenbär
bear	der Bär
bison	der Bison
buffalo	der Büffel
camel	das Kamel

cheetah	der Gepard
chimpanzee	der Schimpanse
cougar	der Puma
coyote	der Koyote / Kojote
deer	der Hirsch, das Reh
elephant	der Elefant
fox	der Fuchs
gazelle	die Gazelle
giraffe	die Giraffe
gorilla	der Gorilla
grizzly bear	der Grizzlybär
hippopotamus	das Flußpferd / Flusspferd
hyena	die Hyäne
impala	die Schwarzfersenantilope
jaguar	der Jaguar
kangaroo	das Känguru
koala	der Koala
leopard	der Leopard
lion	der Löwe
llama	das Lama
lynx	der Luchs
monkey	der Affe
mountain lion, cougar	der Berglöwe
orangutan	der Orang-Utan
panda	der Panda
panther	der Panther
polar bear	der Eisbär
raccoon	der Waschbär
rhinoceros	das Rhinozeros
seal	der Seehund
skunk	das Stinktier
tiger	der Tiger
vicuna	das Vikunja
walrus	das Walroß / Walross
weasel	das Wiesel
wildcat	die Wildkatze
wolf	der Wolf
zebra	das Zebra

Birds, rodents, fish, and reptiles

Vögel, Nagetiere, Fische und Reptilien

alligator	der Alligator
barracuda	der Barrakuda
bat	die Fledermaus
beaver	der Bieber
blackbird	die Amsel
blue jay	der Blauhäher
boa constrictor	die Boa
cardinal	der rote Kardinal
chipmunk	das Streifenhörnchen
cobra	die Kobra
condor	der Kondor
crocodile	das Krokodil
crow	die Krähe
dolphin	der Delfin
dove, pigeon	die Taube
eagle	der Adler
falcon	der Falke
flamingo	der Flamingo
frog	der Frosch
goldfinch	der Stieglitz
guinea pig	das Meerschweinchen
hamster	der Hamster
hawk	der Falke
hedgehog	der Igel
hummingbird	der Kolibri
killer whale	der Orca, der Killerwal
lizard	die Eidechse
mouse	die Maus
orca	der Orca, der Killerwal
ostrich	der Strauß
owl	die Eule
parrot	der Papagei
peacock	der Pfau
pelican	der Pelikan
penguin	der Pinguin
porcupine	das Stachelschwein
python	die Python

quail	die Wachtel
rat	die Ratte
rattlesnake	die Klapperschlange
robin	die Wanderdrossel
salmon	der Lachs
scorpion	der Skorpion
shark	der Hai
snake	die Schlange
sparrow	der Spatz
squirrel	das Eichhörnchen
swallow	die Schwalbe
swan	der Schwan
swordfish	der Schwertfisch
toad	die Kröte
toucan	der Tukan
tuna	der Thunfisch
turtle	die Schildkröte
vulture	der Geier
whale	der Wal
woodpecker	der Specht

Paleontology — Paläontologie

carnivore	der Fleischfresser
carnivorous	fleischfressend
dinosaur	der Dinosaurier
extinct	ausgerottet
fossil	das Fossil
fossil remains	fossile Überreste
herbivore	der Pflanzenfresser
herbivorous	pflanzenfressend
omnivore	der Allesfresser
omnivorous	allesfressend
paleontologist	der Paläontologe / die Paläontologin
skeleton	das Skelett
the Stone Age	die Steinzeit
trace, remains	die Überreste
track	die Spur, die Fährte
Tyrannosaurus Rex	der Tyrannosaurus Rex

Klingen Sie authentisch!

We try to understand the world around us.	Wir versuchen, die Welt um uns herum zu verstehen.
We human beings try to discover shapes and patterns in nature.	Wir Menschen versuchen, in der Natur Formen und Muster zu entdecken.
In an ecosystem, interdependent organisms share the same habitat.	In einem Ökosystem teilen voneinander abhängige Organismen denselben Lebensraum.
The Greeks systematized empirical knowledge.	Die Griechen systematisierten empirische Erkenntnisse.
The English naturalist Charles Darwin developed the theory of evolution by natural selection.	Der englische Naturalist Charles Darwin entwickelte die Theorie der Evolution durch natürliche Auslese.
The blue whale is an endangered species.	Der Blauwal ist eine gefährdete Art.

Ausdrücke, Sprichwörter und Zitate

fresh as a daisy	gesund wie ein Fisch im Wasser
strong as an ox	stark wie ein Ochse
to carry coals to Newcastle (literally, *to carry owls to Athens*)	Eulen nach Athen tragen
to enter the lion's den	in die Höhle des Löwen gehen
to expect the impossible	das Unerwartete erwarten
to fight like cats and dogs	sich spinnefeind sein
to have eyes like a hawk	Adleraugen haben
An old fox understands the trap.	Alte Füchse gehen schwer in die Falle.
The apple does not fall far from the tree.	Der Apfel fällt nicht weit vom Stamm.
You can't milk a bull.	Aus einem Stein ist schwer Öl pressen.
Blood is thicker than water.	Blut ist dicker als Wasser.

„Fügt dem Land, dem Meer und den Bäumen keinen Schaden zu."
NEUES TESTAMENT

„Die Mathematik befriedigt den Geist durch ihre außerordentliche Gewißheit."
JOHANNES KEPLER

„Wissenschaft ist, was wir wissen, und Philosophie, was wir nicht wissen."
BERTRAND RUSSELL

„Der Fortgang der wissenschaftlichen Entwicklung ist im Endeffekt eine ständige Flucht vor dem Staunen."
ALBERT EINSTEIN

„Die Zeichensprache einer Mathematik und die Grammatik einer Wortsprache sind letzten Endes vom gleichen Bau. Die Logik ist immer eine Art Mathematik und umgekehrt."

OSWALD SPENGLER

„Ich stimme mit der Mathematik nicht überein. Ich meine, daß die Summe von Nullen eine gefährliche Zahl ist."

STANISŁAW LEM

„Die Naturwissenschaften braucht der Mensch zum Erkennen, den Glauben zum Handeln."

MAX PLANCK

„Die Computerisierung des Alltags bringt am Ende nicht Kreativität, sondern die große Gleichförmigkeit."

JOSEPH WEIZENBAUM

Übung 100

Complete each German phrase or sentence so that it expresses the meaning of the English phrase or sentence.

1. *the steamboat*   das _____schiff

2. *scientific research*   _____ Forschung

3. *an odd number*   eine _____ Zahl

4. *the Milky Way*   die _____straße

5. *the guinea pigs*   die _____schweinchen

6. *the conservation of matter*   die Erhaltung der _____

7. *one atom of oxygen*   ein Atom _____

8. *multiplication table*   die _____tabelle

9. *in the lion's den*   In der _____ des Löwen

10. *fossil remains*   fossile _____

11. *empirical knowledge*   empirische _____

12. *a rattlesnake*   eine _____schlange

13. *nuclear fission*   Kern_____

14. *the Stone Age*   die Stein_____

15. *a fig tree*   ein _____baum

16. *The Earth revolves around the Sun.*   Die Erde _____ sich um die Sonne.

17. *the center of gravity*   das _____zentrum

18. *environmental sciences*   die _____wissenschaften

19. *He's strong as an ox.*   Er ist stark wie ein _____.

20. *an endangered species*   eine _____ Art

Übung 101

Match each item in the first column with the item in the second column that is related to it.

1. _____ Pasteurisierung   a. Fossilien

2. _____ dreiundzwanzig   b. Kernspaltung

3. _____ Paläontologie   c. Baum

4. _____ Wasserstoff und Sauerstoff   d. Pflanzen

5. _____ Atom   e. die Farm

6. _____ Botanik   f. ungerade Zahl

7. _____ Merkur   g. Erreger

8. _____ Hypotenuse   h. Wasser

9. _____ Stamm und Zweige   i. die Sonne

10. _____ Hennen   j. der Winkel

Übung 102

Choose the word that does not belong in each group.

1. a. Zebra   b. Affe   c. Leopard   d. Pilz
   e. Giraffe   f. Bär

2. a. Eule   b. Hyazinthe   c. Falke   d. Adler
   e. Krähe   f. Flamingo

3. a. Test   b. Division   c. Winkel   d. Verhältnis
   e. Prozent   f. Kompass

4. a. Nelke   b. Tulpe   c. Amsel   d. Gänseblümchen
   e. Narzisse   f. Lilie

5. a. Wüste   b. Waschbär   c. Kap   d. Hügel
   e. Bergkette   f. Hochebene

6. a. Flaschenzug   b. Schwerkraft   c. Komet   d. Mond
   e. Sonnenfinsternis   f. Stern

7. a. Hummel   b. Biene   c. Spinne   d. Käfer
    e. Eidechse   f. Schmetterling

8. a. Pappel   b. Eiche   c. Ulme   d. Schwan
    e. Wacholder   f. Birke

9. a. Schaf   b. Kuh   c. Wal   d. Ziege
    e. Lamm   f. Henne

10. a. Sauerstoff   b. Eisen   c. Quecksilber   d. Wasserstoff
    e. Helix   f. Radium

Übung 103

Give the noun phrase (definite article + noun) that appears in this chapter and is related to each of the following verbs.

1. analysieren   _____

2. klassifizieren   _____

3. kontrollieren   _____

4. entdecken   _____

5. experimentieren   _____

6. quantifizieren   _____

7. addieren   _____

8. beweisen   _____

9. lösen   _____

10. subtrahieren   _____

11. testen   _____

12. beobachten   _____

13. schlußfolgern   _____

14. dividieren   _____

15. multiplizieren   _____

Übung 104

Unscramble the letters in each item to create a word found in this chapter.

1. eibreb   _____
2. arehnpt   _____
3. heeci   _____
4. zilp   _____
5. tolup   _____

6. dawl   _____
7. otteleit   _____
8. luln   _____
9. imtandy   _____
10. reffiz   _____

Übung 105

1. **Sie sind Wissenschaftler/Wissenschaftlerin.** Choose a field—biology, botany, chemistry, geography, paleontology, physics, or zoology—and describe in German what you do; where you work; what you research, analyze, quantify, or classify; what methods you use; and what experiments you carry out. State three questions you hope to answer through your research.

_____
_____
_____
_____
_____
_____
_____

2. **Erfindungen und Entdeckungen.** This chapter lists many of the greatest inventions and discoveries, but the list is hardly exhaustive. What would you add to this list? In German, list ten or more inventions and/or discoveries you consider important. Identify as many innovators as you can.

_____
_____
_____
_____
_____
_____
_____

Übung 106

Translate the following sentences into German.

1. *The researchers use the scientific method to test their hypotheses.*

   _____

   _____

2. *The biochemist does the experiment, observing and analyzing the results in order to arrive at a conclusion.*

   _____

   _____

3. *The children already know how to add and subtract and are now learning to multiply and divide.*

   _____

   _____

4. *The team of microbiologists and pathologists is researching microorganisms.*

   _____

   _____

5. *Benjamin Franklin used a kite* (einen Drachen) *and a key in the experiment that led him to invent the lightning rod.*

   _____

   _____

6. *On the topographical map you* (du) *see the terrain: oceans, mountain ranges, plateaus, and valleys.*

   _____

   _____

7. *The planets closest to the sun are Mercury, Venus, and Earth.*

   _____

   _____

8. *The paleontologists found fossils and dinosaur tracks.*

   _____

   _____

9. *The Indian elephant is an endangered species.*

   _____

Natur und Wissenschaft *Nature and science*   243

10. *There are many maple, oak, elm, and poplar trees all around us.*

_____

_____

11. *We brought them tulips, irises, and carnations from our garden.*

_____

_____

12. *When they were on safari* (auf Safari), *they saw lions, giraffes, chimpanzees, zebras, leopards, and rhinoceroses.*

_____

_____

13. *Do you* (ihr) *have horses, sheep, and goats on the farm?*

_____

_____

14. *Thomas Alva Edison invented the lightbulb, the phonograph, and the alkaline* (alkalische) *battery.*

_____

_____

Cardinal numbers

0	null	31	einunddreißig
1	eins	32	zweiunddreißig
2	zwei	33	dreiunddreißig
3	drei	34	vierunddreißig
4	vier	35	fünfunddreißig
5	fünf	36	sechsunddreißig
6	sechs	37	siebenunddreißig
7	sieben	38	achtunddreißig
8	acht	39	neununddreißig
9	neun	40	vierzig
10	zehn	41	einundvierzig
11	elf	42	zweiundvierzig
12	zwölf	43	dreiundvierzig
13	dreizehn	50	fünfzig
14	vierzehn	60	sechzig
15	fünfzehn	70	siebzig
16	sechzehn	80	achtzig
17	siebzehn	90	neunzig
18	achtzehn	100	hundert
19	neunzehn	101	hunderteins
20	zwanzig	102	hundertzwei
21	einundzwanzig	103	hundertdrei
22	zweiundzwanzig	104	hundertvier
23	dreiundzwanzig	105	hundertfünf
24	vierundzwanzig	106	hundertsechs
25	fünfundzwanzig	107	hundertsieben
26	sechsundzwanzig	108	hundertacht
27	siebenundzwanzig	109	hundertneun
28	achtundzwanzig	110	hundertzehn
29	neunundzwanzig	111	hundertelf
30	dreißig	112	hundertzwölf

113	hundertdreizehn
120	hundertzwanzig
121	hunderteinundzwanzig
122	hundertzweiundzwanzig
123	hundertdreiundzwanzig
200	zweihundert
245	zweihundertfünfundvierzig
678	sechshundertachtundsiebzig
999	neunhundertneunundneunzig
1,000	tausend
1,001	tausendeins
1,002	tausendzwei
1,003	tausenddrei
1,004	tausendvier
1,055	tausendfünfundfünfzig
1,100	tausendeinhundert, (*year*) elfhundert
1,286	tausendzweihundertsechsundachtzig; (*year*) zwölfhundertsechsundachtzig
1,853	tausendachthundertdreiundfünfzig; (*year*) achtzehnhundertdreiundfünfzig
2,000	zweitausend
2,345	zweitausenddreihundertfünfundvierzig
3,000	dreitausend
4,000	viertausend
5,000	fünftausend
10,000	zehntausend
40,000	vierzigtausend
50,972	fünfzigtausendneunhundertzweiundsiebzig
100,000	hunderttausend
392,428	dreihundertzweiundneunzigtausendvierhundertachtundzwanzig
1,000,000	Million

Ordinal numbers

first	erste	*ninth*	neunte	*twenty-second*	zweiundzwanzigste
second	zweite	*tenth*	zehnte	*twenty-third*	dreiundzwanzigste
third	dritte	*eleventh*	elfte	*twenty-sixth*	sechsundzwanzigste
fourth	vierte	*twelfth*	zwölfte	*one hundredth*	hundertste
fifth	fünfte	*thirteenth*	dreizehnte	*six hundred fiftieth*	sechshundertfünfzigste
sixth	sechste	*fourteenth*	vierzehnte	*thousandth*	tausendste
seventh	siebte	*twentieth*	zwanzigste	*millionth*	millionste
eighth	achte	*twenty-first*	einunzwanzigste		

Answer key

Übung 1

1. ein Bekleidungsgeschäft   2. eine Schreibwarenhandlung   3. ein Zoofachhandel   4. ein Obst- und Gemüsehandel   5. ein Lederfachhandel   6. eine Drogerie   7. eine Parfümerie   8. ein Optiker
9. ein Tabakladen   10. eine Fleischerei   11. ein Bürobedarf   12. ein Blumenladen   13. ein Reformhaus
14. eine Tankstelle   15. ein Buchladen   16. eine Bäckerei   17. eine Konditorei   18. ein Weingeschäft
19. ein Baumarkt   20. ein Sportgeschäft

Übung 2

1. f   2. i   3. b   4. g   5. j   6. c   7. e   8. a   9. d   10. h

Übung 3

Answers will vary.

Übung 4

Answers will vary.

Übung 5

1. a   2. c   3. a   4. b   5. c   6. a   7. b   8. a

Übung 6

1. c   2. d   3. b   4. a   5. a   6. d   7. a   8. c

Übung 7

1. Wo ist das Computergeschäft?   2. Das Computergeschäft ist ganz in der Nähe.   3. Gibt es ein Sportgeschäft hier in der Nähe?   4. Ich möchte einen Rucksack kaufen.   5. Was ist in der Brieftasche?   6. Dort ist Geld und ein Führerschein.   7. Es sind Akten in dem Aktenkoffer.   8. Gibt es ein Museum in der Nachbarschaft?
9. In dieser Nachbarschaft gibt es eine Bibliothek, ein Kulturzentrum und ein Fremdenverkehrsamt.
10. Ich kenne die Altstadt und das Einkaufsviertel.

Übung 8

Answers will vary.

Übung 9

1. c   2. a   3. b   4. b   5. d   6. a   7. c   8. d   9. b   10. c

Übung 10

Answers will vary.

Übung 11

1. Mantel   2. Schmuck   3. Bluse   4. Stiefel   5. Schal   6. Gürtel   7. Smoking   8. Schuhe

Übung 12

Answers will vary.

Übung 13

1. Ich muß ein paar Schuhe kaufen.   2. Haben Sie Seidenkrawatten?   3. Ich suche einen schwarzen Wollanzug.
4. Ich bevorzuge einen Rock mit Schrägschnitt.   5. Ich möchte einen marineblauen Mantel mit Gürtel kaufen.
6. Diese gestreifte Krawatte paßt nicht zu dem Hemd.   7. Mir gefällt das Diamantenhalsband.   8. Diese Hose
paßt ihm gut.   9. Mir gefallen diese Ohrringe.   10. Sie trägt einen Rollkragenpullover.   11. Wir möchten
einen Schaufensterbummel machen.   12. Die Designerkleidung ist im Angebot.

Übung 14

Obst   Apfel, Orange, Aprikose, Pflaume, Zitrone
Gemüse   Sauerkraut, Karotte, Rübe, Broccoli, Kartoffel
Fleisch   Lamm, Rind, Wildschwein, Wild, Kaninchen
Fisch   Karpfen, Dorsch, Seelachs, Barsch, Forelle
Geflügel   Truthahn, Hähnchen, Strauß, Wachtel, Ente
Gewürze   Knoblauch, Thymian, Kerbel, Zimt, Nelken
Getränke   Bier, Wasser, Rosé, Magenbitter, Kaffee

Übung 15

1. pochieren   2. schälen   3. schneiden   4. braten   5. schlagen

Übung 16

Answers will vary.

Übung 17

Answers will vary.

Übung 18

1. d   2. b   3. c   4. d   5. a   6. d   7. a   8. b   9. d   10. a

Übung 19

1. Was essen wir zum Frühstück?   2. Magst du Jakobsmuscheln?   3. Was werden wir heute Abend essen,
Fisch oder Geflügel?   4. Dort ist ein französisches Restaurant um die Ecke.   5. Dieses Fleisch ist vergammelt.
6. Die Suppe ist zu salzig.   7. Kannst du die Kartoffeln schälen und die Eier braten?   8. Sie ißt nur vegane
Küche.   9. Laß uns die Spezialität des Hauses probieren!   10. Die Leute essen mehr und mehr Fertiggerichte.
11. Vietnamesische Küche mag ich wirklich gerne.   12. Möchtest du ein Glas Weißwein?

Übung 20

1. j   2. c   3. i   4. h   5. a   6. f   7. e   8. d   9. g   10. b

Übung 21

1. b   2. d   3. a   4. c   5. b   6. d   7. a   8. c   9. d   10. b

Übung 22

1. waschen   2. machen   3. Rasen   4. Altpapier   5. Blumen   6. Staub   7. Müll   8. Küche   9. Wohnung
10. Verstopfung

Übung 23

Answers will vary.

Übung 24

1. eine Bratpfanne   2. ein Handtuch   3. ein Gewächshaus   4. einen Hammer   5. eine Waschmaschine
6. einen Pümpel   7. einen Besen   8. einen Schraubenzieher

Übung 25

1. Es ist ein Leck im Dachboden.   2. Ich brauche einen Hammer und einen Schraubenzieher.   3. Ihr Haus ist einladend und ruhig.   4. Dort ist ein Stück Seife im Arzneischränkchen.   5. Die Konserven sind im Schrank.
6. Das Licht ist ausgegangen. Ich glaube, die Glühbirne ist kaputt.   7. Dieses Haus ist aus Stein.
8. Der Flaschenöffner ist auf dem Weinregal.   9. Das Schlafzimmer ist rechts.   10. Ich muß noch eine Kommode kaufen.

Übung 26

1. Geräte   2. Steuern   3. Markt   4. Nummer   5. Geld   6. Konkurs   7. Tiefen   8. Depot

Übung 27

1. c   2. a   3. d   4. b   5. c   6. d   7. b   8. a   9. c   10. d

Übung 28

Büro   Tacker, Terminkalender, Schreibtisch, Arbeitsplatz, Kopiergerät
Rechner   Bildschirm, Datei, Tastatur, Software, Betriebssystem
Handel   Einzelhandel, Rechnung, Großhandel, Preis, Produkt
Bank   überweisen, Banknote, einzahlen, Zinsen, abheben
Personal   Aufsichtsrat, Geschäftsführer, Berater, Finanzchef, Chef

Übung 29

1. machen   2. starten   3. erhöhen   4. überweisen   5. installieren   6. schicken   7. ausstellen   8. erstellen

Übung 30

1. e   2. j   3. i   4. g   5. a   6. d   7. h   8. b   9. f   10. c

Übung 31

1. Sie müssen alle ihre Dateien sichern.   2. Wir werden unsere Werbekampagne in den sozialen Medien starten.   3. Die Investoren müssen auf die Höhen und Tiefen des Aktienmarkts achten.   4. Die Regierung wird die Steuern erhöhen.   5. Der E-Commerce ist wichtig für das Wachstum des Unternehmens.   6. Unsere Agentur wird eine Werbekampagne für dieses Produkt starten.   7. Es ist nicht viel Geld auf unserem Sparkonto.   8. Der Geschäftsführer und die Berater sind eben gegangen.   9. Das Unternehmen bleibt über die sozialen Medien mit den Kunden vernetzt.   10. Der Finanzchef wird einen Haushalt aufstellen.

Übung 32

1. Fahrplanauskunft   2. Gepäck   3. Internet   4. Fahrkarten   5. Sightseeing   6. Reise   7. Schlittschuh
8. entwerten   9. Altstadt   10. Konzert   11. Schwimmen   12. Hin- und Rück   13. shoppen   14. Tennis spielen   15. mildes und trockenes Klima   16. das Gepäck einchecken/aufgeben   17. im Juli   18. (am) Freitag
19. Hund ausführen   20. reiten

Übung 33

Answers will vary.

Übung 34

Answers will vary.

Übung 35

Answers will vary.

Übung 36

1. hebt ab 2. fahren 3. spielen 4. schwimmen 5. ausüben 6. machen 7. ist 8. an 9. fährt ab
10. ist gestrichen

Übung 37

1. die Landung 2. der Regen 3. der Flug 4. die Reise 5. der Sturm 6. die Wanderung 7. die Verspätung
8. der Blitz 9. das Spiel 10. der Schnee 11. der Start 12. der Spaziergang

Übung 38

1. Sonntag 2. Fahrkarte 3. Flug 4. Nebel 5. Ausland 6. Gepäck 7. Spaziergang 8. Himmel
9. Museum 10. Regen

Übung 39

1. Du solltest die Koffer packen. 2. Hier sind mein Boarding-Paß und mein Ausweis. 3. Das Flugzeug ist gelandet, aber es ist verspätet. 4. Wir haben eine wunderbare, aber sehr lange Reise gemacht. 5. Wenn ich in Hamburg bin, mache ich gerne Sightseeing. 6. Heute ist schlechtes Wetter. Es ist windig, und es hagelt. 7. Wir werden uns in die Schlange am Schalter stellen und eine Hin- und Rückfahrkarte kaufen. 8. Sie wollen Schach spielen. 9. Ich möchte meine Ferien in den Bergen oder auf dem Land verbringen. 10. In meiner Freizeit mag ich campen und angeln gehen.

Übung 40

1. Zahn 2. Fakultät 3. Taschen 4. Blei 5. klingen 6. Notiz 7. wasser 8. aufgaben 9. Lehr
10. knipser 11. tasche 12. Prüfung 13. auf sich aufpassen 14. umziehen 15. seide

Übung 41

1. f 2. h 3. b 4. i 5. c 6. d 7. j 8. a 9. g 10. e

Übung 42

1. schminken 2. zubinden 3. gewaschen 4. anprobieren 5. nutzen 6. bestehen 7. scheiden lassen
8. besorgt sein 9. ziehen 10. lernt

Übung 43

Answers will vary.

Übung 44

1. Fakultät 2. Schule 3. Grippe 4. Architekt 5. Spind 6. Musik 7. Autobahn 8. Zahnbürste
9. Seife 10. Haare

Übung 45

1. Sie gehen gerne spät ins Bett und wachen früh auf. 2. Sie wird ihre Haare mit diesem Shampoo waschen.
3. Die Studenten haben sich eben für Kunstwissenschaften eingeschrieben. 4. Die Schüler müssen jeden Tag zum Unterricht gehen. Sie dürfen nicht den Unterricht schwänzen. 5. Er beabsichtigt, sich mit seinen Freunden zu treffen. 6. Ich interessiere mich sehr für Literatur. Ich werde mich auf ein Stipendium bewerben, um an der philosophischen Fakultät zu studieren. 7. Er steht auf, putzt sich die Zähne, duscht, rasiert sich und zieht sich an. 8. Herr Professor Apitz ist streng und anspruchsvoll, und auch sehr nett. 9. Er hat Jura studiert und ist Rechtsanwalt geworden. 10. Wir werden uns auf der Party sehr gut amüsieren.
11. Du solltest auf dich aufpassen. Sonst wirst du krank. 12. Wann beabsichtigt ihr, in euer Traumhaus umzuziehen?

Übung 46

1. zahn 2. Hilfe 3. Erkältung 4. Mücken 5. Rücken 6. Handgelenk 7. Ernährung 8. ununterbrochen
9. Ziele 10. direkt 11. eingegipst 12. furchtbar 13. Über vergossene Milch 14. belag 15. reich und
krank

Übung 47

1. brechen 2. verstauchen 3. schneiden 4. untersuchen 5. abhören 6. messen 7. verschreiben
8. putzen 9. ziehen 10. ausspülen 11. genießen 12. aufgeben

Übung 48

Answers will vary.

Übung 49

Answers will vary.

Übung 50

1. ein Hausarzt 2. ein Augenarzt 3. ein Geburtshelfer 4. ein Kinderarzt 5. ein Kardiologe
6. ein Hautarzt 7. ein Psychologe 8. ein Zahnarzt 9. ein Internist/Hausarzt 10. ein Chirurg
11. ein Hautarzt 12. ein Zahnarzt

Übung 51

1. Gesicht 2. Allergie 3. Krankheit 4. Hand 5. Migräne 6. Leber 7. Spritze 8. Tablette 9. Virus
10. Grippe

Übung 52

1. Ich gehe zum Arzt, weil ich Rückenschmerzen habe. 2. Welche Symptome haben Sie? 3. Ich fühle mich
nicht gut. Ich habe Bauchschmerzen, und mir ist übel. 4. Der Arzt hat ihm ein Antibiotikum gegeben, weil er
eine Entzündung hat. 5. Ihr Zahnfleisch blutet. Sie sollte zum Zahnarzt gehen. 6. Wie hast du dir die Nase
gebrochen? 7. Die Sanitäter behandeln die Unfallopfer im Krankenwagen. 8. Hast du dir das Handgelenk
verletzt? 9. Ja, ich habe es mir verstaucht. 10. Der Kinderarzt hat eben das Kind geimpft. 11. Henrik geht
an Krücken, weil er sich das Bein gebrochen hat. 12. Sie sind sehr direkt und reden ununterbrochen.
13. Was kann man für eine gesunde Lebensführung machen? 14. Ich versuche, mich ausgewogen zu ernähren
und den Streß zu reduzieren.

Übung 53

1. meine Cousine 2. meine Großmutter 3. mein Schwiegersohn 4. meine Urgroßeltern 5. mein Stiefsohn
6. meine Schwägerin 7. Zwillinge 8. mein Onkel 9. meine Schwiegereltern 10. meine Tante
11. ihr Zwillingsbrüder / ihre Zwillingsschwester 12. meine Enkel

Übung 54

1. Verwandten 2. stand 3. Seelen 4. alt 5. große 6. ein Ei dem anderen 7. Verwandten 8. eingebildet,
egoistisch 9. merkwürdige 10. enge 11. Schwager 12. groß, dunkelhäutig, schön 13. Blut, Wasser
14. Halb 15. grün-braune

Übung 55

1. Junggeselle 2. Waise 3. merkwürdige 4. reiche 5. feige 6. Augen 7. Hochzeit 8. Paar 9. Gold

Übung 56

Answers will vary.

Übung 57

Answers will vary.

Übung 58

1. Cousin 2. Bruder 3. Vater 4. Mutter 5. Pate 6. Großmutter 7. Halbbruder 8. Sohn 9. Enkel
10. Tochter

Übung 59

1. c 2. g 3. m 4. a 5. j 6. e 7. o 8. h 9. b 10. l 11. i 12. d 13. p 14. f 15. k 16. n

Übung 60

1. Ich möchte dich meinen Eltern vorstellen. 2. Du wirst meinen Onkel und meine Tante auf der Party treffen. 3. Die Pateneltern lieben ihren Patensohn und ihre Patentochter sehr. 4. Richard und Erika Schmidt haben eine enge und warme Familie. 5. Ihre Tochter Franziska und ihr Schwiegersohn Moritz haben ein zwei Monate altes Baby. 6. Ihr Sohn Emil ist verlobt. 7. Ihr jüngerer Sohn Arno ist zweiundzwanzig Jahre alt. 8. Anna ist fleißig, großzügig und reizend. Ihr Zwillingsbruder ist faul, egoistisch und lästig. 9. Rita hat mit ihrem Freund Schluß gemacht, weil er Angst vor Beziehungen hat. 10. Wie sieht deine Cousine aus? 11. Sie ist dunkelhaarig, klein, dünn und sehr hübsch. 12. Mein Bruder, meine Schwester und ich haben blaue Augen.

Übung 61

1. bläser 2. Meister 3. acht Uhr 4. Eintrittskarten 5. avantgardistische 6. meister 7. Bühne
8. aufführung 9. gemälde 10. Blech 11. schönen 12. Dirigent 13. Filmstars 14. elf, abends
15. schaft 16. ausländische 17. stück 18. schlager 19. Abend 20. goldenes Zeitalter

Übung 62

1. spielen 2. dirigieren 3. singen 4. anschauen 5. beginnen 6. gewinnen 7. drehen 8. synchronisieren
9. uraufführen 10. malen 11. öffnen 12. können

Übung 63

1. Cello 2. Harfe 3. Klarinette 4. Oboe 5. Posaune 6. Violine 7. Tuba 8. Trompete 9. Viola
10. Waldhorn

Übung 64

1. der Film 2. die Aufführung 3. der Komponist 4. der Applaus 5. der Schauspieler 6. der Interpret
7. die Zeichnung 8. der Maler 9. der Dirigent 10. der Bildhauer

Übung 65

Answers will vary.

Übung 66

1. das Orchester 2. die Galerie 3. die Klarinette 4. die Akustik 5. die Komödie 6. die Tragödie
7. die Melodie 8. der Musiker 9. das Konzert 10. die Gitarre 11. das Theater 12. der Dialog
13. der Kurator 14. die Palette 15. der Fotograf

Übung 67

1. g 2. d 3. a 4. i 5. b 6. c 7. l 8. j 9. e 10. k 11. f 12. h

Übung 68

1. Kannst du Klavier spielen?   2. Das Publikum applaudierte und forderte eine Zugabe.   3. Die Schauspieler werden die Probe um halb zwei beginnen.   4. Wir werden das Theaterstück morgen abend anschauen. 5. Wann schließt die Abendkasse?   6. Gibt es Eintrittskarten für die Vorstellung um neun?   7. Die Produktion ist ein Kassenschlager; sie ist drei Jahre lang gelaufen.   8. Die Kunstkenner mögen diese abstakten Gemälde. 9. Sie drehen einen Film in unserer Stadt.   10. Das Orchester hat die Symphonie letzte Nacht uraufgeführt. Sie ist innovativ aber eingängig.   11. Ich male gerne Landschaften, Portraits und Stilleben.   12. Es gibt eine Ausstellung meiner Gemälde in Klemm's Galerie.

Übung 69

1. englischer Abstammung   2. moderator   3. schweigen ist Gold   4. zweimonatliche   5. versicherung 6. Beamte   7. Osten   8. Vollzeit   9. deutschsprachiges   10. beherrscht   11. Was ist die Hauptstadt 12. Ökonom   13. Tarif   14. Ruhestand   15. Stadt

Übung 70

1. Deutscher   2. Schweizer   3. Japaner   4. Italiener   5. Belgier   6. Polen   7. Thailänder   8. Inderin 9. Iraner   10. Schwedin   11. Spanierin   12. Monegasse   13. Amerikaner   14. Vietnamese/Vietnamesin 15. Engländer

Übung 71

1. England   2. Dänemark   3. den Vereinigten Staaten   4. Norwegen   5. Ungarn   6. Südafrika 7. Argentinien   8. Österreich   9. Frankreich   10. Südkorea

Übung 72

1. Spanisch   2. Persisch   3. Arabisch   4. Tschechisch   5. Deutsch   6. Paschtunisch   7. Thailändisch 8. Portugiesisch   9. Englisch und Französisch   10. Deutsch, Französisch, Italienisch und Rumantsch

Übung 73

1. arbeiten   2. sprechen   3. entlassen   4. gründen   5. streiken   6. gehen   7. auszahlen   8. beherrschen 9. versetzen   10. unterschreiben

Übung 74

1. f   2. c   3. l   4. b   5. h   6. a   7. k   8. g   9. e   10. i   11. j   12. d

Übung 75

Answers will vary.

Übung 76

1. Der Manager beabsichtigt, zwei Buchhalter einzustellen.   2. Die Arbeiter fordern bezahlten Urlaub und eine Berufsunfähigkeitsversicherung.   3. Wenn die Firma den Tarifvertrag nicht unterschreibt, wird die Gewerkschaft streiken.   4. Das Unternehmen entließ zweihundert Angestellte und versetzte weitere dreihundert.   5. Die Physiker und Chemiker arbeiten gemeinsam im Labor.   6. Roland ist Richter, und seine Frau ist Journalistin.   7. Sie ist Französin, mit englischer und spanischer Abstammung.   8. Daniel ist aus der Schweiz. Er spricht Deutsch, Französisch, Italienisch und Rumantsch.   9. Wie heißt diese finnische Schauspielerin?   10. Aus welchem deutschsprachigen Land kommen sie?   11. Sie wollen amerikanische Staatsbürger werden.   12. Beherrschen Sie Chinesisch?

Übung 77

1. Deutschen Einheit   2. feier/party   3. Arbeit   4. Schenken   5. Geschäfts   6. verliebten sich   7. abschied 8. Drei Könige   9. Ehe   10. Christmesse   11. Heilig   12. Benefiz   13. Namens   14. strauß   15. erheben 16. Flitter   17. Kar   18. werk   19. Pfingst   20. vermählten

Übung 78

1. c   2. h   3. f   4. a   5. i   6. b   7. d   8. j   9. e   10. g

Übung 79

1. teilnehmen   2. trinken   3. geben   4. singen   5. wirft   6. fällt   7. verliebt sich   8. wird   9. organisieren
10. erschienen

Übung 80

1. September und Oktober   2. Januar   3. März oder April   4. November   5. August   6. Oktober
7. Mai oder Juni   8. Dezember

Übung 81

1. die Liebe   2. das Geschenk, das Schenken   3. der Kuß   4. der Trinkspruch   5. die Heirat   6. die Feier
7. das Abschiedsfest   8. das Getränk   9. das Essen, das Geschäftsessen, das Arbeitsessen   10. die Verlobung
11. das Weihnachtslied   12. das Ehegelübde   13. die Erinnerung   14. die Hochzeit   15. der Brautstrauß

Übung 82

Answers will vary.

Übung 83

1. Erika ist Samstag dreiundzwanzig geworden.   2. Wir haben eine Überraschungs-Geburtstagsparty für sie
gegeben.   3. Das Geburtstagskind hat sich etwas gewünscht und die Kerzen auf dem Kuchen ausgeblasen.
4. Wir haben alle „Happy Birthday" für sie gesungen, die Gläser erhoben und auf sie angestoßen.
5. Maja und Sebastian haben sich verliebt, verlobt und geheiratet.   6. Die Braut warf den Brautstrauß.
7. Unsere deutschen Freunde wollen, daß wir den Oktober mit ihnen in München verbringen.   8. Sie planen,
Weihnachten in Berlin zu verbringen.   9. Hast du auf der Silvesterparty Spaß gehabt?   10. Die Feierlichkeiten
zum Tag der Deutschen Einheit endeten mit einer Parade und Feuerwerk.

Übung 84

1. Gewalten   2. Artikel   3. antrag   4. Bürgermeister   5. Finanz   6. Umfrage   7. Marine
8. Legislaturperiode   9. berechtigter   10. Amt   11. Kommunal   12. Mitte-Rechts   13. schimmel
14. unveräußerliche   15. Rechtsstaatlichkeit   16. kontroverse   17. Presse   18. Lebenszeit   19. Bestreben
20. Bürger

Übung 85

1. h   2. d   3. a   4. j   5. f   6. b   7. i   8. g   9. e   10. c

Übung 86

1. teilen   2. Zählen   3. besticht   4. zurücktreten   5. verteidigt   6. organisieren   7. stellen   8. berät
9. begehen   10. unterstütze

Übung 87

1. c   2. d   3. a   4. a   5. b   6. c   7. b   8. d   9. a   10. c

Übung 88

Answers will vary.

Übung 89

Answers will vary.

Übung 90

Answers will vary.

Übung 91

1. Im Kongreß gibt es den Senat und das Repräsentantenhaus.   2. Der Präsident ist für eine Legislaturperiode von vier Jahren gewählt.   3. Konrad Adenauer bekleidete das Amt des Kanzlers für vierzehn Jahre.
4. Die Verfassung garantiert die Redefreiheit, die Religionsfreiheit und die Pressefreiheit.   5. Er war General in der Armee und diente seinem Land für viele Jahre.   6. Die Repräsentanten stellten einen Mißtrauensantrag und nahmen einen Gesetzesantrag an.   7. Der Diktator nahm die Macht in einem Staatsstreich.   8. Die Bürger sind gegen die staatliche Verletzung der Privatsphäre.   9. Sie sind nicht nur gegen neue Steuern sondern auch gegen das Stopfen von Steuerschlupflöchern.   10. In der Stadtverwaltung gibt es Skandale und zügellose Korruption.   11. Die Wahl wird am Dienstag stattfinden. Bitte registrieren Sie sich vor der Wahl!
12. Die politischen Parteien haben Umfragen durchgeführt, die das Ergebnis der Wahl beeinflußt haben.

Übung 92

1. Glaube 2. Nachschlage 3. Liebes 4. Theaterstücken 5. Sinn 6. Feinheiten 7. Alphabet 8. Mittel
9. Gebet 10. Heilige 11. Mönchstum 12. monotheistischen 13. Wille 14. vergeben göttlich 15. Böse
16. Beweger 17. segne dich 18. Schrift 19. Erzähl 20. Erkenntnis

Übung 93

1. d 2. j 3. e 4. h 5. b 6. i 7. a 8. c 9. f 10. g

Übung 94

1. c 2. e 3. b 4. c 5. a 6. e 7. b 8. d

Übung 95

1. ist 2. benutzt 3. segne 4. nachdenkst 5. betet 6. beichtet 7. ausgeübt 8. halte 9. lesen
10. teilzunehmen

Übung 96

1. der Begriff 2. die Vergebung 3. die Bedeutung 4. das Gebet 5. das Argument 6. die Beichte
7. die Sünde 8. die Taufe 9. der Glaube 10. die Existenz 11. die Philosophie 12. das Dasein
13. der Erzähler 14. die Dichtung, das Gedicht, der Dichter 15. der Gedanke

Übung 97

1. Wissen 2. Geist 3. Vernunft 4. Glaube 5. Existenz 6. Islam 7. Gott 8. Vokabular 9. Ketzer
10. Nonne

Übung 98

Answers will vary.

Übung 99

1. Die Mitglieder des Lesekreises lesen gerne historische Romane und Kurzgeschichten.   2. Wir haben an einem Workshop für Poesie/Dichtung teilgenommen und Vorlesungen von bekannten Dichtern angehört.
3. Die Sprache dieses Autors ist undeutlich und unverständlich.   4. Er hat eine pragmatische und zynische Erzählperspektive.   5. Viele Menschen denken über das Geheimnis des Lebens nach und versuchen, den Sinn des Lebens zu verstehen.   6. Ich hoffe, sie werden die Feinheiten der Rede verstehen.   7. Die große Mehrheit der Deutschen sind Christen, aber Deutschland hat keine offizielle Religion.   8. Der Kölner Dom, eine gotische Kirche, ist eine der zehn größten Kirchen der Welt.   9. Der Rabbi und seine Gemeinde beten in der Synagoge.
10. Luthertum und Methodismus sind Konfessionen des Protestantismus.

Übung 100

1. Dampf 2. wissenschaftliche 3. ungerade 4. Milch 5. Meer 6. Materie 7. Sauerstoff
8. Multiplikations 9. Höhle 10. Überreste 11. Erkenntnisse 12. Klapper 13. spaltung 14. zeit
15. Feigen 16. dreht 17. Schwerkraft 18. Umwelt 19. Ochse 20. gefährdete

Übung 101

1. g 2. f 3. a 4. h 5. b 6. d 7. i 8. j 9. c 10. e

Übung 102

1. d 2. b 3. f 4. c 5. b 6. a 7. e 8. d 9. c 10. e

Übung 103

1. die Analyse 2. die Klassifizierung 3. die Kontrolle 4. die Entdeckung 5. das Experiment
6. die Quantifizierung 7. die Addition 8. der Beweis 9. die Lösung 10. die Subtraktion 11. der Test
12. die Beobachtung 13. die Schlußfolgerung 14. die Division 15. die Multiplikation

Übung 104

1. Bieber 2. Panther 3. Eiche 4. Pilz 5. Pluto 6. Wald 7. Toilette 8. Null 9. Dynamit 10. Ziffer

Übung 105

Answers will vary.

Übung 106

1. Die Forscher benutzen die wissenschaftliche Methode, um ihre Hypothesen zu testen/prüfen.
2. Der Biochemiker führt das Experiment durch, indem er die Ergebnisse beobachtet und analysiert, um zu einer Schlußfolgerung zu kommen. 3. Die Kinder wissen bereits, wie man addiert und subtrahiert und lernen jetzt zu multiplizieren und dividieren. 4. Das Team von Mikrobiologen und Pathologen erforscht Mikroorganismen. 5. Benjamin Franklin benutzte einen Drachen und einen Schlüssel in dem Experiment, das ihn zum Blitzableiter geführt hat. 6. Auf der topographischen Karte siehst du das Gelände—Ozeane, Bergketten, Hochebenen und Täler. 7. Die Planeten, die der Sonne am nächsten sind, sind Merkur, Venus und die Erde. 8. Die Paläontologen fanden Fossilien und Spuren von Dinosauriern. 9. Der Indische Elefant ist eine gefährdete Art. 10. Um uns herum sind viele Ahornbäume, Eichen, Ulmen und Pappeln.
11. Wir brachten ihnen Tulpen, Iriden und Nelken aus unserem Garten. 12. Als sie auf Safari waren, sahen sie Löwen, Giraffen, Schimpansen, Zebras, Leoparden und Rhinozerosse. 13. Habt ihr Pferde, Schafe und Ziegen auf der Farm? 14. Thomas Alva Edison erfand die Glühbirne, den Phonographen und die alkalische Batterie.

About the authors

David M. Stillman, PhD, is a well-known writer of foreign language textbooks, reference books, and multimedia courses. He is president of Mediatheque Publishers Services, a leader in the development of foreign language instructional materials. He holds a PhD in Spanish linguistics from the University of Illinois, and has taught and coordinated foreign language programs at Boston University, Harvard University, and Cornell University. He is on the faculty of The College of New Jersey, where he teaches French, Spanish, Italian, and linguistics, and coordinates an innovative program of student-led conversation practice. He is a frequent presenter at national and regional conventions of language educators, has consulted on states' K–12 academic standards for world languages, and has been appointed to national committees devoted to the improvement of teacher training.

Daniele Godor, MA, has taught German and Norwegian in colleges and private institutions in Berlin, Germany. He holds one MA in Scandinavian Studies and Modern History and another MA in Romance Studies, both from the Humboldt-Universität zu Berlin and the Freie Universität Berlin. He has written textbooks in Norwegian and Danish, and has published articles on history, music, and politics in international newspapers such as *Le Monde Diplomatique*. He is currently writing a biography on the Swedish opera singer Set Svanholm.

Ronni L. Gordon, PhD, is a prominent author of foreign language textbooks, reference books, and multimedia courses. She is vice president of Mediatheque Publishers Services, a leader in the development of foreign language instructional materials. She holds a PhD in Spanish language and Spanish and Spanish American literature from Rutgers University, and has taught and coordinated Spanish language programs and taught Latin American literature at Harvard University, Boston University, and Drexel University. A foreign language consultant, she has read for the National Endowment for the Humanities, presented at the United States Department of Education, consulted on states' K–12 academic standards for world languages, and presented at conferences on Spanish American literature and foreign language instruction. She is an associate scholar of a Philadelphia-based think tank and is chairman of the board of directors of Dolce Suono Ensemble.

David M. Stillman and Ronni L. Gordon are the authors of the acclaimed *The Ultimate Spanish Review and Practice* and *The Ultimate French Review and Practice*.